D1170929

Wayward Nuns in Medieval Literature

Wayward Nuns
in
Medieval Literature

GRACIELA S. DAICHMAN

SYRACUSE UNIVERSITY PRESS

1986

The paper used in this publication meets the minimum requirements of American National Standard for Information Sciences—Permanence of Paper for Printed Library Materials, ANSI Z39.48-1984. ∞™

Library of Congress Cataloging-in-Publication Data

Daichman, Graciela.
  Wayward nuns in medieval literature.

  Originally presented as the author's thesis (doctoral).
  Bibliography: p.
  Includes index.
  1. Nuns in literature. 2. Literature, Medieval—History and criticism. I. Title.
  PN682.N87D3 1986   809'.9335222   86-14438
  ISBN 0-8156-2372-0 (alk. paper)
  ISBN 0-8156-2379-8 (pbk. : alk. paper)

MANUFACTURED IN THE UNITED STATES OF AMERICA

For
Ricardo

GRACIELA S. DAICHMAN is lecturer in the Spanish and the English departments at Rice University, where she received both her M.A. and Ph.D. She is at present doing research on medieval medicine and superstition in the *Libro de Buen Amor*.

Contents

Acknowledgments

THIS BOOK was born as a doctoral dissertation. The first spark of my interest in medieval nuns was lit by the Archpriest of Hita himself through his own nun. From that point forward, my fascination with the wayward nuns of the Middle Ages took wing. It would not have flown very high, though, without the advice and encouragement of Jane Chance of the English Department of Rice University; to her I am deeply grateful.

I am also indebted to the staff of the Interlibrary Loan Department of Rice University for their help in securing every book I needed; they made it seem like a challenge, not a chore. I also want to thank Jet Prendeville, Rice University Art Librarian, who generously gave her time and expertise to help me find illustrations. Then there are my friends, who did not give up on me all the years I remained buried in the library and shunned their company; among them, Trouta Stoller stands at the head of the list for her loyal support.

To two of my colleagues at Rice University, Deborah Nelson, Chairman of the Department of French and Italian, and Helen Eaker of Spanish, Portuguese, and Classics, I owe an enormous debt. One helped me pick my way through the intricacies of a number of off-color medieval French poems while the other elucidated for me, with marvelous ease, the most puzzling Latin quotes.

A very big thank you goes to my daughter Marcela, radiant presence, who typed my bibliography and never let me give up, and to my son Sean, who shared with me his computer and his love of life. My greatest debt, however, is to my husband Ricardo, staunchest supporter and source of strength, whose unfailing sense of humor, patience, and understanding makes everything possible.

Introduction

'guardas tenié la monja más que la mi esgrima
pero de buena fabla vino la buena cima.[1]
Libro de Buen Amor

(Yet guards she had more than my sword, but guards can't
    ward off crime
And pleasant conversation oft results in merry times.)

Of smal coral aboute hire arm she bar
A peire of bedes, gauded al with grene,
And theron heng a brooch of gold ful sheene,
And after AMOR VINCIT OMNIA.
General Prologue to the Canterbury Tales

T HE LITERARY FIGURE of Doña Garoza, the ambiguous nun of
the Archpriest of Hita's *Libro de Buen Amor* and that of
Madame Eglentyne, the controversial prioress of the *General
Prologue* to the *Canterbury Tales* have been the object of scholarly
scrutiny for a long time, especially in this century. The question
concerns the tone with which each woman is described; is the author
mildly chastising his nun or is he damning her? In the case of Doña
Garoza, critics have interpreted her in three ways: as a gentle, mildly
sinning creature,[2] as a religious failure,[3] and as an—intentionally—
ambiguously drawn character with both characteristics, portrayed
thus to entertain the reader.[4] Interestingly enough, there are also three
ways of intepreting Chaucer's Prioress—as harsh,[5] soft,[6] and ambiguous.[7] However, in order to determine how Chaucer and the Archpriest of Hita regarded their nuns, it is necessary to understand how

xi

the fourteenth century would have regarded them, and whether these nuns were exceptional or typical in their faults. Actually, such apparently ambiguous literary portraits mask satirical portraits of religious women of the fourteenth century. We have attempted to place these portraits in the proper perspective, as heirs to a long and distinguished tradition of literary wayward nuns whose real-life models date back to the beginnings of monasticism. Fourteenth-century audiences would not have expressed shock or even mild surprise at the presence of a possibly wayward nun in a literary work; hundreds of years of exposure to the public as an object of popular ridicule or a target of episcopal wrath had given her clearly defined social and moral features.

In order to situate the wayward nun of the Middle Ages within the literary and social convention that eventually led to the portraits of Doña Garoza and Madame Eglentyne, it is essential to outline the historical background against which medieval nuns lived their lives, and the diverse reasons that led certain women to the cloister. The medieval nunnery was essentially an aristocratic institution open to all females of the upper classes; grieving widows and disconsolate lovers of all ages seem to have been almost as numerous as young novices with a strong vocation. Such unlikely mingling, however, often had disastrous effects, not only on the spiritual aspect of life in the nunnery but also on conventual discipline. Nevertheless, the issue of misconduct in the women's religious houses has been largely ignored by twentieth-century historians.[8] As a result, most contemporary critics of medieval literature have failed to perceive the presence of the wayward nun in the "chanson," the fabliau, and the satire—three genres where her figure chiefly appears in the literature of medieval Europe—as in any way related to her historical existence.[9] Despite this, though, the salacious sisters of the fabliaux, as well as the unwilling nuns of the "chansons de nonne" and the dishonest ones castigated by the churchmen in lengthy tirades, are the direct descendants of those religious women whose improper, and often indecent behavior was recorded by the bishops in their visitation reports of the convents in their dioceses.

Because of its remarkable social composition, the medieval nunnery witnessed transgressions that were a constant source of anxiety for the Church that, beset with incidents of monastic abuse, had come to regard scandal as worse than sin by the fourteenth century. The sins of the medieval nun seem to have ranged from the trivial—

being late to chapel—to the cardinal—incontinence and childbearing. To support the contention that, far from being an isolated literary occurrence, the wayward nun in medieval literature is the reflection of the one in the nunnery, special attention is given to those works where profligate nuns seem to have been drawn almost directly from the pages of the episcopal reports. Different from the studies offering a general picture of the life of the professed woman in the Middle Ages,[10] our emphasis is on the evidence of immodest or dishonorable behavior in the convent observed through the centuries by those who felt it their duty to record it, reprove it, or mock it.

Chapter 1, which furnishes the historical background, takes a look at collections of medieval wills that show how women of every age were forced into the convent. Such collections of wills as the *Testamenta Vetusta* (London: Nichols and Son, 1826), the *Testamenta Eboracensia* (Surtees Society, London, 1836), and the *Calendar of Wills Proved and Enrolled in the Court of Husting,* edited by R. Sharpe (London: John C. Francis, 1889) reveal how well-to-do fathers provided for their daughters by assigning them either to a suitor or a nunnery, both of which required an equally generous dowry. As to the girls themselves, though for some young women the religious life was certainly a true vocation, for others it simply offered an honorable alternative to matrimony. Another group of women, all of them young and just as numerous, seem to have entered the nunnery at the behest of their families and entirely against their will. Then, there were the widows and older women seeking shelter from the turmoil of a dangerous and often violent world in the convent, a haven where they could spend the rest of their lives in safety and seclusion. Such studies of medieval monastic life as Lina Eckenstein's *Woman under Monasticism* (Cambridge: University Press, 1896) and especially G. G. Coulton's impressive *Five Centuries of Religion* (Cambridge: University Press, 1952) disclose one startling fact: not only were religious women no longer paragons of Christian duty and devotion but, near the end of the Middle Ages, the centuries-old monastic impulse itself appeared dangerously on the wane.

Chapter 2 surveys the works of the moral and satirical writers of the period, who provide the Archpriest of Hita and Chaucer with models for tone and attitude toward their nuns. The French moralists of the thirteenth and fourteenth centuries, like Guiot de Provins and Hughes de Berzé in their *Bibles* and Matheolus in his *Lamentations,* indignantly denounce the unchaste behavior of religious women whom they accuse of concealing their boundless concupiscence with an aura of spirituality and devotion. In order to satisfy their evil desires, says Matheolus, nuns are constantly looking for reasons to go outside the convent, a charge echoed by numerous ecclesiastical authorities throughout the Middle Ages. It is, in fact, this failure to remain loyal to their claustration vows that prompts religious women to commit all sorts of horrible crimes, according to the bishops in charge of the well-being of their souls. One after the other, the spiritual leaders of the Church chastise certain nuns for leading sinful lives with complete disregard for religion or even propriety. To illustrate further the concern of those interested in preserving—or rather, restoring—to conventual life its original pristine quality, cited in this chapter are certain works of the churchmen in praise of virginity, as well as some books of devotion or admonition addressed to nuns. The former, though, are not considered in detail since they do not really concern themselves with the actual life of a professed woman.

Chapter 2 also examines certain satiric parodies on the conduct of profligate nuns. Written mostly in a jocular vein, the humor, however, is sometimes rather somber in these, as in Langland's *Piers Plowman* and Matheolus's *Lamentations,* for instance. Langland refers to a convent in which very dishonorable events take place and whose prioress "had childe in chirityme," while Matheolus's book contains an entire section devoted to religious women whom, he believes, should not be trusted because they cannot control their appetites. In the *Spill* or *Libre de les dones,* the Portuguese Jacme Roig gives a detailed picture of a medieval nunnery where vices and corruption are rampant, much like the section in Nigellus Wireker's *Speculum Stultorum* in which, half seriously and half in jest, the decay of the female monastic order is exposed. The chapter ends with an analysis of the anonymous *Concilium in Monte Romarici,* a Latin "jeu d'esprit" describing in a typically medieval tone of good-humored blasphemy a large gathering of nuns at Remiremont. Here, "de solo negotio Amoris tractatum est" (the only business is love) and the debate centers on the merits of clerks and knights as lovers, all actually an impudent parody of Ovid's *Ars Amatoria,* as well as of the openly unchaste behavior of certain religious women.

Chapter 3 reviews the medieval "chanson de nonne" and the fabliau, two literary forms in which the figure of the wayward nun plays a very significant role, and which provided the Archpriest and

Chaucer with models for their nuns. Though the "chanson de nonne" is the plaint of the nun unwillingly professed, her wishful thinking is often highly indecorous and most of the "chansons" have an air of almost irrepressible frivolity. The earliest known ancestor of the "chanson de nonne" that has come down to us is the twelfth-century "Planctus monialis," published for the first time in 1922 in *Studi Medievali*, I (1904). The "Planctus" is unusually sorrowful, however, while in general the "chansons de nonne" sound more like this one from *L'Ancienne Chanson populaire,* edited by J. B. Weckerlin (Paris: Garnier Frères, 1887):

> Mon père n'a fille que moy
> Il a juré la sienne foy, guoy,
>
> . . . .
>
> Que nonnette il fera de moy,
> Et non feray, pas ne voudray, guoy.
>
> . . . .
>
> J'aimerois mieux mary avoir,
> Qui my baisast la nuit trois fois, guoy
>
> . . . .
>
> L'une au matin et l'autre au soir,
> L'autre à minuict, ce sont les trois, guoy.

(My father has no other daughter; he has sworn a hundred times that he will make me a nun, but I will not be one and I do not want to. I would rather have a husband who would kiss me in the night three times, once in the morning and once at night, once at midnight; these are the three.)

The other medieval literary form discussed in Chapter 3 is the fabliau, where the figure of the wayward nun also plays a prominent role. The same stories used by the Church for edifying purposes were used by the jongleur, although his aim was not to edify but to provoke laughter. Thus, the reprobate nun was the target of countless ribald tales that eventually found their way into vernacular verse; scurrilous and unredeemed by any sense of moral decency, the fabliaux mock the immoral habits of certain religious women with total impunity. In Italian literature, probably the most notorious—and indecent—nun stories are those in the Decameron, where religious women are held up to ridicule in tale after tale of unrelenting debauchery.

The stage is now set for Chapter 4. The Archpriest of Hita's Doña Garoza and Chaucer's Madame Eglentyne are no longer literary types; in them the content of the "chansons de nonne" merges with the tone of the satires on nuns. Sharing the "vertwes" and "vyces" of most medieval nuns, Doña Garoza and the Prioress stand out as the polished end-products of a long line of prototypical wayward nuns going back many centuries in European literature. The tradition to which they belong was already an old one by the Archpriest's and Chaucer's time; it is, however, the poets' exceptional achievement that, from the composite satirical figure that had begun to emerge hundreds of years before, each was able to create a fascinating and enigmatic literary character. The ambiguity of the two portraits explains the centuries-old critical controversy surrounding them.

Wayward Nuns in Medieval Literature

The Nunnery as a Social Institution

"Nec omnes virginis sunt, mihi crede, quae velum habent."[1]

(All the veiled aren't virgins, believe me.)

T HE WAYWARD NUN of the Middle Ages is a product of the social, economic, and political climate of an era in which the Church was going through some of the most eventful moments in its history. This was particularly true of the fourteenth century, when a divided papacy was causing a schism in the Christian world that threatened to become permanent. Obviously, the changes taking place in the structure of the Church itself had to affect all of its institutions, among which monasticism was one of the strongest. By this time, the centuries-old monastic impulse that had inspired so many devoted men and women to enter the religious life was apparently on the wane, and incidents of misconduct in the religious houses were alarmingly frequent, if we are to trust the historical documents of the period. Among these, the reports and injunctions written by the bishops after visits to the convents of their dioceses provide the most thorough evidence of such misconduct in the women's houses. It is precisely through these visitation reports on conventual scandals, rumored or confirmed, and the bishops' subsequent injunctions, that something like a catalogue of sins and sinners of the nunnery has come down to us. Sometimes dire and menacing, often forgiving and almost always understanding, the medieval bishops took their mandate to act as guardians of the Church's sons and daughters with the zeal of true spiritual fathers, whose tolerance seems to have been greatly abused by certain religious women.[2] The sins of the medieval

3

Monasticon Anglicanum,

SIVE

Pandectæ

COENOBIORUM

Benedictinorum
Cluniacensium
Cisterciensium
Carthusianorum

A primordiis ad eorum usque dissolutionem

Ex MSS. Codd.

Ad Monasteria olim pertinentibus;

Archivis

Turrium Londinensis, Eboracensis;
Curiarum Scaccarii, Augmentationum;

Bibliothecis

Bodleianâ; Coll. Reg. Coll. Bened.
Arundellianâ, Cottonianâ, Seldenianâ, Hattonianâ
aliisque digesti

per { ROGERUM DODSWORTH, Eborac.
{ GULIELMUM DUGDALE, Warwic.

LONDINI
Typis *Richardi Hodgkinsonne,*
M. DC. LV.

Title Page. *Monasticon Anglicanum: A History of Abbies and other Monasteries, Hospitals, Frieries and Cathedral and Collegiate Churches with their Dependencies in England and Wales.* Sir William Dugdale, editor. London: James Bohn, 1846.

nun apparently ranged from the trivial to the cardinal, from failure to attend services to incontinence[3] and child-bearing.[4]

Although some of the erring sisters[5] come from the smaller, more poorly endowed houses, others belong to the wealthiest, most prominent abbeys such as Shaftesbury, Godstow, and Amesbury. Therefore, even though it would be unfair to level a charge of generalized immorality against any particular nunnery, since in all of them there must have been many devout and high-principled women, some communities seem to have had more wayward nuns than others. Interestingly enough also, it was this small group of dishonest nuns who caught through the centuries the attention of the ecclesiastical authorities striving to return order and morality to the monastic world. Thus, reports of immoral behavior in the convent date as far back as the early twelfth century, although they do not become common until the beginning of the fourteenth, increasing in number and severity throughout the entire fifteenth century, almost to the end of the medieval period. The reported cases of errant behavior in the nunnery are far too numerous to list in their entirety. Profligate nuns were not a rare phenomenon in the Middle Ages; they were, instead, a matter of intense concern—also dismay and disgust, even—to the guardians of the spiritual life and the laughingstock of countless others.[6]

An early example of immorality in the convent is that of certain nuns of Amesbury, one of the oldest and most prestigious houses in England, which fell into bad times in the last quarter of the twelfth century. According to the records, this convent was dissolved in 1189 after the abbess was said to have given birth three times and a large number of the sisters were found to be leading sinful lives: "The nuns of Amesbury (Ambresbiria), some 30 in number for the turpitude of their life, the dissolution of their order, and public scandal (infamia), were, by the mandate of Pope Alexander, with assent of his father king Henry and by the care of Richard archbishop of Canterbury, . . . removed from their monastery and placed in other monasteries."[7] Another nunnery whose name is mentioned in connection with the scandalous conduct of some of its inmates is Godstow where, near the end of the thirteenth century there seems to have been a contoversy regarding the probity of the sub-prioress. Although the archbishop speaks on her behalf—"la tenouns por nette e pur chaste kant a tote charnalité" (we regard her as pure and chaste, as to any carnal desires)[8]—he makes strong recommendations concerning conduct at Godstow: "nule nonein ne parle a nul homme seculer, si deus autres noneins bones et de bon renoun oient kant ke len li dirra" (no nun should talk to any layman, unless another nun of good renown can hear what she says).[9] Injunctions, however, no matter how severe, did not seem to prevent the transgressions.[10] Incidents involving sinning sisters were also reported in some of the smaller, less richly endowed houses such as Cannington and Easebourne, for instance. A document signed by two commissioners of the Archbishop of Shrewsbury states that at Cannington, "two of the Nuns, Matilda Pulham and Alice Northlode, . . . were known, to the violation of their monastic vow and the shame of their sex, to keep company with, and too frequently to admit, sundry suspected women . . . and by their sensuality brought disgrace upon their vow and a scandal on their House."[11] At Easebourne one of the nuns testified during a 1422 visit that sister Philippa King had had relations with "a certain 'brother William Cotnall'" and that, together with sister Joan Portsmouth, a chaplain, and one of the Earl of Arundel's retainers they had left the convent after giving birth to one or more children each.[12]

Many more examples of immoral conduct in the nunnery are mentioned in the sections on religious houses of the *Victoria History of the Counties of England,* where the nature of the sins and the circumstances under which they were committed are often given in full detail. An example is the following excerpt from Archbishop Thoresby's *Register:* "On 8 December 1358" Alice de Reygate, a nun of Hampole, "with weeping countenance, had prostrated herself at his feet, confessing that she had broken the vow of her profession and been guilty of immorality with an unmarried man."[13] At the same nunnery, Isabella Folifayt had been found guilty of incest[14] with Thomas de Raynevill in 1324, and at Arden Priory Archbishop Greenfield had "dealt with the case of Joan de Punchardon, one of the nuns, who had become a mother" in 1306.[15] Incidents of monastic abuse were just as frequent in German nunneries. In the fifteenth-century convent of Sonnenburg in the Pusterthal, in Bishop Nicolas Cusanus's diocese, "the young daughters of the Tyrolese nobility led the freest and most luxurious life under cover of the veil,"[16] and in an Augustinian monastery in Friesland, priests and lay brothers were accused of "'keeping nuns with them . . . with whom they slept and sometimes begat children.'"[17]

As we review more examples of lewd conduct in the nunnery and before investigating the reasons for such behavior, it may help us understand it to consider the identity of the nuns' lovers, and whether perhaps some of the sisters fell to the charms of a seducer without fully weighing the consequences of such a reprehensible act. While the latter may have been the cause on some occasions, most of the evidence, however, seems to indicate that only seldom was a religious woman seduced or forced to submit to sexual advances by either a priest or a civilian; the punishment imposed by the Church on those found guilty of violating a bride of Christ was severe enough to discourage most would-be assailants. It was considered a very serious crime by the state as well as the Church, and under a law passed by Edward I, the ravisher of a nun had to make restitution to the convent somehow and could also be condemned to three years in prison. If the accused failed to prove his innocence before the bishop by submitting the required number of witnesses that could attest to it, he would be excommunicated if unrepentant, or given a penance if remorseful. In such cases, the punishment could range from fairly mild to quite severe as may be seen from the following two excerpts: "For committing the sin of incest with Isabella Folifayt, nun of Hampole . . . Thomas de Raynevill was to stand, wearing a tunic only and bareheaded, holding a lighted taper of a pound weight of wax in his hand."[18] Dated 1286, this fragment of a letter taken from the Register of Godfrey Giffard, Bishop of Worcester, discloses the penance imposed by the Bishop of Salisbury on his relative, Sir Osbert Giffard, accused of abducting and seducing two nuns of Wylton:

> The bishop enjoined upon him that he should restore the aforesaid sisters and all goods of the monastery withdrawn and should make all the satisfaction that he possibly could to the abbess and convent. And that on Ash Wednesday in the church of Salisbury, the said crime being solemnly published before the clergy and people, he should humbly permit himself to be taken to the door of the church, with bare feet, in mourning raiment and uncovered head, with other penitents and should be beaten with sticks about the church on three holy days and on three Tuesdays through the market of Salisbury and so often and in like manner about the church of Wylton and through the market there; and he should be likewise beaten about the church of Amesbury and the market there and about the church of Shaftesbury and the market there. In his clothing from henceforth there shall not appear any cloaks of lamb's wool, gilt spurs or horse trappings, or girdle of a knight, unless in the meantime he should obtain special grace of the king, but he shall journey to the Holy Land and there serve for three years.[19]

Aware, then, of the consequences that a love affair with a nun could bring to the men involved in it, we wonder even more at the kind of man who would approach a sister with such a purpose in mind. Who were these men willing to lead—or follow—into sin a "Sponsa Dei?" For the most part they were naturally those with whom the nuns could have frequent and easily disguised contact, such as a married boarder at the convent,[20] or the bailiff of a manor,[21] or maybe one of the workers who were allowed into the inner cloisters for needed repairs (a nun of Watton made the acquaintance of one of the lay brothers who were engaged in repairing the women's dwelling "and the two contrived to meet frequently out of doors until at last the nun's condition became obvious"[22]), or perhaps even a wandering minstrel[23] whose art and whose charm may have captivated the heart of an amorous sister. The most common liaison, however, seems to have been between nuns and priests, since the vicars, chaplains, and chantry priests who moved about the convent had perfectly easy and justified access to the sisters. Furthermore, because these men were all under the same vow of celibacy as the nuns, they knew very well how to break it, and they could practically tempt and absolve a sinner in the same breath. There is very strong evidence in the historical documents and the literature of the Middle Ages that priestly corruption was rampant, and the affairs between religious men and women aroused the fury and condemnation of every guardian of monastic morals. In the fourteenth century, the Franciscan Alvarus Pelagius fulminates against the "causes and matters of unchastity to Religious": "Another cause is conversation with nuns. For in the convents they have their lady-devotees—'devotas suas'—with whom they too often talk too long without witnesses, extorting rather than obtaining leave from the superiors. There are undisciplined laughter and ogling glances exchanged; there are words of levity and vanity and carnality, and amorous touches; there are hearts aflame with fire, and every window open to the deadly things around (Jerem. ix, 21). The rest is indecent [for me] to write; but it is most wicked [for them] to do."[24]

Sometimes the priestly lover did not belong to the nunnery but lived in a nearby village, where he might be a clerk, a chaplain or a vicar. At the priory of Villa Arcelli in 1249, for instance, Archbishop Eude Rigaud of Rouen found, among other irregular activities that,

> prior de Gisorcio frequentat domum pro ipsa Idonia. Philipa de Rothomago, de presbytero de Suentre, Carnotensis diocesis. Marguerita, thesauraria, infamata est de Richardo de Genevilla,

clerico. Agnes de Fonteneio infamata de presbytero de Guer-
revilla, diocesis Carnotensis. La Tooliere infamata de domino
Andrea de Monciaco, milite. Omnes nutriunt comam usque ad
mentum; ponunt crocum in peplis. Jacquelina recessit gravida de
quodam capllano qui propter hoc eiectus fuit de domo. Item,
Agnes de Monte Securo infamata est de eodem.[25]

(the Prior of Gisorcium is always coming to the house for Idonia.
Philippa de Rouen is suspected with a priest of Suentre, of the
diocese of Chartres; Marguerita, the treasuress, with Richard de
Geneville, a clerk, Agnes de Fontenei, with a priest of Guer-
reville, diocese of Chartres; La Tooliere with Andrea de Monciaco, soldier. All wear their hair improperly and perfume their
veils. Jacqueline came back pregnant from visiting a certain
chaplain, who was expelled from his house on account of this.
Also, Agnes de Mont Sec was suspected with the same.)

At Nunkeeling Priory in York, "Avice de Lelle was strictly
forbidden to go outside the inner cloister of the house, in any manner,
or to talk to Robert de Eton, chaplain, or any other secular person
whomsoever. She had confessed incontinence." At Keldholme Priory,
also in York, "Archbishop Melton wrote to the prioress and convent
directing them to compel Mary de Holm to undergo the penance
enjoined her for the vice of incontinence by her with Sir William Lyly,
chaplain."[26] At Swine Priory in 1310, Archbishop Greenfield wrote a
letter to Roger de Driffield, abbot of Meaux, "concerning Brother
Robert de Merflet and Stephen de Ulram his fellow monks, who had
been guilty of incontinence and incest with Elizabeth de Rude, nun of
Swine."[27] One of the worst offenders seems to have been John
Stafford, Archbishop of Canterbury, accused of having children by a
nun when he was Bishop of Bath and Wells in 1443: "existens genuit
filios et filias ex una moniali"[28] (procreated a son and a daughter by a
nun). Their office naturally gave these priests easy access to the
convent, while at the same time it allowed a nun to arrange for visits
to different locations where she could meet her lover away from the
eyes of the indiscreet.[29] A nun of Catesby Priory, for instance, reported, "priorissa consueit sola accedere ad villam de Catesby ad
gardinas cum vno solo presbytero, nomine Willelmo Taylour"[30] (the
prioress is wont to go by herself to the town of Catesby to the
gardens with one man alone, a priest by the name William Taylour).
    A few pages back we mentioned the punishment often given by

the Church to those men found guilty of a liaison with a nun; if we compare it with the measures taken by the same ecclesiastical authorities against an erring sister we notice a disparity at once. This, in fact, may seem to soften, somehow, what could be seen as typical antifeminine bias in the church's handling of incidents of monastic misconduct. When a nun committed a carnal sin, the punishment was not overly severe provided she repented and returned to the convent. The penance for a lapse or two was actually rather light in view of the crime, probably because the Church, beset with incidents of monastic abuse had come more and more to regard scandal as worse than sin and, therefore, attempted whenever possible to conceal a nun's misdeed. It was usually not too difficult to do this since the episcopal visitations which took place every few years were the only occasions when grievances, disturbances, and sinners were exposed either by the prioress or the other sisters. Thus, rumors of an illicit affair could be kept secret within the convent or its existence even denied for a while, except when a sister became pregnant as a consequence of her trespass.[31] There are few official records of any abortions that might have been performed in the medieval convents,[32] and the reports are extremely hazy as to what happened to the children born to religious women. Although according to a thirteenth-century priest, the reverend Augustus Jessop, they were immediately disposed of—"et proles obiit immediate post"[33] (the offspring died immediately after)— certainly not all of them could have died.

As mentioned above, the punishment for a crime of such magnitude as moral turpitude seems to us extremely benign; a guilty nun, for instance could be made to sit last among all her sisters or walk at the head of a solemn procession of the convent on Sunday dressed in white flannel and wearing no veil. A recalcitrant sister might be "shut up in a room by herself, and on no account go outside the convent precincts for a year,"[34] or perhaps in extreme cases, "be bound by the foot with a shackle (ad modum compedis), but without hurting her limbs or body."[35] In the case of Johanna Trimelet, a nun of Cannington Priory who "had been frequently guilty of incontinence, and had given birth to a child," the bishop's deputies in charge of the inquiry "enjoined that the said Johanna should remain for a whole year imprisoned in one house within the precinct of the Monastery; that, with a view of repressing her youthful ardours, 'suos calores macerans juveniles,' she should fast on bread and water on Mondays, Tuesdays and Fridays, and that on all other days during the time aforesaid she should have for her maintenance bread, pottage, and ale only."[36]

In addition to the punishments just described, a nun found guilty of immoral behavior was automatically barred from holding any office in the nunnery, but even this injunction sounds more forbidding than it actually was. Since many of the sisters came from influential court-related families, a dispensation annulling the ban was often arranged. The reason for the leniency of the Church's measures against some religious women's transgressions was probably that most bishops preferred to bring their erring daughters back to religion rather than lose them to a world always too ready to heap condemnation on the entire Church every time a sheep left the fold.

There was one sin, however, which the Church was reluctant to pardon, and this was apostasy or abandoning the nunnery to return to the world. An apostate nun broke all monastic vows. If she was allowed to do so with impunity, there was a danger her example might be followed by other nuns who were subject to the same pressures and the same temptations even if they resisted for the moment. In order to prevent apostates from remaining in the world unpunished and free, the Church reached out with a mighty arm and through a combination of threats and pleas generally succeeded in luring them back to the nunnery. When these efforts failed, though, the bishops resorted to more forceful means by enlisting the help of the state's machinery to regain their hold over a sinner. Such was the case of Elizabeth Arundel, for instance, who ran away from her house in 1382, and whose arrest was ordered by the king at the petition of the prioress of Halliwell, in the diocese of London, and also of Joan Adeleshey, a nun of Rosney who became an apostate in 1400.[37] The records indicate that both Elizabeth and Joan were apprehended by the king's men and forcefully returned to their nunneries. The same fate was suffered by Mary de Felton, of the Minoresses Without Algate; in 1385, the king "ordered his serjeant-at-arms to arrest . . . Mary de Felton and deliver her to the abbess for punishment."[38]

Despite the fact that the odds were against her when a nun left the convent, the list of apostates is quite long and between the years 1290 and 1360, for example, the names of eleven out of thirty-four houses in the diocese of Lincoln appear in the records. One of the nuns was from Wothorpe (1296);[39] another from Sewardsley (1300);[40] one from Goring (1358), who "had apparently fled with someone who was also under a vow of celibacy, as her sin is called 'incest';"[41]

one from Markyate (1336),[42] and one from St. Leonard's (1337).[43] At
the Abbey of Delapré in Northampton, things were in a very bad
state for a while between 1300 and 1311 with four nuns denounced
for apostasy in that period,[44] and at Ankerwyke Priory in 1441,
Bishop Alnwick notes that "vj moniales recesserunt a domo in apos-
tasia" (six nuns have now left the house in apostasy).[45] Among the
recorded cases of apostasy which have come down to us in considerable detail, one of the most colorful and complex ones is probably
that of Agnes de Flixthorpe, also known as Agnes de Wissendun, a
nun of St. Michael's, Stamford, whose tragic story begins to unravel
in 1309, when Bishop Dalderby excommunicated her for apostasy.
Brought back to the convent by the sheriff of Nottingham, Agnes
refused to repent and by order of the bishop was then placed in a
room with her legs fettered as punishment. In 1312, after a year's
confinement in a remote little Devonshire priory, Agnes broke down
and declared her repentance but was still kept in solitary confinement
until 1314, at which time she was considered "cured" and allowed to
return to Stamford. Two years later, however, Agnes was once more
out in the world, having again left the veil that she obviously should
never have adopted. Nothing more is said about the unfortunate
Agnes in the records, and how she spent the rest of her life is left to
the imagination.[46]

What could possibly be the reason for such heinous breaches of
monastic—and moral—law among women who had vowed to devote
their lives to Christ? The answer must lie in the variety of motives that
led certain medieval women to take the veil and, despite their dif-
ferences in education, taste, and temperament to live together as
members of a community ostensibly dedicated to the glorification of
God's love. The circumstances under which these women entered the
cloister were precisely the determining factor for their behavior once
inside. Those who became nuns of their own volition because of a
strong religious vocation, still found the fourteenth-century nunnery
the ideal place for a spiritual communion with God that it had been
when St. Jerome founded the first convent in Rome around the year
400. There were other women, however, forced into the nunnery for
social, economic, or political reasons and often totally unsuited for
the religious life who seem to be the ones guilty of the immodest or
indecent behavior described above. Among these are the nuns who
took the veil much too young to be able to decide on a religious
vocation for themselves, but who were forced into the convent by

relatives, either out of a genuine desire to protect them[47] or merely to dispose of them: "daughters of noble families, dumped into a convent because the medieval world had no other place for them."[48] An entry in Dugdale's Monasticon for the year 1298 says that "Robert de Albini and Cicely his mother placed Amice, a little maid, the sister of Robert and daughter of Cicely, in this Cell, to serve God continually,"[49] and during a 1441 visit to Ankerwyke Priory, Bishop Alnwick observed that three nuns "sororibus Isabella Coke, Elizabetha Londone et Elena Moretone, propter etatis teneritatem et discrecionis simplicitatem, cum vltra tresdecim annos etatis non transcendat senior earum"[50] (sisters Isabel Coke, Elizabeth Londone and Ellen Moretone were of tender age and slender discretion, seeing that the eldest of them is not more than thirteen years of age). Sometimes young girls were also sent to the nunnery in an attempt to deprive them of an inheritance that was rightfully theirs. Such was the case of the daughter of Sir Philip de Covele, Isabel, kept from her share of her mother's inheritance in 1293 because she was a professed nun at Sewardsley,[51] while at Ankerwyke Priory, "'A. the daughter of W. Clement'," fifteen years old when professed, in 1197 "was bold enough to claim a share in her father's property on the ground that she had been forced into the monastery against her will by a guardian who wished to secure the whole inheritance."[52]

Other circumstances probably contributed to increase the number of young girls made to enter the convent without much regard for their particular inclination. One was, perhaps, the fact that it was an almost established custom in large families for one or more daughters to become nuns,[53] and the other the concern of well-to-do fathers about their daughters' future—enough to inspire a popular proverb of the time: "aut virum aut murum oportet mulierem habere"[54] (a woman ought to have either a husband or a wall). The latter made it imperative for the fathers to make provision in their wills to assign the girls' dowries for marriage either to an earthly lord or to Christ. This last circumstance is evident in entries from the collections of medieval wills from the last centuries of the Middle Ages which are a veritable "Who's Who" of the medieval nunnery.[55] Nevertheless, the reasons why this practice of sending to the cloister the young unmarried females of means appears to have flourished during the Middle Ages was not only social—it offered a suitable arrangement to their parents—but also economic. Because the nunneries were always in need of financial support,[56] they welcomed the

wealthy women who could contribute to the usually depleted conventual treasury. For a similar economic reason older women, generally widows with considerable incomes and often vast estates, were
also received with gratitude as they endowed the nunnery of their
choice with grants of money or land.[57] It may be interesting to note
here that the practice of demanding a fee from postulants was severely
condemned by the Church as "simoniacal depravity" but that the
nunnery, by neglecting for economic reasons to observe this dictum,
contributed more and more to the change in its own character. Thus,
by continuing to accept as novices only women of the upper classes,
the convent consistently encouraged the presence within its walls of a
number of females lacking the basic ingredient for the life of a nun,
that is, a religious vocation. These were the women who would
obviously find it extremely hard to adapt to the almost unrelieved
monotony of a day punctuated solely by the singing of the litany of
the divine services.[58]

    Besides the overriding external concerns mentioned above and
because of which vocation had apparently ceased to be an impelling
force for the religious life by the fourteenth century, there was another economic factor affecting the character of the nunnery which
had begun to make itself felt about two hundred years before. This
was the firmly established existence of a class of "nouveaux riches"
who also often opted to send their daughters to the nunnery. Proof of
this phenomenon are some of the wills of the enriched tradesmen of
the time, such as John Syward and William Wyght, "stok-
fisshmongers" of London, for example, who left the following in-
structions: "To Dionisia his daughter forty pounds sterling for her
advancement, so that she either marry therewith or become a religious, at her election" and "to each of his daughters Agnes, Margaret,
Beatrix, and Alice, fifty pounds sterling for their marriage or for
entering a religious house." The will of William Marowe (1504) leaves
"to Elizabeth and Katherine his daughters forty pounds each, to be
paid at their marriage or profession."[59] At Ludlow, the Palmers' gild
declared, "if any good girl of marriageable age cannot have the means
found by her father either to go into a religious house or to marry,
whichever she wishes to do . . ." and at Berwick-on-Tweed the gild
established that "if any brother die leaving a daughter true and
worthy and of good repute, but unendowered, the gild shall find her a
dower, either on marriage or on going into a religious house."[60]
There is no specific record of how many of these young women

conducted themselves with the proper decorum once professed, but quite clearly, as in the case of the daughters of the upper class, only those taking the veil in response to a genuine spiritual calling could have become true religious women.

Besides the girls who took their vows because they had no alternative, there was in the nunnery another group of women often equally unsuited for the religious life. Sometimes older, and definitely more seasoned, these women were thrust into the convent by external circumstances either social, political, or economic.[61] Among them were the widows, wives, or daughters of vanquished enemies placed in the convent by the victor;[62] "immured" for all time, the women could never become rallying forces for any supporters of their defeated lords who might still refuse to give up the fight. They were often joined by the illegitimate offspring of the higher classes or even of the clergy themselves; thus, the 1346 will of Hugh de Tunsted, rector of Catton, leaves "vnum lectum integrum cum tapeto" (a bed, complete with hangings) to his niece—"dominae Johannae, . . . Sanctae Moniali de Wilburfosse"[63] (dame Johanna, a holy nun of Wilberfosse)—while one of Cardinal Wolsey's own children was a nun of Shaftesbury at the time of the Dissolution. Also sent to the nunnery to wither away were those girls afflicted by some deformity or an incurable disease, for whom there was no hope of marriage and whose families could not—or would not—provide care.

> Now earth to earth in convent walls
> To earth in churchyard sod.
> I was not good enough for man,
> And so am given to God,[64]

sings a girl in an anonymous medieval song. In 1441, the prioress of Ankerwyke Priory was accused by one of the sisters before Bishop Alnwick of accepting as novices "quasi idiotas et alias inhabiles"[65] (some that are almost witless and others that are incapable). It is probably right to assume that only a few of these nuns would actually become truly devoted religious women. Such a possibility was probably quite as remote for those older women who came to the nunnery of their own volition but prompted by motives other than a religious vocation. These were the widows and inconsolable lovers who took the veil hoping to find in the cloister a refuge from their sorrow or

their shame, like Abelard's own Heloise, one of the most famous
among them. The list contains many other illustrious names, such as
the Earl of Warwick's widow, Margaret Beauchamp; Katherine, wife
of John de Ingham, and the daughter of Ralph de Neville, Eleanor
Lady Scrope, among others.[66] It is important to note here that these
well-endowed ladies were always received enthusiastically at the convent because of the usually considerable dowry they brought with
them. At the same time, however, they imported into the nunnery
something much less desirable, that is, some of the turbulence and
excitement of the outside world which still lingered in their attitudes
and behavior after a lifetime spent in a position of influence and
superiority. Thus, quarrels frequently arose between self-willed and
domineering widows and certain equally forceful abbesses, a circumstance that led to the formation of factions among the nuns and that
could only have had a detrimental effect on conventual discipline as a
whole. At Wroxall Priory in 1323, for instance, Bishop Cobham
attempted to settle the quarrel between the prioress, Agnes de Ales-
bury, and Isabel, Lady Clinton of Maxteke, widow of the priory's
patron, who had taken the veil there. The bishop "found grave
discord existing between the Prioress and dame Isabel Clinton, some
of the sisters adhering to the one and some to the other."[67]

It seems evident, then, that misconduct among religious women
ranged from petulance and minor infractions to the most heinous
crimes such as sexual contact in and outside the cloister. In order to
understand, not only the diversity of the transgressions but also the
apparent ease with which some were committed by the sisters, we
should perhaps look into the character of some of the women ap-
pointed to lead such communities of nuns and to provide role models
for their followers—even in their transgressions. Who were, then,
these ladies chosen as heads of a convent on the basis of their alleged
spiritual and moral fortitude? Medieval abbesses appear to have been
mostly aristocratic, temperamental, often indomitable women,[68]
whose influence on the community under their care was of the utmost
importance and whose conduct set the norm for the rest of the nuns.
Most of the time, the abbess was "a woman of some social standing in
her own right."[69] Once in office she was vested with all the authority
and powers of an abbot, that is, she was the landlord of the estates and
properties belonging to the convent and if her house held these by
feudal tenure, she actually became a feudal "lord." As a lady of noble
blood, the abbess

wielded notable power and influence. The apogee of authority was reached in the tenth and eleventh centuries by the abbesses of royal nunneries in Saxony who reigned over vast tracts of land; as barons of the king they summoned their own armed knights to war, and they held their own courts. The abbesses of Quedlinburg and Gandersheim struck their own coins. Royal abbesses were even called to the Imperial Diet. . . . Sometimes these abbesses took an active part in politics, like German emperor Otto III's aunt, Matilda, abbess of Quedlinburg, who served unofficially as regent.[70]

An abbess remained in office for life or until she resigned or was removed under some extraordinary circumstance, such as embezzlement of conventual funds or clearly immoral behavior. Although the majority of medieval abbesses and prioresses were obviously women of strong moral principles, some of them deviated from the right path and were not even too circumspect about what they did. Prioress Denise Lewelyck of Markyate "was accused of having broken her vow of chastity, to the very evil example of her sisters,"[71] and was forced to resign after a board of inquiry found her guilty of consorting with Richard, the steward of the priory. Joan de Barton, prioress of Moxby, resigned from her post and the records indicate that "the reason for resignation is apparent from a penance enjoined upon her for having been guilty 'super lapsu carnis' (of a lapse of the flesh) with the chaplain, Laurence de Systeford."[72]

As the mother superior of a convent in charge of the physical and spiritual well-being of her daughters (and sometimes her sons too, since in the few dual monasteries that existed for a while in the early Middle Ages the head was usually a woman),[73] the medieval abbess enjoyed, among other things, incredible freedom of movement as well as the power granted by the control of the nunnery's treasury. Unfortunately, sometimes she would abuse one or the other. This was the case at Easbourne, for instance, where in 1441 the bishop found that "the prioress' extravagance had run the house into debt. . . . She was constantly out of the convent, feasted sumptuously wherever she went, and wore a mantle . . . [with] fur trimmings."[74] Bishop Alnwick's records indicate that in 1441, also at Ankerwyke Priory, "priorissa vitur anulis aureis quamplurimum sumptuosis cum diuersis gemmis et eciam zonis argentatis et deauratis et cericis velis" and "habet in collo vnum longum ligamen

Fontevrault. Romanesque Abbey, eleventh century. Loire Valley, Southeast of Saumur. Photo courtesy of Jet Prendeville.

anglice lace pendens vsque inferius pectore et in eo vnum anulum aureum cum j diamaunde"[75] (the prioress wears golden rings exceedingly costly with divers precious stones, and also girdles silvered and gilded over and silken veils . . . and has on her neck a long silken band, in English a lace, which hangs down upon her breast, and theron a golden ring with one diamond.) Naturally, moral turpitude was a much more serious charge against a prioress or an abbess than indulgence in rich clothes and delicacies, or even the throwing of lavish parties for her friends and relatives as some were in the habit of doing.

As we already know, most instances of misconduct in the nunnery came to light during episcopal visitations which were followed, whenever there were any serious accusations, by an investigation conducted by the bishop's own deputies. After a visit to the Priory of Redlingfield in Suffolk, for example, there was an inquiry into the conduct of the prioress, Isabel Hermyte, who confessed among other things, that "she had been alone with Thomas Langelond, bailiff, in private and suspicious places, such as a small hall with windows closed, "and sub heggerowes;" that no annual account had been rendered; that obits had been neglected; that goods had been alienated, and trees cut down and sold without knowledge or consent of the convent; and that she was not religious or honest in conversation."[76] A twelfth-century abbess of Amesbury "was accused of incontinence and her evil ways were followed by the nuns;"[77] around 1274 Pope Gregory X deposed Bishop Henry of Liège and accused him of taking a Benedictine abbess for his "public concubine," and of having "one (or two?) other abbesses and a nun . . . among his concubines."[78] In 1316, Alice de Chilterne, prioress of Whitehall "stood publicly charged with the crime of incontinence with John de Passelewe, chaplain,"[79] and during an episcopal visit in 1396 the nuns of Arden, Yorkshire, said that their prioress "was defamed with a certain John Beaver, a married man, that they had slept together in a house at night, and that on one occasion they lay alone together within the priory, in the prioress's chamber."[80] As we review the list of names of certain abbesses and prioresses and their crimes, we cannot help but wonder what effect such reprobate behavior had on the community in their charge. According to the records, the bad example set by their leader would not only confer a bad name on that particular nunnery, but often led some sisters to violate their own sacred vows in emulation of the head of the house. Thus, Joan Tates, a nun of Redlingfield, upon "being questioned as to incontinence, [she] said that it was provoked by the bad example of the prioress."[81]

Confronted with so many abuses in the convent, the church authorities searching for an answer to the seemingly unsolvable problem appear to have coincided throughout the centuries that the "radix malorum" of conventual misconduct was the nuns' habit of wandering outside the cloister: "It would have been no unusual circumstance . . . to meet a sister of Canyngton or Buckland in the busy streets of Taunton or Bridgwater. . . . Actually some of the sisters . . . were accustomed to wander through the streets and lanes of Ivelcestre, . . . and sometimes, which was worse, did without scruple or fear enter into the houses of secular and suspected persons, . . . to the scandal of holy religion and the manifest peril of their own souls."[82] Nuns allowed to leave the convent on justifiable errands often stayed out longer than their permission granted and spent too much time engaged in worldly pursuits. On a 1303 visit to Greenfield Priory, for example, Bishop Dalderby heard that the prioress "had been absent from the house for two years,"[83] while Dame Isabel Morgan, Prioress of Ramsey Abbey in the early thirteenth century, complains that "the nuns frequent taverns, and continually go into town without leave," so she asks the bishop "that they may not go outside the monastery without her leave."[84]

In vain did the Church exhaust her power and resources to keep its daughters within the cloister. Evidently those who had chosen a life of seclusion in the nunnery out of a true spiritual vocation needed no encouragement to persevere in their vow of claustration. It was the others, however, for whom the lure of the world seems to have been too strong, who disregarded episcopal injunctions through the centuries to remain loyal to the rule of enclosure. The nuns' motives for abandoning the quiet of the convent for the bustle of the outside world were valid most of the time. The account rolls of their houses, for example, show some of them out collecting tithes from farmers who forgot to pay or rents from tenants who were remiss, while others went to market to buy what their land did not produce or to sell what it did. The conventual records and the bishops' visitations' reports note that the nuns went on visits to sick relatives, business trips, and pilgrimages; sometimes they went to weddings, christenings, and funerals, all of which meant renewing those ties with the world that many seemed to find difficult to break.

Because the need to secure an income for the community and to buy and provide for it was so pressing, the enforcement of enclosure became extremely complicated. The sisters were constantly requesting permission to leave the convent, and although this was usually granted with many restrictions, it was up to each individual nun to abide by them. In January of 1320, Bishop Stapeldon sent a pastoral letter to the prioress and convent of Polslo, near Exeter, in which sundry regulations for the better government of the house are given. The following, setting up travel restrictions on visits, are evidence of one bishop's concern on this matter:

> That any religious who had leave to visit her friends in a certain place was not to go to any other without express permission; that any Nun who should take refreshment in Exeter, or elsewhere, should return the same day, or the day following at the very furthest, together with her companion, and that the Chaplain, or some esquire of good name and fame, should be appointed by the Prioress as their escort; that, while in Exeter, they were not to wander from house to house, to the dishonour of their estate and

religious profession; that, should the family or friends whom the Nun was to visit reside at a greater distance, the duration of absence was to be regulated by the circumstances of the case and the command of the Prioress; and that, in the event of any disobedience to this rule, the punishment should follow of enclosure for two years within the outer gate of the Priory.[85]

Inevitably, the fear that wandering in towns or spending too much time at friends' or relatives' houses would lead to greater abuses elicited from the bishops countless injunctions, the tenor of which whether in English or Latin was always the same: "It is forbidden to eat, drink or spend the night in the town of Ramsey;" "No nun is to go out except in staid company, nor is she to stay with secular folk beyond three days;"[86] "volumus et ordinamus quod nulla monialis vel soror monasterii claustrum exeat sine licencia priorisse"[87] (we wish and ordain that no sister of the monastery leave the cloister without permission from the prioress).

Sometimes, the bishops' worst fears were confirmed; in 1442, for example, a nun of Catesby Priory

> pernoctauit apud fratres Augustinianos Northamptonie et ibidem cum ipsis saltauit et citherauit vsque mediam noctem, et nocte sequenti pernoctauit cum fratribus predicatoribus Northamptonie consimiliter citherisando et saltando, etc.[88]

> (did pass the night with the Austin friars at Northampton and did dance and play the lute with them in the same place until midnight, and on the night following she passed the night with the friars preachers at Northampton, luting, and dancing in like manner.)

By the end of the thirteenth century the situation had deteriorated to such a degree despite previous papal fulminations, that in 1298 Pope Boniface VIII proclaimed his famous statute on monastic claustration based on the sixty-sixth chapter of the Benedictine Rule. The text of the bull was widely quoted throughout the next two hundred years as a deterrent to monastic wandering, specifically the section beginning:

> Periculoso et detestabili quarundam monialium statui que honestatis laxatis abenis et monachali modestia sexusque verecundia

impudenter abjectis extra sua monasteria nonnunquam per habitacula secularium personarum discurrunt et frequenter infra
eadem monasteria personas suspectas admittunt in illius cui suam
integritatem voluntate spontanea devoverunt grave offensam religionis opprobrium et scandalum plurimorum proinde sa-
lubriter cupientes presenti constitucione irrefragabiliter valitura
sanccimus universas et singulas moniales presentes atque futuras
cuiuscumque sint religionis vel ordinis in quibuscunque mundi
partibus existentes sub perpetua in suis monasteriis debere de
cetero permanere clausura ita quod nulli earum religionem tacite
vel expresse professe sit vel esse valeat quacumque racione vel
causa, nisi forte tanto et tali morbo evidenter earum aliquam
laborare constaret quod non posset cum aliis absque gravi pe-
riculo seu scandalo in simul commorari, monasteria ipsa deinceps
egrediendi facultas nulli aliquatenus inhoneste persone nec et
honeste, nisi racionabilis et manifesta causa existat ac de illius ad
quem pertinuerit speciali licencia, ingressus vel accessus pateat ad
easdem ut sic a publicis et mundanis conspectibus separate om-
nino Deo servire valeant liberius et laciviendi oportunitate su-
blata eidem corda sua et corpora in omni sanctimonia diligencius
custodire.[89]

(Desiring to provide for the perilous and detestable state of
certain nuns, who, having slackened the reins of decency and
having shamelessly cast aside the modesty of their order and of
their sex, sometimes gad about outside their monasteries in the
dwellings of secular persons, and frequently admit suspected
persons within the same monasteries, to the grave offence of
Him to Whom they have, of their own will, vowed their innocence, to the opprobrium of religion and to the scandal of very
many persons; we by the present constitution, which shall be
irrefragably valid, decree with healthful intent that all and sundry
nuns, present and future, to whatever order they belong and in
whatever part of the world, shall henceforth remain perpetually
enclosed within their monasteries; so that no nun tacitly or
expressly professed in religion shall henceforth have or be able to
have the power of going out of those monasteries for whatsoever
reason or cause, unless perchance any be found manifestly suffering from a disease so great and of such a nature that she cannot,
without grave danger or scandal, live together with others; and
to no dishonest or even honest person shall entry or access be
given by them, unless for a reasonable and manifest cause and by
a special licence from the person to whom [the granting of such a

licence] pertains; that so, altogether withdrawn from public and mundane sights, they may serve God more freely and, all opportunity for wantonness being removed, they may more diligently preserve for Him in all holiness their souls and their bodies.)

The injunction that nuns should remain within their convents which was repeated through the following centuries may actually be seen as the most powerful indication of its failure. If to keep the nuns inside the nunnery, tightly enclosed in what the Church saw as their safe cocoon had become almost impossible by the fourteenth century, to shut out the world entirely was even harder, as it kept intruding in the form of a multitude of visitors—"the grete and contynuelle accesse and recourse of seculere and regulere persones."[90] Their presence provided for the nuns a constant reminder of the life they had left or had perhaps been made to leave behind. In an attempt to avoid this, the episcopal injunctions against conventual visitors mingling with the nuns in the dorter (the sisters' dormitory) ranged from mild admonitions—"inter sorores autem mulieres jacere nolumus seculares"[91] (we do not want secular women to lie among the nuns)—to vivid threats of excommunication against transgressors:

> Because of the continual soujourn of seculars, we find the tranquillity of the nuns to be much disturbed and scandals to arise in your monastery, ordered (on pain of excommunication and deposition of the Abbess, Prioress, and greater officials of the Convent, if they be found disobedient or negligent in this), that secular women, married and single ("coniugatas et solutas"), staying there, from the time of the receipt of the presents, shall be wholly removed from the Abbey without hope of return.[92]

All the efforts, however, seem to have been in vain, and again the evidence provided by the episcopal visitation records, as well as numerous entries in other historical documents, shows that the stream of noble visitors remained unabated during the twelfth, thirteenth and fourteenth centuries, eliciting complaints from some of the less worldly sisters. In 1363, for instance, the Augustinian canoness of Campsey in Norwich asked to be allowed to transfer to another monastery "in order to escape the number of nobles coming to Campesse,"[93] and in 1375 "Beatrice, the prioress, and the majority of the nuns of the Benedictine monastery of North Berwick . . . [were] much molested by the neighbourhood and visits of nobles and other secular persons."[94] Since many of the nuns came from the upper class, they had friends about the Court who could, under various pretexts, obtain leave to visit and lodge in the convents for a while. The fourteenth-century *Calendar of Papal Letters* records a large number of "indults" granted to such noble ladies and gentlemen to enter different religious houses,[95] where their visits not only burdened the meager resources of the nunnery but must have played havoc with conventual discipline as well. This was probably what happened in October 1391, for example, when Queen Anne was given "indult to enter as often as she pleased with a suite of fifty honest persons of either sex, any monastery of enclosed religious women and to eat and drink therein."[96] It was, somehow, unavoidable that the visitors should exert a pernicious influence on the nuns' morale, as they brought unbearably close to them the temptations of a life which, for their own individual reasons the women had vowed—or been forced—to renounce. Furthermore, even more harmful to the physical and spiritual peace of the cloister than the high-living style of such guests as earls and countesses or various members of the royal family was the presence in the nunnery of their train of assorted followers. At Nunburnholme Priory, for example, scandal having arisen from the frequent gossiping between certain nuns and the secular persons who accompanied the noble visitors, both men and women, "the prioress and sub-prioress were ordered by the Archbishop not to allow such access to the nuns."[97] In an attempt to curb the possible abuses involved in entertaining noble company, the bishops continually issued new injunctions or refurbished old rules that had been allowed to expire. One of these was the 1295 Cistercian statute which established that nuns were forbidden to eat with secular guests "on account of the perils which beset cloistered persons if they live among the gentiles, and lest their good manners be corrupted by evil communication."[98] It was, perhaps, a mild reproof masking the extreme fear of the much more serious consequences of such an intimacy.

One thirteenth-century bishop who was absolutely adamant about not allowing any secular women to lodge in the nunnery[99] was Johannis Peckham, whose indefatigable zeal produced several volumes of injunctions on monastic conduct; also one of the *Praecepta Recte Vivendi* of the twelfth-century bishop Robertus de Arbrisello steadfastly maintains that "ut nullus extraneus recipiatur in conventum fratrum absque licencia abbattissae"[100] (that no outside person be received into the convent without permission from the abbess). As in the case of the wandering nuns, however, the restrictions and the punishment imposed on the congregation for receiving visitors did not stop the practice, and as Theobald lamented before the Council of Constance in 1417, the convents were frequented "not without very great scandal, as if they were public places, even more than the theatres, and even by great folk."[101] Another circumstance revealed by the records is that even if the visitors were not allowed to sleep in the dorter or enter the inner cloisters, the nuns apparently found a way to enjoy a little gossip with them by occasionally slipping out to the guest house. During Alnwick's visitation of Heynings in 1440, sister Alice Leget reported to him "quod moniales exercent potaciones serotinas in ly gestchaumbre eciam post completorium, potissime cum earum amici ad eas declinauerint" (that the nuns do hold drinkings of evening in the guestchamber even after compline, especially when their friends come to visit them). While visiting Catesby Priory in 1422, sister Margaret Wavere complained to the bishop "quod seculares habent frequentem accessum ad cameras monialium infra claustrum et ibi fiunt colloquia et solacia [priorissa] ignorante" (that secular folk have often recourse to the nuns' chambers within the cloister, and talkings and junketings take place there without knowledge of [the prioress).[102] This situation and others like it naturally brought on more injunctions from the bishops, all along the lines of Alnwick's to the nuns of Heynings Priory in 1440:

> For as muche as we founde [that] there are vsede late drynkynges and talkyng by nunnes as wele wythe yn as wythe owte the cloystere wythe seculeres, where thu[rgh] som late ryse to matynes and some come not at thayme, expressely agayns the rule of your ordere, we charge you[w and] yche oon singulere that fro this day forthe ye neyther vse spekyng ne drynkyng in no place aftere complyne, but [that] after collacyone and complyne sayde ych oon of yow go wythe owte lengere tarying to the dormytorye to your rest[e.][103]

What really concerned the ecclesiastical authorities, however, was not so much to keep the visitors out of the convent, since this seemed to have become a losing battle, but to keep them out of certain parts of the house and during certain hours. Thus, regulations were passed forbidding any secular person from entering after sunset or curfew, while at the same time the most elaborate arrangements were made to lock and unlock the doors of specific times. At Esholt and Sinningthwaite, for instance, Archbishop Lee commanded that the prioress should furnish enough locks and keys for the convent doors, "incontinent after recept of thies injunctions and that the same doores surely be lockid every nyght incontinent as complane is doone, and not to be unlocked in wynter season to vij of the clock in the mornyng and in sommer vnto vj of the clock in the mornyng; and that the prioresse kepe the keyes of the same doores, or committ the custodie of them to such a discrete and religious suster, that no fault nor negligence may be imputed to the prioresse, as she will avoyde punyshment due for the same."[104] After a visit to Catesby Priory in 1442, one of Bishop Alnwick's injunctions to the prioress was "that in dwe tyme, specyally whan complyne is saide, ye do close and sperre alle the dorres of your kyrke and cloystere and dortour, and kepe the keyes of thise dorres to your selfe vnto dwe tyme on the next morne, so that in the meen tyme no man ne womman come yn ne go owte wythe owte your specyalle leve askede and had, and for a resonable cause."[105]

Sometimes the ordinances became so strict that the nuns must have felt like prisoners, locked in too early on summer evenings when nature was most appealing, but the wise bishops obviously knew how the warm air and the fragrance of the new flowers could affect the cloistered sisters and they would not relent. An example of such disciplinary action is the following injunction from 1441: "To prevent the Benedictine nuns (of Augsburg) from receiving friends in their convent and from going out as freely as though they had not been cloistered, the iron railings had to be replaced by walls, and then the walls had to be built higher and guarded by town soldiers."[106]

No matter what measures were adopted, though, it seems to have been almost impossible to keep the world from penetrating the cloister; therefore, attempts were made through regulations to prevent, at least, any secret communication between nuns and secular persons in secluded corners and passages or through darkened windows. Such a plan naturally involved blocking up certain doors which could give access to undesirable visitors and with this purpose,

Dean Kentwode of St. Helens enjoined the prioress and convent there,

> that noone of yow speke, ne comone with no seculere persone; ne sende ne receyve letteres myssyves or geftes of any seculere persone, with oute lycence of the prioresse: and that there be an other of yowre sustres present, assigned be the prioresse to here and recorde the honeste of bothe partyes, in suche commynication; and such letteres or geftes sent or receyvyd, may turne into honeste and wurchepe, and none into velanye, ne disclaundered of yowre honeste and religione.[107]

Once visitors were admitted to the nunnery, the rules established that before speaking with them the nuns had to request permission from the head of the house, and they could only engage in conversation with them in the locutorium or parlor or perhaps in the abbess's hall. Most important of all, at least one other nun of "sound character" or even two had to be present during the meeting and, furthermore, the conversations should not last too long. Archbishop Peckham admonished the sisters of Romsey Abbey:

> Nec alicui moniali liceat colloquia cum quocunque homine protelare, nisi vel in locutorio vel in latere ecclesiae versus claustrum. Et ut omnis suspicio sustollatur imposterum, ordinamus ut quaecunque monialis cum quocunque homine locutura praeter casum confessionis, secum habeat duas socias colloquium audituras ut vel aedificentur verbis utilibus si tractentur, vel verba mala impediant ne corrumpant mala eloquia bonos mores.[108]

> (To hold converse with any man save either in the parlour or in the side of the church next the cloister. An in order that all suspicion may henceforth be removed, we order that any nun about to speak with any man, save in the matter of confession, have with her two companions to hear her conversation, in order that they may either be edified by useful words, if these are forthcoming, or hinder evil words, lest evil communications corrupt good manners.)

Even more disruptive to the nuns' peace of mind than the temporary contact with the visitors, however, must have been the constant presence in their midst of the secular boarders and corrodians[109] who lived in the nunnery. Sometimes the ladies residing there, whether permanently or for a brief period of time, brought their servants or gentlewomen with them. In 1328 Lady Margery Treverbyn went to Canonsleigh as a boarder accompanied by a "certain priest, a squire and a damsel,"[110] and in 1398 the widow of the Earl of Warwick had an indult from the Pope to live at the Minoresses Without Algate "with three matrons as long as she pleased."[111] A thirteenth- and fourteenth-century list of boarders at Carrow Priory which mentions a number of ladies and their servants, also includes the names of several men, a circumstance that was rather unusual but quite possible as the much publicized case of the Paston family proves. When Margery Paston fell in love with her brother's bailiff, Richard Calle, and against her family's wishes became engaged to him, her mother shut her out of the Paston home. The bishop then seems to have placed her in the same nunnery where Richard was staying because Margery's brother John says about him in a subsequent letter: "As to his abiding it is in Blakborrow nunnery a little fro Lynn and our unhappy sister's also."[112]

The boarders' presence in the convent must have been very disrupting not just because they were there all the time, but also because, on occasion, they seemed to assert themselves through somewhat eccentric behavior. Lady Augley, for instance, a lodger at Langley, had an array of dogs living with her at the priory, and the beset prioress complained to Bishop Alnwick on a visitation that,

> domina de Audeley ibidem perhendinans habet magnam multitudinem canum, in tantum quod cum venerit ad ecclesiam sequuntur eam xij canes, qui faciunt magnum strepitum in ecclesia, impediendo psallentes, et moniales ex hoc redduntur attonite.[113]

> (Lady Audley has a great abundance of dogs, insomuch that whenever she comes to church there follow her twelve dogs, who make a great uproar in church, hindering them in their psalmody and the nuns hereby are made terrified.)

Another lady, Margaret Ingoldesby, a boarder at Legbourne was accused of sleeping in the dorter with the nuns, "adducens secum volucres, per quorum strepitum silencium rumpitur et quies monialium turbatur"[114] (bringing with her birds, by whose jargoning silence is broken and the rest of the nuns is disturbed). It is rather amusing to imagine the bleary-eyed sisters trying to stay awake at prime after a sleepless night filled with cackling and cawing! Not all the disturbances caused by secular boarders were quite as innocent, though, and at times they seemed to have been the reason for grave scandal, particularly in the case of male boarders. During a 1478 episcopal visit to Easebourne, it was proved that "a certain Sir John Senoke much frequented the priory or house, so that during some weeks he passed the night and lay within the priory or monastery every night, and was the cause . . . of the ruin of two nuns."[115] It is obvious that the episcopal injunctions and prohibitions failed to eliminate an extremely serious problem because the nuns refused to cooperate, since they. could not afford to lose the money they received from their boarders.

The reason why such an income was probably so important to the nunneries generally stemmed from economic circumstances beyond their control. Sometimes, however, they found themselves in financial straits through mismanagement of conventual funds, a situation that also affected the men's houses and which could not have enhanced life in the cloister. Such was the case, for instance, of the nunnery of Whitehall, Ilchester, "reduced to beggary" after the regime of an unscrupulous prioress and two wardens at the beginning of the fourteenth century,[116] and of the abbeys of Romsey and St. Mary's where, in 1351, Bishop Edyndon of Winchester had to come to their aid. At the time, the nuns, "overwhelmed with poverty, . . . were brought to the necessity of secret begging."[117] Another extreme case was that of the nuns of Cheshunt Priory, who had previously appealed to Edward III for assistance and who "represented their extreme want to him again in 1367, saying that they had often had to beg in the highways,"[118] a practice not only demeaning for the sisters, but one which must have increased the danger of their breaking their already tenuously held claustration vows. Paradoxically, therefore, poverty was one more deterrent to maintaining the celibate ideal of the monastic life intact in an environment actually designed precisely with the purpose of shunning all worldly comforts and possessions.

The historical evidence, then, leaves very little doubt that, as we approach the end of the Middle Ages, everything that had conspired to make the monastic ideal hard to attain at the beginning of Christianity was still troubling the religious life. Intended originally as

Fontenay, Cloister. Cistercian Abbey, twelfth century. Burgundy, Northwest of Dijon. Photo courtesy of Jet Prendeville.

enclaves of peace and devotion during one of the most turbulent periods of mankind, the medieval convents as well as the Church were torn by inner struggles reflecting the turmoil of the times. The same social, political, and economic forces at work in society affected life in the nunnery, casting together the young and the old, the saintly and the sinful. Although at times it may seem that the latter were a majority, it must be remembered that only incidents of bad behavior are signaled out in the visitation reports. However, since the actions of the truly dedicated sisters are taken for granted and nothing is said about them officially, the reader may feel inclined to concur with a historian's remark, "happy the nunnery that has no history."[119]

Moral and Satirical Literature

"La piours amors c'est de nonnains."
Thirteenth-century proverb[1]

(A nun's love is the worst kind of love.)

*H*AVING ESTABLISHED the historical presence of the wayward nun in the convents of the Middle Ages, we turn now to her literary presence in the works of certain moralistic and satiric writers of the twelfth through the fifteenth centuries. We continue, thus, tracing a pattern of the attitudes toward the profligate nun leading up to the Archpriest of Hita's and Chaucer's own nuns. The existence of dishonest sisters in the nunnery is confirmed by the work of the moralists, because their aim is precisely to single them out as examples of reprehensible conduct among the religious. The satirists, on the other hand, also with an ideal in mind, promote it through mockery of improper behavior in the nunnery. Satire was a method that had become very popular by the end of the twelfth century, and medieval writers knew only too well how to use it: overtly to provoke laughter and subtly to condemn what they saw as immoral and corrupt in the life of the Church. Furthermore, the satirical pieces serve a double purpose; they not only provide evidence of the diffusion of the literary theme of the wayward nun, but also very appropriately lead the way to the topic in our last chapter, the ambiguous portraits of Doña Garoza and Madame Eglentyne.

As we review the work of the moralist and the satirist who wrote about profligate nuns we find that, whether attacked by one or mocked by the other, the wayward nun of the Middle Ages comes to life in the complaint and the parody as a type of "femme fatale," and her conduct and her "amors" are alternately extolled and condemned depending on the writer's point of view. It is true that both the moralist and the jongleur tell the same tale, but while the purpose of the latter is to provoke laughter, the moralist is interested in drawing edifying conclusions; it is not the story that matters to him but the ideas it allows him to set forth. Thus, in tones that range from mere animosity to deadly wrath, the moralist conducts his campaign against

> des faulx religieux
> Des félons et malicieux
> Qui l'habit en veullent vestir
> Mais leur cueurs ne veullent matir.[2]

> false, felonious nuns
> Malicious ones who would the habit wear
> But never would subdue their evil hearts.

The tirades vary in length and virulence, although they generally agree that it is the ease with which some nuns are allowed to come and go, more often and more freely than they should, that is responsible for the licentiousness of their morals. Among the fiercest castigators of ecclesiastical sins, specifically those attributed to women, are some of the best-known church figures in the last four centuries of the Middle Ages, a period in which moral turpitude among the religiously professed stood side by side with the most pristine examples of apostolic purity. In the practically endless register of monastic offenders, however, the nuns seem to have occupied a prominent position. Although in the misogynistic world of the Middle Ages the mere fact of their sex already made them prey to the worst possible faults—"more envious then a sarpent; more malysceous than a tyrante; and more deceytfulle then the devylle"[3]—their often loose behavior was censured harshly. Because of the vastness of the material in this chapter it becomes necessary to approach it from a somewhat unorthodox point of view. Rather than a more conventional chronological sequence, the guiding principle for the order of the works quoted is the degree of indignation or animosity evidenced by the authors in their outlook. This is precisely what sets the tone for the Archpriest of Hita's and Chaucer's approach to their nuns.

To the men and women directly involved in the religious life as

well as to the lay moralists of the period, the alleged misconduct in
the nunnery was only one symptom of the vice and corruption
threatening to destroy the old monastic order. The pamphlet, the
poem, and the pulpit all carry the same message: condemnation of
breaches in conventual discipline running from the trivial to the
infamous, from lateness at chapel to unchastity. In tirades that display
their feelings of either anger, despair, or disgust a number of high-
minded ecclesiastics lash out at those wicked sisters who break their
sacred vow and abandon the love of the Heavenly Spouse to embrace
the world instead. One of the most acerbic castigators of monachal
iniquity is St. Catherine of Siena who thinks nuns lead a wanton life,
engaging in sexual relations with the monks assigned to the nunnery
as spiritual advisors:

> Non sta molto colorato col colore della devozione; anco subbito
> appariscono e' frutti delle loro devozioni: prima si veggono e'
> fiori puzzolenti de' disonesti pensieri con le foglie corrotte delle
> parole, e con miserabili modi compiono e' desidèri loro. E' frutti
> che se ne vegono, bene lo sai tu che n'ai veduti, che sonno e'
> figliuoli.[4]

> (It does not long maintain this colour of devotion; therefore it is
> not long before their devotions bear fruit. First appear the stink-
> ing flowers of unhonest thoughts, with the rotten leaves of
> words; and in miserable fashion they fulfill their lusts; and the
> fruits which appear are such as I know well you have seen,
> children to wit.)

Equally caustic in his comments is the early fifteenth-century
churchman and chancellor of the University of Paris, Johannes Ger-
son, who urges those either ignorant of the situation, or pretending
to be, to open their eyes and see whether the convents had become
"brothels of harlots." Johann Nider, the fifteenth-century Dominican
prior of Basel observes with the bitterness of a prelate dealing with a
painful subject that "sometimes nuns prostitute themselves abominably," while in the same century, Dionysius the Carthusian laments:
"How many sins and scandals have arisen and do constantly arise
from the fact that nuns go forth from their cloister and visit secular
folk, and that they permit men to enter their cloisters and converse
with them." In anguish, he then exclaims: "Would that this were not

proved by their swelling wombs, and the proofs [of their sin] that walk about on the earth!"[5] In fourteenth-century Spain, observing life with a keen eye, Juan Ruiz, Archpriest of Hita is a harsh critic of dissolute morality among the religious, both men and women, particularly the latter, whom he accuses of infinite wiles. In turn this leads to the bitter remark "religiosa non casta es podrida toronja"[6] (an unchaste nun is worse than rotten fruit).

Somewhat less severe in his criticism of monachal misconduct is the fourteenth-century churchman Giraldus Cambrensis. Giraldus, a Welsh archdeacon whose work evidences a stern attitude toward any form of corruption whether political, ecclesiastical, or royal shows considerable moderation in his denunciations of the alleged profligacy of religious women. In his *Gemma Ecclesiastica* there are many edifying stories of monks, priests, and nuns who were sometimes able to resist temptation or were punished for succumbing to it, but none displays the extreme bitterness evident in some other writers.[7] Another eminent churchman, the thirteenth-century Caesarius of Heisterbach, author of the *Dialogus Miraculorum,* a collection of religious miracles from various sources, is not a very acrimonious critic either. In most of the tales in the *Dialogus* involving a nun she either repents and is forgiven, or is "cured" of her lust through reasonable means as in the example that follows. There was once a young sister in a community in England over which a holy man presided:

> In cuius contemplatione iuvencula quaedam illius congregationis adeo coepit tentari, et tam gravissime stimulis carnis agitari, ut verecundia postposita passionem suam illi aperiret.

> (By often gazing upon him, [the young nun] began to be so tempted that at last she put away all modesty and opened to him her passion.)

He tried in vain to dissuade her with reminders of her monastic vow until in the end he agreed to meet her, only to show her that the body she coveted was "vermibus corrosum, cilicio attritum, scabiosum atque nigerrimum illi ostendens"[8] (eaten with vermin, scarred with the hair shirt, covered with sores and black with grime). Upon seeing this, she no longer felt any desire for the monk and threw herself at his feet asking for forgiveness.

Even less fulminating in his comments regarding nuns than Giraldus or Caesarius is a certain thirteenth-century monk of Cluny called Guiot de Provins, author of the *Bible Guiot,* written sometime between 1204 and 1224. Although the first four lines proclaim that the Bible will be an outright denunciation of "dou siecle puant et orrible . . . / Por poindre et por aguilloner / Et por grant essample doner"9 (the fetid and horrible world . . . to sting and prod and set a good example), Guiot's object seems to have been to amuse rather than to edify his courtly audience, and he comes across throughout the book as "gossipy rather than thunderous, and more grumbling than indignant."10 He does, however, speak of certain monks and nuns, weak and infirm and with mishapen bodies, who keep with them their ill-begotten offspring merely to use them as lures for the alms-giving folk:

> Moines retraiz, Noneins retraites
> Ont trop et contraiz et contraites:
>
> . .   .   .
> S'il feissent contraïraz,
> Que des enfanz ont-il assez;
> Touz li païs en est pueplez.11

(Cloistered monks, cloistered nuns, have mishapen bodies plenty: they pretend to be crippled and have lots of children; the entire country is populated by them.)

"Ont les Nonains et li colon: / Ne tienent pas lor maison nete,"12 (nuns are like pigeons: they keep an untidy house), he says later on, possibly referring to affairs of the heart and not of the home:

> Je n'aim pas où mostier la plume
> Ce colomp, por l'orde costume,
> Ne poil de fame rooingnie,
> Se la costume n'est changie
> Dont l'ame est en si grant dotance:
> Por la mauvaise acoustumance
> Rent-en le droit qui en aquite,
> Ainz encombre bien est maudite,
> Que de ce que rendent encombre,
> Nuz forz nombriers n'en set le nombre,

Por ce que c'est rente qui trouble,
Qant en la tient et ele double.[13]

(I like neither the place where, ordinarily, this pigeon shows its
feathers, nor the woman with clipped hair; if the custom that
endangers the soul does not change: by that wicked custom[?]
and the nuns are not made to adopt once more the habit they
have left, pregnant and despised are so many that we lose count,
because it is the wandering that turns one into two.)

There were certain moralists who were able to strike a position
midway between unrestrained bitterness and only light concern;
among them is Gilles li Muisis, abbot of St. Martin-de-Tournai, who
began to record around 1350 his reflections on the life and morals of
the time in a "registre." In it he observes that in earlier times religious
houses were under very strict rules but that now things have deteriorated entirely. As to the nunneries and their inmates, in a long section
entitled *Les Maintiens des nonnains*,[14] li Muisis comments that the
permissiveness present in the life of some religious women is due to
the ease with which they are allowed to leave their convent and
wander abroad:

je le voie aler souvent, dont moult m'anoie;
Se plus closes estoient, moult joyans en seroi.
. . . .
Et s'en osteroit-on un grandment de diffames. (pp. 213–14)

(I see them go out often, something which greatly displeases me;
if they stayed cloistered more, I would be very pleased. Many
scandals could be avoided.)

Nowadays, he says, the "très douches nonnains" (the very sweet
nuns) behave like noble ladies in the world do and,

Ès maisons de nonnains aucun sont bien venut,
Et as gens festyer n'a nul règne tenut;
On y va volentiers et souvent et menut,
Mais mieuls son festyet jovène que li kenut. (p. 215)

(In the houses of the nuns everyone is welcome, and there is no restraint on entertaining men; they go willingly and often and eagerly, but the young are even more welcome than the old.)

This situation often leads to love affairs but, should they abandon the love of God for a man?—"Doit-on l'amour de Dieu pour un homme laissier?," asks li Muisis.

> Tel amant font samblant de tenir leur couvent,
> S'envoient messagiers et menut et souvent;
> Tost sont nonnains levées, s'elles sont en couvent,
> Car leurs coers leur volette comme coches dou vent.
>
> A ches messagiers prendent lettres ou tavelettes;
> Là dedens sont escriptes parolles d'amourettes.
> Hé! très-doulces nonnains, vous toutes qui chou faites,
> Wardés que ne perdés del honneur vos florettes.
>
> .   .   .   .
>
> Au jour d'ui ces nonnains voelent yestre moult cointes;
> Toutes sont loyemières, se font pluseurs accointes;
> Se fait-on des amours des ordenances maintes:
> Hélas! jadis estoient des nonnains pluseurs saintes. (p. 216)

(These lovers pretend to be faithful to their vows, they send one another messages eagerly and often; the nuns rise early if they are at the convent, for their hearts spin like weathercocks in the wind. From the messengers they take letters or notes and there are words of love written on them. Ah! sweet nuns, all of you who do this, beware, lest you lose the flower of your honor. . . . Today, the nuns want to be worldly; they love easily and make themselves available; they turn their love affairs into a career: Alas! formerly the nuns were saintly.)

A little later, li Muisis continues,

> Dames religieuses, blankes, noires et toutes,
> Vous donnés à parler à ches gens et des doubtes;

> Car quand on voit de vous hors de vos lieus les routes,
> Li fol ont tantost dit: "Or rewardés ches gloutes!" (p. 217)

(Religious ladies, white, black and all, you cause these people to talk and to doubt; when they see you leaving your places, fools then say, "See now, these wantons!")

Li Muisis thinks that "the Pope would do well to enforce claustration"—[15] "Li Papes feroit bien, se tost les enclooit" (p. 218), and he also points out the importance of abbesses as role models for the nuns in their charge, some of whom were admitted to the convent much too young, a matter of grave concern to the Church authorities as we know:

> Abesses ont grand coulpes en ces désordenanches,
> Par leur congiés légiers et par leurs grans souffrances,
> Pour chou que convenir les laissent dès enfances:
> Nonnains en congiés prendre font moult de décevances. (p. 229)

(Abbesses are much to blame in these disorders, with their easy leaves and their great permisiveness, because they let them in as children: nuns on leave from their house are prone to give in to deceit.)[16]

It is useless, however, to preach to these reckless women:

> On poroit tous les jours à ches nonnains praiechier,
> Et poroit-on user une langhe d'achier,
> Anchois qu'on puet les cuers d'aucunes resachier
> Dou siècle: là se vont, quand pueient, enlachier. (pp. 230–31)

(One could preach to these nuns every day, even if one used a tongue of steel one could not wrench their hearts from the world: they will go there to immerse themselves in trouble whenever they can.)

However sparing, *Les Maintiens des nonnains* is by far the longest, most detailed literary denunciation of the misconduct of nuns in the Middle Ages that has come down to us; each stanza seems to corroborate different pieces of the historical evidence cited earlier on.[17] Written in a calm and dignified manner, this indictment by a French abbot stands as a superb example of the response evoked in some of the less irate moralists of the Church by the presumably wanton behavior of certain religious women.

Among the lay critics of unchaste behavior in the nunnery, the fifteenth-century Italian writer Tommaso Guardato, known as Masuccio il Salernitano is one of the most acerbic ones. As a careful observer of the contemporary scene, Masuccio spares no one in his bitter attack on the licentious practices of some religious men and women. In his book of stories, *Il Novellino,* he accuses certain nuns of unrestrained concupiscence and of bringing into the world "de gentils moinillons" (little monks) whom they often destroy while still unborn—"elles se font avorter" (they give themselves abortions). Aware that some people might doubt his word on such an abominable practice, Masuccio suggests that,

> si quelq'un était tenté de soutenir que cela n'est pas vrai, il n'a qu'a fouiller dans les cloaques des couvents de nonnes, et il y trouverá une quantité d'essements d'enfants, à peu près comme à Bethléem au temps d'Herode.[18]

> (If one were tempted to maintain that that is not true, he has only to search in the sewers of the nunneries, and there he will find many baby skeletons, the same as in Bethlehem during Herod's time.)

Considerably less gruesome and forbidding is a Frenchman writing around 1220, Hughes de Berzé, "seignor" of a manor and noble lord who "takes up his pen in all seriousness to offer a lesson to his world."[19] With the quiet gravity of a thinker whose spirit has already been tried by the crusades and the fall of emperors, de Berzé writes about the spiritual decadence of his time and the vice and corruption that gnaw at the moral order. His natural austerity, however, is tempered by a tolerance for the weaknesses of others, even though he shows little mercy for the sins of those who only pretend to be pure, such as some men and women of religion. A large number of them, it is true, "font bien" (behave well) but there are many others who deserve condemnation, like certain nuns, says Berzé, because

> eles ont mesons plusors
> Où l'en parole et fet d'amors
> Plus c'on ne fet de Dieu servir.[20]

(They have many convents where there are more words and acts
of love than of service to God.)

"Ecce sonat in aperto / vox clamantis in deserto"[21] (Behold,
there rings out clear / the voice of one crying in the desert), wrote St.
Thomas à Becket two hundred years before and the feeling is echoed
in the somber tones of Gower's *Vox Clamantis,* where man is the
microcosm that reflects the evils of society's three classes: knights,
peasants, and clergy. In a tone of gentle rebuke rather than anger,
Gower forgives women's trespasses:

> Si tamen in claustris fragiles errent mulieres,
> Non condigna viris culpa repugnat eis;
> Nam pes femineus nequit vt pes stare viriles.[22]

(If weak women in the cloister go astray, their unchastity does
not militate against them equally with men; for a woman's foot
cannot stand as steady as a man's can.)

Also religious women were often led astray by their own confessors,
a very old and deplorable situation: "Graviore autem sunt animadver-
sione plectendi, qui proprias filias spirituales, quas baptizaverint vel
semel ad confessionem admiserint, violaverint"[23] (to be punished
severely are those who have violated their own spiritual daughters, or
those they have once admitted to confession).

It is interesting—and distressing—to note that the problem still
existed in the sixteenth century, as evidenced by a story in one of
Erasmus's *Colloquies.* In it two nuns attending a dinner party behave
in the most indecorous manner, and their drinking and laughing
shocks the narrator: "Sed plane vereor, ne quid ea nocte patratum sit
parum virgineum, nisi me fallebant prooemia; lasciui, lusus, nutus et
suauia"[24] (But I'm very much afraid what was done that night was
hardly virginal, unless the preliminaries, the sexy games, nods and
kisses, deceived me). The interlocutor's comment further confirms
the bad reputation attributed to confessors: "Istam peruersitatem non
tam imputo virginibus, quam sacerdotibus earum curan gerentibus"[25]

(I don't so much blame the nuns for that waywardness as I do the priests in charge of them).

Gower again chastises reprobate nuns in a section of the *Mirour de l'omme,* a long poem dealing with the conflict between the Seven Deadly Sins and the Cardinal Virtues in society. This time the indictment is harsher than in the *Vox Clamantis,* however. Though promised to God only, says the poet-moralist, religious women often allow their flesh to lead them to luxury:

> Incest est fole de Nonneine,
> Celle est espouse au dieu demeine,
> Mais trop devient sa char salvage
> Qant son corps a luxure meine.[26]

(Incest is madness in a nun, she is the spouse of God himself, but her flesh becomes wild when her body is lustful.)

In the *Rimado de Palacio,* a fourteenth-century poem by the Spanish moralist Pero López de Ayala, nuns are accused of the same sin, also called here incest, the name applied to adultery among the religiously professed:[27]

> Es de muchas maneras éste, feo pecado:
> en él es adulterio que es de omne casado,
> otro es el incesto de monja de sagrado,
> del santo monesterio que Dios está fundado.[28]

(This is, in many ways, an ugly sin: one is adultery by a married man, the other is incest by a professed nun from the sacred monastery founded in God.)

The tone is considerably milder in a story in *El Libro del Caballero Cifar* by another Spanish author of the time. Here, a young girl whose father is upset at her knowledge of the world confesses having learnt everything "en los monasterios mal guardados" (the poorly guarded monasteries) where those nuns who can read and write are worse than the others because they do not need intermediaries or messengers to arrange gentlemen's and admirers' visits to them— "ciertas de éstas que saben escribir y leer no han menester medianeros que les procuren visitadores y veedores."[29]

A long fifteenth-century English poem entitled "Why I Can't Be a Nun"[30] also expostulates against those religious women who do not abide by the rules of chaste behavior enjoined by their order but, again, as in the case of Gower and the two Spanish poets, the author merely expresses mild reproach:

> And a nother lady was there wonnying
> That hyȝt dame loue vn-ordynate,
> In that place bothe erly and late
> Dame lust, dame wantowne, and dame nyce,
> They ware so there enhabyted, . . .
> . . . few token hede to goddys servyse.
> Dame chastyte, I dare welle say,
> In that couent had lytelle chere,
>
> .   .   .   .
> Sche was so lytelle beloved there.
>
> .   .   .   .
> Such bene the nunnes in euery warde,
> As for the most part, I say not alle,
>
> .   .   .   .
> For sum bene devowte, holy and towarde
> And holden the ryȝt way to blysse;
> And sum bene feble, lewde, and frowarde,
> Now God amend that ys amys! (ll.233–318)

(And another lady was living there, called Dame Excess, in that place, both early and late, Dame Lust, Dame Wanton, and Wantonness herself lived there, . . . few paid attention to God's service. Dame Chastity, I dare say, in that convent had very little joy, . . . she was loved so little there . . . Thus are the nuns in every word, as for the most part, I do not say all of them . . . because some are devout, holy, and demure and stay on the right path to bliss; and some are weak, lewd, and wicked, now may God amend what is wrong!)

The poem is generally attributed to a woman because it concerns a woman's experiences and seems to have been written by someone not attached to a nunnery, but with precise knowledge of the religious life. It is actually an adaptation of the legend of the "Ghostly Abbey," a popular medieval literary device whereby a religious house is peopled with personified virtues and vices. In the case of "Why I Can't Be a Nun," though, those living in the convent are mostly vices.

"Paradise" (predella panel). Giovanni di Paolo (Giovanni di Paolo di Grazia) (Italian, born c. 1403, died 1482–83). Tempera and gold on canvas, transferred from wood. 06.1046. Courtesy, The Metropolitan Museum of Art, Rogers Fund, 1906.

Life in the nunnery, then, as reflected in some of the moralistic literature of the Middle Ages was far removed from the ideal that had inspired the great monastics centuries before. Whatever motives they might have had for abandoning their sacred vow of chastity, the nuns who strayed usually come across as wicked and debauched in the most accusing portraits or as merely dishonest and weak in the mildest. The tainted virtue of certain religious women is made the rallying cry for all those who would wish to see the Church proud of every one of its children once again.

There is another group of works, written in its entirety by churchmen filled with consternation at the ruinous moral condition prevalent in so many convents, one more symptom of what Walter de Chatillon saw as a time when

> Iacet ordo clericalis
> in respectu laicalis,
> Sponsa Christi fit mercalis.[31]

(The ecclesiastical order lay lower than the laic, and Christ's bride was for sale.)

These men's concern found expression in poems and manuals praising virginity and books or treatises in which nuns are either admonished or encouraged to keep their monastic vows intact. The fact that this kind of literature existed, that religious men and women had to be reminded constantly of the vital importance of remaining pure both in thought and deed could be taken as further evidence of the need for such advice in religious communities presumed guilty of immoral conduct.

Although addressed to religious women in general and not intended specifically for those either accused or suspected of committing sins of the flesh, three thirteenth-century English poems in praise of heavenly love are examples of what could be called "roundabout" attempts to inspire young women to follow the path of religion. In *A Luue Ron, Of Clene Maydenhod,* and *Hali Meidenhad* earthly love is presented in varying degrees of undesirability from unfulfilling to abject. The tone in the three poems also covers a wide emotional range with each author revealing himself as tenderly solicitous, poetically inspired, or rudely vociferous in his approach.

The basic theme of *A Luue Ron,* written by the Franciscan Thomas Hales at the request of a nun—"A Mayde cristes me bit yorne / þat ich hire wurche a luue ron" (one of Christ's maidens entreated me to make a love song)—is that "þis worldes luue nys bute o res" (the love of this world is false and fickle). After a long section in which heavenly love is said to be the fairest and truest and the only one that may bring total happiness, the author tells us that Jesus has given religious women a treasure more valuable than silver or gold which they must guard with total devotion because, once lost, it can never be recovered: "þis ilke ston. þat ich þe nemne. / Mayden-hod icleoped is"[32] (this precious stone that I name is called virginity).

Of Clene Maydenhod is an anonymous poem dedicated to a maiden who must learn how to love Christ. Although poetically inferior to *A Luue Ron,* it also compares heavenly and earthly love much to the disadvantage of the latter, and it encourages young women who wish to devote their life to Christ to please Him above all else, by remaining chaste:

> ᵹif þou wolt þi lemmon qweme
> And to his brihte boure be brouᵹt,
> In Chastite kep þou þe clene.[33]

(If you want to become His mate and to His bright bower be brought, in Chastity remain pure.)

The last composition of this group, *Hali Meidenhad* is an alliterative homily seeking to persuade young women to enter the religious life by describing it as the sweetest of all, one which may be led in the most absolute spiritual ease: "Whatsoever God sees will be of advantage to þem. Nor may any worldly mishap bereave þem of þeir weal, for þey are rich and wealðy wiþin þe heart."[34] At the same time, to emphasize the undesirability of earthly love, and possibly by contrast to stress the perfect spiritual joy awaiting those who refrain from any carnal contact, the author offers a singularly twisted and brutal picture of matrimony and childbirth: "Now þou art wedded and from so high estate alighted so low: from being in likeness of angels, from being Jesus Christs leman, from being a lady in heaven (fallen) into þe filð of þe flesh, into þe manner of life of a beast. . . .

When it comeð to þat at last, þere is þe sore sorrowful anguish, þe strong piercing pang, þe comfortless ill, þe pain upon pain, þe miserable wail."[35]

Similar in tone to *Hali Meidenhad,* though not so violent in its portrayal of the sorrows of a woman who chooses the married state over virginity, a twelfth-century poem by the canon of Bayeux to a nun named Muriel also offers a bleak picture of conjugal life:[36]

ferrea iura subit mulier quo tempore nubit;
non vacat a poena, quia lex premit hanc aliena.

(A woman must submit to iron laws when she marries, and she
never lacks punishment, as she must abide by someone else's
rule.)

This is followed by some lavish praise of the religious life where peace
and security abound, and then a stern injunction to choose the enduring love of Christ instead of the temporary love of man: "elige quod
durat, nil te quod praeterit urat"[37] (choose that which is lasting,
nothing that passes by should disquiet you).

The pressing need to admonish religious women to value chastity above all else was already evident in the eighth century. In *De
Virginitate,* written for Abbess Hildelith and some of her nuns in the
monastery at Barking, Essex, Aldhelm starts by praising their virtues
and comparing them to bees who go about gathering knowledge
from different sources. He exhorts the nuns to chastity in the manner
of the Church Fathers and then urges them to beware of the sin of
luxury into which they may be led by "gaudiness of dress." "In
Apocalipsi," he quotes,

"Mulier illa amicta erat pallium purpureum et coccineum.
Fugiant castae virgines et pudicae incestarum cultus,
habitus impudicarum, lupanarum insignia, ornamenta
meretricum!"

("And the woman [i.e., the whore of Babylon] was clothed
round about with purple and scarlet" [Apoc. xvii, 4]. Let chaste
and modest women flee from the dress of adultresses, from the
appearance of strumpets, from the furbelows of prostitutes and
the trumperies of whores!)[38]

From a survey of works concerned with the good life that a
religious woman was supposed to lead but often did not, we proceed
now to other works whose authors are also troubled by reports of
dishonorable behavior in the nunnery. Their attack on monastic
corruption, however, is carried out in the satirical mode. "Occasionally they use the gay satire of the writer of fabliaux; their condemnation is an undercurrent beneath a lightly flowing stream, their

moral is implicit, they poke fun at the erring monk or nun, rather than chastise them."[39] This is the case of *The Land of Cokaygne,* for example, a thirteenth-century English poem quoted as follows in an Anglo-Irish version.[40] Cokaygne is an incomparable place:

> Vnder heuen n'is long iwisse.
> Of so mochil ioi and blisse.
> . . . .
> Þer beþ riuers gret and fine
> Of oile, melk, honi and wine.
> . . . .
> Al is solas and dedute.
> Þer is a wel fair abbei.
> Of white monkes and of grei.
> Þer be bowris and halles.
> Al of pasteiis beþ þe walles.
> Of fleis, of fisse, and rich met.[41]
> Þe likfullist þat man mai et.
> Fluren cakes beþ þe scingles alle.
> Of cherche. cloister. boure. and halle. (ll. 23–58)

(Under heaven there is no land like this, of so much joy and bliss. There are rivers great and fine, of oil, milk, honey and wine. . . . . All is solace and delight. There is a very beautiful abbey of white and grey monks. There are bowers and halls. The walls are all made of pastries, of flesh, of fish and rich meat, the most pleasing that man may eat. Flour cakes are the shingles of the church, the cloister, the bower, and the hall.)

There is a cloister made of glass where the monks live in absolute comfort, busy at times with prayer or else seeking diversion elsewhere. To make everything more pleasant even,

> Anoþer abbei is þerbi.
> For soth a gret fair nunnerie, (ll. 147–48)

(Another abbey is nearby, truly a great beautiful nunnery)

where all is just as splendid and there is an equal abundance of riches and of ease. Down the river of milk,

> Whan þe somer-is dai is hote.
> Þe ȝung nunnes takith a bote.
> And doth ham forth in that riuer.
> Bothe with oris and with stere.
> When hi beth fur from the abbei.
> Hi makith ham nakid for to plei.
> And lepith dune in-to the brimme.
> And doth ham sleilich for to swimme.
> Þe ȝung monkes þat hi seeth.
> Hi doth ham up, and forþ hi fleeþ.
> And commiþ to þe nunnes anon (ll. 151–61)

(When the summer day is hot, the young nuns take a boat and come forward on that river both with oars and by steering. When they are far from the abbey they strip themselves naked to play and jump down into the water and go slyly for a swim. The young monks that see them come up and run forward and go to the nuns at once.)

The same spirit of unmitigated mockery of monastic corruption is evident in a thirteenth-century French poem called *L'Ordre de Bel Eyse*.[42] In it all the vices associated with each religious order are combined into the fabulous "Order of Fair Ease,"[43] open to all fair ladies and gentlemen but which, like real life monastic orders does not accept anyone of low birth.

> en cet Ordre de Bel-Eyse
> Ne doit fossé ne mur aver,
> Ne nul autre destourber,
> Qe les freres à lur pleysyr
> Ne pussent à lor sueres venyr,
>
> . . . .
> Jà n'i avera ne lyn ne launge
> Entre eux, e si le peil y a,
> Jà pur ce ne remeindra. (p. 67)

(In this Order of Fair Ease there should be neither ditches nor walls, nor any other obstacles to keep the brothers from their pleasure, from coming to their sisters.[44] There will be neither linen nor lingerie between them and, thus, the flesh will not remain pure.)

After such a startling requisite there follows a long list of the orders from which that of Fair Ease will adopt certain traits, such as the Secular Canons—"que dames servent volenters" (who willingly serve ladies)—from whom the brethren must learn:

> Si est, sur eschumygement,
> Comaundé molt estroitement
> Que chescun frere à sa sorour
> Deit fere le giw d'amour
> Devant matines adescement
> E après matines ensement. (p. 71)

(Since it is commanded very strictly on pain of death that each brother must always play this game of love with his sister before matins and after matins in the same way.)

The next section of the poem shamefacedly insists on this activity by poking fun at the Grey Monks who are in the habit of going to matins without breeches—[45] "Quar à matines vont sans breys" (p. 72). With merry piquancy, the point is pursued even further by encouraging the brethren of the Order of Fair Ease to emulate this custom of the Grey Monks so as to be more at their ease:

> E quant il fount nul oreysoun,
> Si deyvent estre à genulloun,
> Pur aver greindre devocioun.
>   .   .   .   .
> . . . no sueres deyvent envers
> Gysyr e orer countre-mount,
> Par grant devocioun le fount. (p. 72)

(When they are at prayer, they must be on their knees for greater devotion. . . . Our sisters must, on the contrary, lie and pray on their backs.)

After more of the same coarse humor, the poem ends with the reminder that,

E c'est l'Ordre de Bel-Eyse,
Qe à plusours trobien pleyse! (p. 77)

(It is this Order of Fair Ease that pleases so many very well.)

The satirical perspective from which monastic abuses were often viewed is also found in a long thirteenth-century poem, the *Gesta Regum Anglorum*. Here, William of Malmesbury claims that William of Aquitaine founded at the castle of Niort an abbey of prostitutes—

Denique apud castellum quoddam, Niort, habitacula quaedam quasi monasteriola, construens, abbatiam pellicum ibi se positurum delirabat; nuncupatim illam et illam, quaecunque famosioris prostibuli esset, abbatissam vel priorem, ceterasve officiales instituturum cantitans.[46]

(Finally, at a certain castle, Niort, building little rooms like little cells, he raved that he would establish there an abbey of prostitutes, and that he would install by name so and so and so and so, whoever was of a rather notorious brothel as abbess or prioress and not only she, but also other officials.)[47]

One of the most prolific French satirists of the reign of Louis IX was the poet Rutebeuf, whose work covered a wide range of subjects from the historical to the frivolous. It was only natural, then, that he too should express concern at the deterioration of religious ideals that marked his age. In his long satirical poem *La Vie du monde* there is a section on the Church and the monastic orders called "L'Eglise, les ordres mendiants, l'université"[48] in which, after ridiculing the friars, Rutebeuf comments with sardonic humor on the dangerous consequences of an inveterate custom of certain religious women: wandering outside the convent:

Quant ces nonnains s'en vont par le paÿs esbattre,
Les unes à Paris, les autres à Monmartre,
Teiz fois en moinne hom deulz c'on en ramainne quatre. (ll. 109–11)

(When these nuns amuse themselves around the countryside, some going to Paris, others to Montmartre, they leave in groups of two but come back as four.)[49]

Also included in *La Vie du monde* are a few verses on the beguines—women who lived in communities consecrated to the performance of good works and acts of devotion without taking vows. The poet again conveys a most unfavorable opinion of outwardly pious women with inwardly profane longings, jokingly but pointedly accusing them of doing under their long robes things that they do not talk about:

> Beguines à ou mont
> Qui larges robes ont;
> Desous lor robes font
> Ce que pas ne vous di.[50]

(There are worldly beguines who wear long robes; underneath their robes they do what they do not tell you.)

Though a much lesser work than *La Vie du monde,* the fourteenth-century "Satire on the People of Kildare," written by a friar Michael of Kildare also ridicules friars, monks, and nuns as well as the other two estates of medieval society:

> Hail be ȝe, nonnes of seint Mari house,
> Goddes bourmaidnes and his owen spouse,
> Ofte mistredith ȝe ȝur schone, ȝur fete beth ful tendre,
> Datheit the sotter that tawith ȝure lethir.[51]

(Hallowed be the nuns of Saint Mary's, God's bower maidens and His own spouses, they often wear the wrong shoes, their feet are too tender for them, therefore, a curse on those who tanned the leather.)

In the light of the rest of the satire, a good-humored catalogue of the foibles of the people of his town, it is probably safe to interpret these verses as the poet's mild indictment of the nuns of Kildare who, like

Chartres Cathedral. Photo by author

so many others of the time "wore the wrong shoes for their tender feet," that is, did not have the spiritual strength required to be brides of Christ.[52]

There is another type of satire on the subject of wayward nuns, caustic rather than mild, unrelenting and acrimonious. Imbued with a magnificent wrath, its authors lampoon the weak and the corrupt with the true fury of the righteous. One such writer is William Langland in whose *Piers Plowman* there is a description of a convent where Wrath is cook and his aunt the abbess, and where some highly dishonorable things seem to be happening:

Iohanne was a bastard
And dame Clarice a kniჳtes douჳter, ac a kokewolde was hire
    syre,
And dame Peronelle a prestes file; priouresse worth she neuere,
For she had childe in chirityme, al owre chapitere it wiste.

(Mother Joanna was an illegitimate child,
[And] sister Clarice might be a knight's daughter, but her
    mother was no better than she should be,
And sister Peacock had an affair with a priest—"She'll never be
    Prioress" . . .
"She had a baby last year in cherry-time; it's the talk of the
    Convent!"[53]

In just four lines we are given a picture of conventual life in a work of
fiction which seems to come directly from the pages of an episcopal
visitation report. Here is a nunnery where parents can send an unwanted child, and where there is a prioress guilty of the same sins as
those real-life dishonorable prioresses whose names come up so often
in the historical documents reviewed.[54]

Slightly more sardonic even is the passage on religious women
in *Les Lamentations,* an antifeminine poem by Matheolus, an obscure
thirteenth-century clerk from Boulogne-sur-Mer whose work eventually became a symbol of French medieval misogyny. According to
Matheolus, nuns may appear very devout but they are as much prey
to sexual appetites as other women and they are always thinking of
excuses to go out in search of "carnal knowledge." One of their
favorite subterfuges is that their relatives are in bad health and sometimes about to die; this often allows them to roam the countryside in
total freedom from monastic restraint. Matheolus believes nuns cannot be trusted because they "pluck and fleece" other people more than
robbers do:

> Les nonnains, les religieuses
> Se tiennent pour trop precieuses
> Par leur espirituaulté.
> Mais assés y a cruaulté,
> Pour ce que de char ont deffaulte.
> Peu en y a, basse ne haulte,
> En toute la religion,
> Qui n'ait charnel affection

> De soy conjoindre charnelment.
>
> . . . .
>
> Nonnains feingnent peres et meres,
> Cousins, parens et suers et freres
> Languereus et en maladie.
> Elles le font, quoy que l'on die,
> Afin d'issir hors de leur cloistre,
> Pour faire charnelment congnoistre
> Leur "quoniam" et leur "quippe."
> Tout est par elles dissipé;
> Par le païs s'en vont esbattre.
>
> . . . .
>
> Mieulx sera plumés et tondus
> Que se les larrons le tenoient.[55]

(The nuns, the religious women, regard themselves as really precious because of their devotion. However, there is much cruelty because they do not have physical relationships. There are few, high or low in the world of religion who do not feel the carnal impulse to engage in sex. . . . Nuns pretend that fathers and mothers, cousins, relatives, and brothers and sisters are melancholy and ill. They make them seem about to die, no matter what the truth may be, so that they can leave the cloister to let someone have carnal knowledge of their "cunts" and their "pussies." Everything is spoilt by them; they like to amuse themselves about the countryside. . . . They will pluck and fleece you more than robbers would.)

Nuns are also much too fond of receiving gifts from their lovers:

> Ne vous priseront une prune,
> Se vous ne leur donnés souvent;
> C'est l'usage de leur couvent.
> Dons veult avoir la messagiere,
> La maistresse et la chamberiere,
> Et la matrone et la compaigne. (ll. 1758–63)

(They will not promise you more than a prune if you do not give them enough gifts; that is the custom of their convent. Gifts are expected by the messenger, the mistress, and the chambermaid, the matron and the companion.)

Much stronger than *Les Lamentations* in its attack on the vices and corruption of the monastic orders in his time is the *Speculum Stultorum* (Mirror of Fools), a long Latin poem by Nigellus Wireker. Its hero, Brunellus the Ass is supposed to represent the monastic order—"Asinus iste monachus est, aut vir quilibet religiosus in claustro positus, qui, tanquam asinus ad onera portanda Domini servitio est mancipatus"[56] (This ass represents a monk, or any religious person who lives in a monastery and who, like the ass, is obliged to bear burdens in the service of the Lord). Nuns in the *Speculum* are divided into two startlingly simple categories—"quaedam steriles et quaedam parturientes" (some bear no children and others do)—and "virgineoque tamen nomine cuncta tegunt" (they hide it all beneath the virgin's name). A few lines before, Wireker describes them in typical anti-feminine fashion:

> Vocibus altisonis adeo modulamine dulci
> Cantant, sirenes quod cecinisse putes.
> Corpore serpentes, sirenes voce, dracones
> Pectore . . .[57]

(In high-pitched tones they chant, ringing so sweetly, you would think that they were sirens singing. Slender in shape as serpents they appear, they bear the serpent's wisdom in their hearts.)

The *Doctrina y reprehensión de algunas mujeres* and the *Coplas de Vita Christi* are two Spanish poems of the fifteenth century written by priests whose anti-monastic satire surpasses that in any of the works just quoted. The *Doctrina,* by fray Ambrosio de Montesino, is wholly dedicated to castigate vices in women, and the section addressed to the sisters once again reveals the bitterness felt by a representative of the Church at the immoral conduct allegedly prevalent in the nunnery. Fray Ambrosio calls the religious women "monjas lisonjeras, / De entrincados apetitos" (flattering nuns, with twisted appetites) and wonders,

> ¿Qué vale el encerramiento
> De los cuerpos enclaustrados,

Cuando está el entendimiento
En las cortes y poblados?[58]

(Isn't it useless to lock up the [nuns'] cloistered bodies when their
thoughts are in the courts and towns?)

In the *Coplas de Vita Christi,* fray Iñigo de Mendoza is even more
acerbic in his comments on the behavior of some religious women.
Suggesting that they "circumcise" or excise their particular vices, fray
Iñigo castigates certain nuns severely for their sins:

¡O monjas!, vuestras merçedes
deuen de çircunçidar
aquel parlar a las redes,
el escalar de paredes,
el continuo cartear,
aquellos çumos y azeytes
que fazen el cuero tierno,
aquellas mudas y afeytes,
aquellos torpes deleytes
cuyo fin es el infierno.[59]

(Oh, nuns! You ladies must [circumcize?] excise those conversations through the mesh [?], the wall climbing, the constant
letter writing, those perfumes and ointments that make the skin
tender, those clothes and cosmetics, those crude pleasures that
lead to hell.)

By far the most merciless—no matter how exaggerated—
medieval satire of the seemingly profligate life of the nunnery is
included in the Catalan *Spill, Libre de les dones* or *Libre de consells* by
Jacme Roig.[60] The entire book is an open attack on the female sex,
with two episodes in Book II dealing specifically with several wicked
nuns. In the first one (Book II, part two) the narrator plans to marry a
beguine—"la vil beguina"—[61] who turns out to be totally corrupt
and whose crimes range from idolatry to adultery and abortion; in the
second episode (Book II, part four) he marries a novice who has not
yet taken final vows. This young woman, educated in a convent and
without knowledge of the world, has learned the most gruesome
things in the nunnery. Her fellow nuns have given her advice on

practically every aspect of conduct and each suggestion is equally abominable. The prioress tells her:

> si fill paris,
> m'ensenyorís,
> may no m prostras;
> masque m mostras
> un tant altiva,
> no m fes cativa
> de marit vell. (ll. 5985–91)

(If I bore a child I would be arrogant, I would never humble myself; I would rather appear lofty, not make myself the captive of an old husband.)

The sacristan says nursing a child should be avoided:

> car lo criar
> fills alletar,
> prest fa envellir, (ll. 6015–17)

(because to nurse a child and to raise it makes you grow old too soon)

and the abbess advises her—"pretend to be ill"—"que me fes malalta" (l. 6025)—adding to that a few tips on how to fool the doctor:

> ab una agulla
> te pots punchar
> lo paladar
> secretament,
> poras sovent
> ab sech tossir
> sanch escopir. (ll. 6084–90)

(With a needle you can prick your palate in secret; you will often cough and spit blood.)

An old nun teaches her how

> fer avortir'
> saber fingir
> virginitas, (ll. 6123–25)

(to induce a miscarriage and to fake virginity,)

while another sister offers her cell for any trysts:

> e si volreu
> guardat vos sia,
> la cambra mia. (ll. 6280–82)

(If you want I will lend you my room.)

Regardless of how much of the above may have been written tongue-in-cheek, the description of all these perversities certainly combines to evoke one of the most infamous pictures of conventual life in the late Middle Ages.

We finish this bird's eye view of the satirical literature aimed at medieval wayward nuns with a commentary on a little known twelfth-century Latin poem. Written in a typically medieval tone of good-humored blasphemy, *The Council of Remiremont* presents a debate on love among the nuns of Remiremont. It is not spiritual love that occupies them, however, but rather the kind of love whose rewards are temporary no matter how satisfying. The poem, regarded as a prototype of the "débats du clerc et du chevalier" (debates of clerks and knights) that flourished near the end of the medieval period appears without a title in the original manuscript and was published for the first time in 1849 by Georg Waitz with the name *Das Liebesconcil*.[62] The *Council* is probably the "work of a clerk, a poor Latinist but a spiritual libertine, . . . one of those that a few years later became known as Goliards."[63] It is an impudent parody of a church council designed to entertain the nuns of Remiremont themselves or perhaps the poet's own friends with a description of something which had in all probability never taken place. However, the *Council* cannot be dismissed as pure fantasy only since the records report alleged dissolute practices at Remiremont from early times. By the twelfth century it is obvious that morals had become so lax at the abbey that a bull of Pope Eugene III dated March 17, 1151 assails the nuns of Remiremont for engaging in "carnal exchanges":

quod ille jam pridem conversatione carnalis subventionis vestre indignas exhibuerunt, quam quod sacre religionis cultum in eodem loco credimus processu temporis reformandum et "peccati [lascivi]am in [ar]dorem spiritalibus convertendam . . ."[64]

(because they have for a long time been engaging in carnal exchanges unworthy of any support, because we believe that the observation of sacred religion should be reformed in due time and that the lasciviousness of sin should be converted into spiritual fervor . . .)

The action of the *Council* takes place in spring—"Veris in temporibus, sub aprilis idibus"[65] (in spring, at the time of the Ides of April)—and the council is meeting with a most singular purpose:

> In eo concilio, de solo negotio
> Amoris tractatum est, quod in nullo factum est. (ll. 7–8)

(In this council the only business is love, something which has never been in any council.)

Except for some "honeste clerici" (honorable clerks) from the diocese of Toul, all men are excluded from attending and also excluded are older women:

> Veterane domine arcentur a limine,
> Quibus omne gaudium solet esse tedium. (ll. 20–21)

(Banned from the assembly are older women for whom every joy usually becomes boring.)

The gospel of Ovid, master of the "ars amatoria" is substituted for that of the Church at this gathering:

> Lecta sunt in medium, quasi evangelium,
> Precepta Ovidii, doctoris egregii, (ll. 24–25)

(Read like a gospel in the midst of them all are the teachings of Ovid, that noble master) and in charge of the reading is Eva de Danubrio, "potens in officio / Artis amatorie" (able in the performance of the art of love).

The session is opened by the "cardinalis domina" (lady in charge), delegate of the god of love for the occasion, who has come dressed in resplendent robes and glittering jewels:

> Hec vestis coloribus colorata pluribus,
> Gemmis fuit clarior, auro preciosior,
> Mille maii floribus hinc inde pendentibus. (ll. 39–41)

(She is dressed in resplendent clothing, adorned with many colors, more dazzling than precious stones, more precious than gold, with a thousand May flowers hanging from her dress.)

She proceeds to question the nuns on their deportment and promises—"It is up to me to chastise or to pardon"—"Meum est corrigere, meum est et parcere" (l. 57). This is followed by Elizabet de Granges' speech in the name of the entire congregation:

> Nos, ex quo potuimus, Amori servivimus:
> . . . .
> Sic servando regulam, nullam viri copulam
> Habendam eligimus, sed neque cognovimus,
> Nisi talis hominis, qui sit nostri ordinis. (ll. 58–63)

(Whenever we have been able to, we have served Love: . . . In accordance with the rule we have not accepted the company of any man; we are not acquainted with anyone who is not of our order.)

Elizabet de Falcon explains the reasons for such a preference:

> Clericorum gratiam laude[m] et memoriam
> Nos semper amavimus, et amare cupimus,
> . . . .
> Quos scimus affabiles, gratos et amabiles;
> . . . .
> Amandi periciam habent, et industriam;
> Pulchra donant munera, bene servant federa,
> Si quid amant dulciter, non relinquunt leviter. (ll. 64–74)

(We have always loved the grace, the praise, and the re-
membrance of the clerks, and we wish to love them more . . .
The clerks, we know, are affable, gracious, and amiable . . .
They have experience and talent in love; they give us beautiful
gifts and keep their promises; the woman that they love tenderly
they do not willingly leave.)

As to the love of knights, it is well known that "detestable, ill-fated
and short-lived" are the words to describe it—"detestabilis, quam
miser et labilis" (l. 81)—therefore, no nun should ever love a knight;
she should only love clerks who follow

> Amor, deus omnium, juventutis gaudium,
> Clericos amplectitur . . .
>
> . . . .
>
> Tali vita vivimus, in qua permanebimus. (ll 95–98)

(Love, the god of all men, the joy of youth the clerks follow . . .
Such is the life that we shall continue to live.)

Despite this declaration of allegiance to clerks, however, there
are some sisters present at the council who prefer the love of knights:

> Audaces ad prelia sunt, pro nostri gratia,
> Ut sibi nos habeant et ut nobis placeant,
>
> . . . .
>
> Eorum prosperitas est nostra felicitas,
>
> . . . .
>
> Nostrum illud atrium est, et erit pervium. (ll. 110–22)

(They are bold in combat to be agreeable to us, to possess us and
please us . . . Their prosperity is our happiness . . . Our house is
always open to them and will always be.)

The clerks' supporters are adamant, though, and they promise they
will "give them all the pleasures that a woman owes a man"—
"Quotquot oblectamina viro debet femina" (l. 133). In exchange, the
nuns say, the clerks

Laudant nos in omnibus rithmis atquae versibus,
Tales, jussu Veneris, diligo pre ceteris,
Dulcis ami[ci]cia, clericis est et gloria. (ll. 140–42)

([They] praise us in every rhythm and in all forms of verse, thus,
by order of Venus, I love them above all others; there is with the
clerks sweet friendship and glory.)

The majority agrees and the "cardinalis domina" now commands:

eas in consorcio
Nostre non recipiant, nisi satisfaciant:
Sed si penituerint, et se nobis dederint,
Detur absolucio, et talis condicio,
Ne[c] sic peccent amplius, quia nil deterius.
Uni soli serviat, et ille sufficiat. (ll. 167–74)

(That our companions do not receive their opponents if they do
not make amends: but if they repent and return to us, we give
them absolution, on condition, however, that they do not sin any
more, that each of you serve only one and no more.)

No nun should ever allow a knight to touch her "body," her "neck"
or her "thigh" (!)—"Tactum nostri corporis, vel colli vel femoris" (l.
180). There follows a fierce threat of excommunication[66] for the
disobedient with all manner of sorrow and pain to be visited upon
them by order of Venus herself:

Maneat confusio, terror et contricio,
Labor, infelicitas, dolor et anxietas,
Timor et tristicia, bellum et discordia,

.   .   .   .
Pudor et ignominia vobit sint per omnia.
Laboris et tedium, vel pudoris nimium. (ll. 210–29)

(May you suffer confusion, terror, and remorse, [have] labors,
sorrow, pain, and anxiety, fear and grief, war and discord, . . .
that in everything you should feel shame and humiliation, an
aversion to work and much dishonor.)

"Two Monks." Master of the Amsterdam Cabinet, c. 1480. Drypoint. LI68, LII 70. Courtesy, Rijksprentenkabinet, Rijksmuseum, Amsterdam.

The poem ends amid a chorus of "Amens" from the nuns and an amused smile from the twentieth-century reader for whom such satire has lost much of its edge.

It is always difficult to draw a precise line between history and satire. Experience tells us that an event of which there is no documentary proof may not have taken place, and that exaggeration and ridicule are the tools of the satirist. Yet, no matter how extravagant some of the examples just quoted may seem, the historical evidence cited earlier can easily corroborate most of them. The same is true of the selections in the next chapter, where we get one step closer to identifying the possible sources for the enigmatic portraits of the Archpriest of Hita's Doña Garoza and Chaucer's Madame Eglentyne.

"Chanson de Nonne" and Fabliau

Il était une religieuse
Fort amoureuse;
Son père l'avait mise au couvent,
Parc' qu'elle aimait trop son amant.[1]

(There once was a very amorous nun; her father put her in the
convent because she loved her lover too much.)

ACCORDING TO one prestigious French critic, the question of
the allegedly indecorous behavior of the medieval nun is "a
commonplace of the love literature of the Middle Ages."[2]
The wealth of material available to illustrate the presence of the
wayward nun in the popular literature of the medieval period is
overwhelming; sheer volume, therefore, makes selectivity an imperative. In the attempt to identify the common elements linking the
"chansons de nonne" and the "fabliau" to the portraits of the Prioress
and Doña Garoza, a powerful—and largely ignored—literary convention emerges whose influence is evident in the characters of the
two nuns. Since this literary convention was still strong one hundred
years later (and for many centuries to come too) and because they
serve to confirm its lingering presence and influence in medieval
literature, some of the examples reviewed go beyond the Archpriest's
and Chaucer's time well into the fifteenth century. There is mention
of profligate nuns throughout the entire popular literature of the
Middle Ages; the "chanson de nonne" and the fabliau, however, are
the two genres which best illustrate the literary presence of the
wayward nun.

"CHANSONS DE NONNE"

The socio-economic background against which the historical models
for the nuns of the songs and the tales lived, as well as some of the
reasons that led medieval women to the cloister have already been
explored. Since the women of the lower classes were barred from a
career in the Church, the people probably did not look upon such a
profession with kindness. Nevertheless, if we consider the songs
themselves, the dislike does not seem to extend to the nuns, particularly those forced into the convent without any regard for their
preference and whose plight invariably elicits from the singers a
sympathetic response. This is what the people sing:

> Mariez-vous, les filles,
>
> .   .   .   .
>
> Avecque ces bons drilles,
>
> .   .   .   .
>
> Et n'allez jà, les filles,
>
> .   .   .   .
>
> Pourrir derrièr les grilles.[3]

(Marry your daughters to some jolly fellows, and do not let your
daughters rot behind a convent grille.)

> Une jeune fillette de noble coeur
> contre son gré l'on at rendu nonette.
> Point ne le vouloit estre, par quoy vit en langueur.[4]

(A young girl with a noble heart was made a nun against her will;
she did not want to be one because she pines away.)

Most of the medieval "chansons de none," "Klosterlieder," or
"Nonnenklagen" deal with the nun forced into the convent against
her will or the nun who regrets her decision to enter the religious life.
The songs never attempt a philosophical justification of the singer's
attitude, and since they reflect the viewpoint of the people, the
emphasis is usually on the merry and the materialistic. The origin of
the "chansons de nonne" is to be found in the plaint of the nun
unwillingly professed, common in French romances and German
lieder of the thirteenth century on. The "chansons de nonne" record

the emotions of the nun unwillingly professed as she alternately cries and questions, laments and endures, seemingly never losing all hope. Pining away in the nunnery for the pleasures of the world or the arms of a lover, the nuns of the "chansons" are often plotting to escape or actually running away from the cloister, much like the real ones seem to have done. Although all the "chansons" express the same feeling of frustration at the loss of physical freedom that the cloistered life entails, the tone in which such a feeling is conveyed varies widely. Thus, the selections that follow have been arranged to display the assorted moods of the singers, from bitter resentment through benign resignation, to almost blatant raciness.

The oldest version of the nun's complaint that has come down to us is the twelfth-century "Planctus monialis," contained in a Vatican manuscript and printed for the first time by an Italian scholar at the beginning of the twentieth century.5 The following are Latin and English versions of the "Planctus":

> Plangit nonna, fletibus
>   inenarrabilibus
> condolens gemitibus—
> que consocialibus:
>   Heu misella!
> nichil est deterius
>   tali vita!
> Cum enim sim petulans
>   et lasciva,
>
> Sono tintinnabulum,
> respeto psalte[rium],
> gratum linquo somnium
> cum dormire cupere[m]
>   —heu misella!—
> pernoctando vigilo
>   [cum] non velle[m];
> iuvenem amplecterer
>   quam libenter!
>
> Fibula n[on] perfruor,
> flammeum non capio,
> strophium [as]sumerem,
> diadema cuperem,
>   heu misella!—

monile arriperem
  si vale[r]em
pelles et herm[inie]
  libet ferre.

Ago trabe circulum,
pedes volvo per girum,
flecto capu[d] supplicum,
[non] ad auras tribuo,
  heu misella!

Manus dans, [in] c[or]di[bu]s
  rumpo pec[tus],
linguam [te]ro dentibus
  verba promens.

Lectus es in pissinis,
filtris non tappetibus,
cervical durissi[mum],
subter filtrum palea—
  heu misella!
[Vin]cor lance misera
  et amara,
[e] succis farinule
  et caseo.

Tunica tet[er]rima,
interula fetida
stamine conposit[a];
ceno[sis] obicibus
  —heu misella!—
[f]lex cupedes adolens
  inter pilos,
atque lens per[fe]ritur,
  scalpens carnes

Iuvenis, ne moreris!
faciam quod precipis;
dormi mecum! s[i non v]is,
tedet plura dicere
  —heu misella!—
atque magis facere
  perdens vit[am]—

cum possim e[r]u[e]r[e]
memetipsan.[6]

(A nun is lamenting with unutterable tears and moans, grieving deeply on behalf of her companions: Woe is me, nothing is
more degrading than such a life! for, though I am made for love
and play,

I have to ring the chapel-bell, to chant the psalter over and
over, to leave my dear dreams when I long to sleep—woe is me—
and stay awake all night against my will. How gladly would I fly
into a lover's arms!

I have no brooch to enjoy, can wear no bridal-veil; how I'd
long to put on a chaplet or tiara, woe is me—I'd get hold of a
necklace if I could—and what joy to wear ermine furs!

I pace the floor, walking round and round, I bow my head
submissively, not raising it heavenwards, woe is me; giving in,
my heart bursts with grief, but as the words come out I bite my
tongue.

My bed is a pitchy place, with felt, not coverlets; the pillow
very hard, under the bedding—straw, woe is me! I am defeated
by the wretched, bitter fare, tasting of a little flour and cheese.

The shift I wear is grim, the underwear unfresh, made of
[coarse] thread; within these muddy walls—woe is me—there's a
stench of filth in my delicate hair, and I put up with the lice that
scratch my skin.

Young man, please don't delay! I'll do your bidding; sleep
with me! If you don't want to, there's no more to say, woe is me,
and no more to do, wasting my life—since I can still destroy
myself.)[7]

From the very beginning, then, the bitter and the wanton
mingle in the nun's complaint; the resentment and the pent-up desire
to share once again in the life outside the convent walls become
intolerable and find expression in song. There is almost unbearable
sorrow in the lament of the nun, but there is also anger at the memory
of all she has been forced to leave behind, therefore, no matter how
mournful the song, the longings of the flesh still come through;
"cupiditas" will not be vanquished by "caritas." This is precisely the
attitude evident in the following ten songs from the thirteenth and
fourteenth centuries which have come down to us from many different regions of medieval Europe.

"Ki nonne me fist, Jesus lou maldie"[8]—"May Jesus curse the one who made me a nun"—sings the maiden in the first song from Southern France, while a new nun in Angoumois cries:

> Maudit soit le faiseur de toile,
>   Qu'a fait mon voile!
> Maudit ciseaux si dangereux
>   Qui ont coupé mes blonds cheveux![9]

(A curse on the weaver of the fabric that made my veil! Cursed be the scissors so dangerous that have cut my blond hair!)

In this fourteenth-century Italian song a nun, constrained by reasons of domestic interest to remain in the cloister, regrets the life she must lead:

> Soleva vestir camisa
> bianca, morbide e sotile;
> or vesto tenga bissa
> de stamegna, ed è sí vile;
> la mia carne bianca e umile
> è fata aspra, zala e verde,
> e ogno bel color perde;
> vunde mi despererazo.[10]

(I used to wear a white shirt soft and supple; now I wear a coarse tunic made of burlap and very ugly; my skin, white and fresh, has turned rough, yellow, and greenish, and it is losing all its beautiful color; for this reason I despair.)

Very similar to this bitter lament are those of the novice in a Catalan song of the fourteenth century and the nun in a German lied of the same period:

> Lassa, mays m'agra valgut
>   que fos maridada,
> o cortes amich agut
>   que can suy mongada.
> Monjada fuy a mon dan,
>   pecat gran

han fayt seguons mon albir;
mas cels qui mesa mi han,
    en mal an
los meta Deus e ls ayr.
Car si yo u agues saubut,
mas fuy un poch fada,
qui m donas tot Montagut
    no ych fora entrada.[11]

(Alas! if I had married
Or had a courtly lover—
But I became a nun.
A nun to my lasting sorrow
And great the sin
Of those who put me here.
And those who put me in
Great sorrow,
May God's wrath do them in!
For if I had ever known
—But then I was a fool—
Though they gave me all Montagut
I'd never have gone in!)

Gott geb im ein verdorben jar
der mich macht einer nunnen
un mir den schwarzen mantel gab,
den weissen rock darunten![12]

(May God send a lean year to the one who made me a nun and
put on me a sooty mantle and a cassock white!)

In a tone almost as bitter as that of the previous five singers, a
religious woman in the Spanish poem *Las doze Coplas Moniales* (The
Twelve Verses of the Nun) complains about the desolate life she must
lead in that "prison" where she lies buried. She was made a nun much
too young to know what her fate would be, like so many unfortunate
real life novices[13]:

Derelicta sum cautiva,
in florenti etate mea,
en esta cárcel esquiva

Benedictine Nun. *Monasticon Anglicanum: A History of Abbies and other Monasteries, Hospitals, Frieries and Cathedral and Collegiate Churches with their Dependencies in England and Wales.* Sir William Dugdale, editor. London: James Bohn, 1846.

do viviré cuanto viva
dolorosa afflita y rea.

Sepultada estoy aquí
do muero hasta que muera.
Desventurada de mí . . .

. . . .

> Yo, desque monja metida,
> inocente de mi daño
> hasta después de crescida.[14]

(I am a prisoner abandoned in the flower of my life in this harsh cell where I will remain as long as I live, in pain, suffering and a captive. I am buried here where I will keep on dying till the day I die. Woe is me . . . I was made a nun unaware of my misfortune until I became a woman.)

The same feeling of unrelieved sorrow and loss is evident in the next German lied, where an older sister laments that she must bear her grief in secret:

> Awe meiner jungen tage,
> waffen meiner senden clage
> daz man mich wil in ain closter twingen!
> da gesich ich nimmer me
> laup, gras, plümen noch grünen cle,
> noch gehor der clainen fogelin singen;
> daz ist ain not, mein freude ist tot
> daz man mich wil schaiden
> von den lieben freunden mein
> und stirbe ouch in dem laide.
>   waffen waffen meiner clage
>   die ich tougenlichen clage![15]

(Alas for my young days, alas for my plaint. They would force me into a convent! Nevermore then shall I see the grass grow green and the green clover flowers, nevermore hear the little birds sing. Woe it is, and dead is my joy, for they would part me from my true love, and I die of sorrow. Alas, alas for my grief, which I must bear in silence!)

The following two fourteenth-century "chansons de nonne" come very close in spirit to the "Planctus monialis." In the first one, a young novice from Germany wishes only unhappiness to the one who would force her to become a nun:

> gott geb dem klässer unglück vil
> der mich armes mägdlein
> ins kloster haben wil![16]

(God give much unhappiness to the one who wants to put me in the cloister.)

The second song is the complaint of an Italian nun who feels entombed in the monastery, just like the Spanish sister of *Las doze Coplas Moniales* quoted above:

> Estava en quello monasterio
> Com' una cossa perduta:
> Sense nullo reffrigerio;
> Non vedia, ni era veduta.
> Non vol'essere più monequa.[17]

(I was in that monastery like a lost thing; without solace, neither seeing nor seen. I do not want to be a nun any more.)

Judging from the words of the next two songs, sometimes the years of enclosure in the convent, meant to curb rebellious spirits, seemed to have the opposite effect on certain young women. On occasion, in fact, the enforced claustration appears to have strengthened their resolve never to accept what they saw as an unjust fate. Thus, the nun in this old French song can still lash out at the world that forced her into the cloister when she was much too young:

> Par may foy, dist Robinette,
> Je fu mise trop joeunette
> Nonnain en religion,
> Et pour ce prophession
> Ne sera ja par moy faite.
>
> . . . .
> Ou l'en doit rendre contrette
> Ou corps de rude façon,
> Femme borgne ou contrefette,
> Non pas fille joliete,
> Qui scet baler du talon.[18]

(By my faith, says Robinette, I was made a nun too young and this profession will never be for me. . . . Cloistered should be the bodies that are crippled, women with only one eye or deformed, not a dainty young maiden who knows how to dance.)

.Equally defiant is the attitude of the girl in the second song, also professed against her will, who tells her mother:

> Si je suis renfermée,
> Ah! c'est bien sans raison
>
> . . . .
>
> Ah! mère téméraire,
> Qui m'en veut à la mort,
> Achève ta colère,
> Punis mon triste sort.
> Je suis donc la victime
> Que l'on ne nomme plus.
> Si l'amour est un crime,
> Vaut mieux que tu me tues.[19]

(If I am cloistered, ah! it is quite without reason. . . . Ah! reckless mother who hates me to death, put an end to your wrath, punish my sad lot. I am, then, the victim that has a name no more. If love is a crime, it will be better if you kill me.)

Sometimes the resentment of the nun unwillingly professed is much less obvious, and although in the following selections the singers still complain about their fate, their tone is no longer bitter, but rather wishful and in some cases even frivolous. The sister in this fourteenth-century Italian song, for instance, has been in the cloister a long time now—"Ancora non avea deze ani / che fu' serata e streta in quela mura" (I was barely ten years old when I was locked up within these walls)—yet she can still imagine the joys of an earthly love she will never know:

> Stagando sola sola sul mio leto
> un dolze sono alora me vignía:
> credando ch'el fose el mio dileto
> che in le soe braze streta el me tegnía;

e in quel dolze tenpo che volea
conpir nostro desío,
oi me! dolor mio . . .[20]

(Alone, alone in my bed a sweet dream came to me: thinking that
my loved one was holding me tight in his arms, and right then
wanted to fulfill our desire. Oh, me! My sorrow . . .)

Even lighter in spirit is a song from Provence in which a novice curses
not only the father who put her in the convent, but also everyone else
who had anything to do with her becoming a nun:

La mounget' a maudich soun pero,
    que la fourceio
a n'en quittar soun bel amic
per pendre lou voil' et l'habit.

La mounget' a maudich la tiblo
    qu'a fach l'egliso;
e lou maçoun que l'a bastid',
les manobros que l'ant servit.

La mounget' a maudich lou pretro
    que'a di la messo,
et les clerzons que l'ant servid'
et lou monde que l'ant ausid'.

La mounget' a maudich la toilo
    qu' a fach lou voilo,
et lou courdoun de Sant Frances
que n'en pouerto à son coustat drech.[21]

(The nun cursed her father who forced her to give up her lover to
take the religious habit and the veil. The nun cursed the crew that
erected the church, and the mason who built it, and the laborers
that helped. The nun cursed the priest who said the mass, and the
clerics who were in it, and the people who heard it. The nun
cursed the fabric out of which her veil is made and the rope of St.
Francis that they hung from her right side.)

Even more frivolous in spirit is the fourteenth-century chanson where a nun sees a monk coming her way as she stands one day in church lamenting her fate. "Wait a while," she says, promising him

> Se plus suis nonette,
> Ains ke soit li vespres
> Je morai des jolis malz.[22]

(If I am no longer a nun before vespers I will die of pleasurable pains.)

The tone, then, as pointed out earlier, varies from bitter to frivolous in the "chansons de nonne." A few songs, however, seem to stand in the middle of this scale of feeling, as it were, and in them the singer, though lamenting her fate, is neither resentful nor flippant about it. One such song is this thirteenth-century Bavarian lied in which the nun's mournful question to her sisters—"Swester, lieben swester mîn, / sullen wir gescheiden sîn / von der werlt. . . ?" (Sisters, my dear sisters, shall we be parted from the world?)—is followed by a mere sigh of regret at all the wonderful things that are no longer theirs:

> Swester, lieben swester mîn,
> sullen wir gescheiden sîn
> von der werlt, daz ist mîn meistiu swaere.
> Sol ich nimmer schapel tragen,
> sô muoz ich wol von schulden klagen,
> wan ich gerne bî der werlde waere.
> Ein schapel klâr ûf mînem hâr
> trüeg ich für den wîle
> als man siht die nunnen tragen
> zeiner kurzewîle.
> wâfen wâfen mîner klage,
> die ich tougenlîchen trage.
> Ich muoz der werlde ein urloup hân,
> wan ez wil an ein scheiden gân:
> elliu freude muoz mir sêre leiden.
> Tanzen springen, hôher muot,

vogele singen, meigen bluot—

. . . .

Trüegn vogelîn den jâmer mîn,
möhten si wol swîgen
in dem walt und anderswâ
    ûf dem grüenen swîge.
wâfen wâfen mîner klage
die ich tougenlîchen trage.[23]

(Sisters, my dear sisters, must we be parted from the world?
Deepest woe it is, since I may never wear the bridal wreath and
must make moan for my sins, when I would fain be in the world
and would fain wear a bright wreath upon my hair, instead of the
veil that the nuns wear. Alas, alas for my grief, which I must bear
in secret! I must take leave of the world, since the day of parting
is come. I must look sourly upon all joy, upon dancing and
leaping and good courage, birds singing and hawthorn bloom-
ing. If the little birds had my sorrow well might they sit silent in
the woods and upon the green branches. Alas, alas for my grief,
which I must bear in silence!)

The next group of songs, from Spain now, again illustrates the
wide range of feeling usually found in the "chansons de nonne." In
these songs, certain young maidens forced to enter the convent
against their will are determined not to do it meekly, however, and in
tones ranging from the plaintive to the defiant refuse to accept their
fate. They wish to remain in the world free to love and be loved; there
is no tinge of bitterness in their song, though, only regret at the
thought of all that they will lose if they become nuns. One girl
complains:

¿Agora que sé d'amor me metéis monja?
¡Ay Dios, qué grave cosa!
Agora que sé d'amor de caballero,
agora me metéis monja en el monesterio.
¡Ay Dios, qué grave cosa![24]

(Now that I know of love you make me a nun? Oh, God what a
terrible thing! Now that I know of a man's love, now you make
me a nun and put me in the convent. Oh, God what a terrible
thing!)

Another girl protests:

> Agora que soy niña
> quiero alegría,
> que no se sirve a Dios
> de mi monjía.[25]

(Now that I am a young girl I want joy; I will not serve God as a nun.)

The same determination not to be a nun may be prompting the maiden in the next song to warn everyone:

> Aunque me vedes
> morenica en el agua
> no seré yo fraila.[26]

(Though you see me dark in the water [perhaps a reference to the black habit of a religious woman], I will not be a nun.)

The singers in the next four songs also refuse to become nuns. They are more explicit, however, as to their reasons: they already have lovers and will not think of exchanging such joy for a life of religious devotion. Thus, while one simply wants to be left alone:

> No quiero ser monja, no,
> que niña namoradica so.
> Dejadme con mi placer
> con mi placer y alegría,
> dejadme con mi porfía,
> que niña malpenadica so,[27]

(I do not want to be a nun, no, for I am a girl in love. Leave me with my pleasure, with my pleasure and my joy, leave me with my stubborn ways for I am a girl in love,)

another girl pleads with her mother to understand: she cannot serve God because love "follows" her:

¿Cómo queréis, madre,
que yo a Dios sirva,
siguiéndome el amor
a la contina?[28]

(How can you expect me to serve God, mother, when love
follows me all the time?)

and a third one is ready to be married and will not take the veil:

Monja yo no entiendo ser
aunque mi padre lo quiera:
. . . .
Yo soy moza casadera.[29]

(I do not intend to be a nun though my father wants me to. . . . I
am a girl ready for marriage.)

In the last of the four songs the tone is actually flippant, even though
seemingly firm, and to a mother who has vowed to put her in a
convent—"pues para monja profesa os prometí y mandé" (I vowed to
make you a professed nun)—the daughter responds with complete
nonchalance:

Aquel caballero, madre,
tres besicos le mandé,
cresceré y dárselos he.[30]

(To that man, mother, I sent three kisses. I will grow up and give
them to him.)

Similar in tone to the Spanish songs and with the singers displaying an equal disregard for parental wishes, the girls in the next
two songs clearly—and merrily—announce that the convent is not for
them. One has no desire at all to be a nun:

On me veut doner un cloître,
Mais point d'envie ne m'en prend;
Ma mère m'en parlé,

> Et plusiers de mes parents.
> Point de couvent je ne veux, ma mère,
> Point de couvent je ne veux, maman.[31]

(They want to put me in a convent but I have no desire to go; my mother has talked to me and many of my relatives too. I do not want the convent, mother, I do not want the convent, mother.)

The other girl, already a novice, "a le cuer joly" (has an amorous heart)—and would like to marry and have a husband—"avoir mary"—and never have anything to do with the nunnery again:

> Adieu le moniage:
> Jamais n'y enterrai;
> Adieu tout le mainage
>
> . . . .
> Plus ne seray nonnette.[32]

(Goodbye to the convent: I will never enter it; good-bye to all the nuns . . . I will not be a nun any more.)

A variation of the theme of the nun unwillingly professed has her proclaim to the world her true feelings, actually just like the sister in the original "planctus" does. The refrain from a thirteenth-century French song, for instance, unabashedly declares the singer's motives for not wanting to be a nun:

> Je sant le douls mals leis senturete
> malois soit de deu ki me fist nonnete.[33]

(I feel the sweet pain below my waist; cursed be the one who made me a nun.)

The novice in this song from the Gascon region experiences the same longing and she yearns for something she cannot have in the convent: some white apples and a young man:

> Il y a une nonne
> malade dedans.

—Dites-moi, nonnette,
De quoi avez-vou faim?

De pommes blanchettes,
Et d'un garçon jeune.

(There is a nun sick inside. "Tell me, little nun, what are you
hungry for?" "Some white apples and a young man".)

The song, as is the case with all the "chansons de nonne" is
sympathetic to the young nun, and although this particular song does
convey a warning to someone who strays—even if only in her mind—
it is all done in the same spirit of lighthearted banter that is the
distinguishing feature of so many of the chansons. The nun is cautioned:

—N'en mangez pas, nonnette.
On vous enterrait,

Pas dans une église
Ni meme au couvent.

Mais au cimetiere,
Avec les pauvres gens.[34]

("Do not eat, little nun, we will bury you neither in a church
nor in the convent, but in the graveyard with the poor folk.")

The tone becomes even more frivolous in a few songs where the
feelings conveyed speak more openly of the desires of the flesh that
some unfortunate sisters cannot—or will not—repress. In a highly
irreverent display of dishonest thoughts, a nun in a thirteenth-century
song clearly explains the reasons why she feels she does not belong in
the nunnery—she likes a good life full of pleasures and love much
more than she does prayers:

J'amaixe trop muels moneir bone vie
Ke fust deduissants et amerousete.[35]

(I love my good life that had charm and love in it too much.)

In an old Spanish song, a prioress whose noble lover now disdains her, begs him to grant her his favors once more:

> Gentil caballero,
> dédesme hora un beso,
> siquiera por el daño
> que me habéis fecho.[36]

(Kind gentleman, give me a kiss now, at least to make up for the harm you did to me.)

In the next three songs, first found in what appear to be fifteenth or sixteenth-century versions, the spirit remains consistently light. In the first one a girl laments she has lost her lover because she was too coy, and now it is too late as her father wants to put her in a convent:

> Mon père n'a fille que moy,
> Il a juré la sienne foy, guoy,
> Trépignez-vous, trépignez,
> Trépignez-vous comme moy.
>
> Il a juré la sienne foy
> Que nonnette il fera de moy, guoy,
> Trépignez-vous, . . .
>
> J'aimerois mieux mary avoir,
> Qui my baisast la nuit trois fois, guoy,
> Trépignez-vous, . . .[37]

(My father has no other daugher, he has sworn a hundred times, guoy, dance like me. He has sworn a hundred times that he will make me a nun, guoy . . . I would prefer to have a husband who would kiss me in the night three times, guoy . . .)

In the second song a maiden rejects the life of the nunnery with complete assurance and for a very good reason: she has a lover:

le
deuinaille
entraille
a maille
lozvaille
it fans faille
ozriers
fcuiers
eftriers

cau de iolattrue vont il grieu prote prenoze
ges cil ont bon talent. quil la veulent deffendze
s espees dachier loz font venu contendze
aulus point le cheual grans faus li fait porprendze
fiert lacanoz que lescu li fait fendze
e plus hardi des loz z si eftoit le mendze
les ert othelerie el champ le fift eftendze
ı la mozt abatu lame li eftuct rendze
a fes vaches garder ne porra mes entendze

A monk and a nun playing a ball game. Flemish, fourteenth
century. MS. Bodley 264, folio 22recto. Whole lower border.
Courtesy, Bodleian Library.

Derrière chez mon père,
il est un bois taillis
(serai-je nonnette, oui ou non?
serai-je nonnette? Je crois que non).

Le rossignol y chante
et le jour et la nuit.

Il chante pour les filles
qui n'ont pas d'ami.

Il ne chante pas pour moi,
j'en ai un, dieu merci.[38]

(Behind my father's house there is a thick wood; should I become a nun, yes or no? Should I become a nun? I guess not. The nightingale sings night and day, he sings for the maidens who do not have a lover. He does not sing for me for I have one, thank God.)

The girl in the third song, from the region of Poitou, playfully asks her parents to wait a year before sending her to the convent because, she says,

> Peut-être au bout de l'année,
> Trouverai-je un pauvre amant.

(Perhaps at the end of the year I will find a poor lover.).

Then she goes on with considerable irreverence:

> Il vaut mieux conduire à vèpres
> Son mari et ses enfants,
> Que d'être dedans ces cloétres,
> A faire les yeux doulents;
> Point de couvent, je ne veux, ma mère,
> C'est un amant qu'il me faut vraiment.
>
> . . . .
>
> A jeûner tout le carême,
> Les quatre-temps et l'avent:
> Et coucher dessur la dure
> Tout le restant de son temps;
> Point de couvent, . . .
> . . . .
>
> Serais-je pas plus hereuse
> Dans les bras de mon amant,
> Il me conterait ses peines,
> Ses peines et ses tourments.
> Point de couvent, . . .[39]

(Much better to take to vespers a husband and children than to stay in the cloister with sad eyes; I do not want the convent, mother, a lover is what I truly need. To fast all through Lent, the Four Seasons and Advent also, and to lie on the hard floor the rest of the time. I do not want the convent. . . . Wouldn't I be happier in the arms of my lover, he would talk to me of his pain and his torment. I do not want the convent . . .)

The last song merely hints at what the dissatisfied young woman singing would like instead of the religious life that may be forced upon her, but the next selection tells with remarkable audacity the story of the recent love affairs of an Italian nun with three different men. First there was a priest,

> è son sì desventurata
> Che per una più bella
> intra a la santa favella!

(and I am so unfortunate that for a more beautiful one he entered into holy speech!)

Afterwards there was a friar from a minor order:

> El me portava poco amore,
> sempre stava a dio pregare,
> Non savea che cosa é amore,
> se non laldar el dio beato.

(He gave me little love, he was always praying to God; he did not know what love is except praising holy God.)

Last was a hermit friar, the only true lover:

> ben m'ebe contentata
> del mio gran dolore.[40]

(he assuaged my great pain well.)

If the last song is a grim reminder of how abominably certain real-life religious women conducted themselves, the next two songs are also reminiscent of a historical situation discussed earlier: the plight of the high-born woman once she reached a certain age. A matter of social and economic concern to her parents, to the people it was a matter of song:

> Que ferons-nous de tant d'argent?
> Nous mettrons nos fill's au couvent.
>
> . . . .
>
> Si nos fill's ne veul point d'couvent
> Nous les marierons richement.[41]

(What shall we do with so much money? We shall put our daughters in the convent. . . . If our daughters do not want the convent at all, we shall marry them richly.)

Again in a cruel but fitting mockery of the medieval practice of marrying rich young daughters either to God or to a feudal lord,[42] the father in this Italian song from the thirteenth or fourteenth century announces with obvious disrespect for the ancient institution of monasticism:

> Io lascio la mia fia cara
> al monester de Santa Clara
> et se non li piace de stare in quelo
> vada a stare a l[o] bordelo. Testamento.
> L'altra mia figliattina
> laso a santa Catarina,
> ch'ella stia nel monestero
> fazza stento e vitopero.[43]

(I leave my beloved daughter to the monastery of St. Claire, and if it does not please her to stay there, she should go to a bordello. My will. My other little daughter I leave to St. Catherine's; let her be in the convent in hardship and shame.)

We have until now only reviewed those "chansons de nonne" where a religious woman laments her fate expressing either sorrow or outrage at what the world has done to her and vowing, sometimes, to abandon a life for which she knows she is not suited. Much more common, however, than the theme of the nun leaving the monastery by herself—though this was common enough in real life, as we know—are the songs dealing with a nun's escape from her convent-prison. The flight is usually accomplished with the aid of a lover who, through a clever disguise or a well-worn ruse manages to get past the portress and reach the cell of his loved one. Naturally, the tone is one of unrestrained frivolity, as we see in the next three selections which have come down to us in either French or Italian versions. In the first one a young nun is rescued from the cloister by her lover who enters the abbey posing as a gardener:

La mère abbesse va se promener, la jeune fille à son côté.
"Quel accent oh! il travaille! belle, demandez-lui une fleur."
La belle et le monsieur, tous deux n'on changé de couleur.

Tout en prenant le bouquet, lui dit: "Vous viendrez me trouver,
A minuit, dedans ma chambre, prendrai mes habillements;
Sans dire adieu à mes compagnes, nous irons abbattre les
    champs."[44]

(The mother abbess goes for a walk, the young woman by her side. "What ardor, oh! he works! Beautiful one, ask him for a flower." The beauty and the man did not show any emotion. While picking the bouquet, he says, "You will come to meet me at midnight in my room. I will get my clothes; without saying goodbye to my comrades we will go across the fields.")

Another version of the same song is slightly more serious, as it ends with a promise from the young nun placed in the convent "sans demander son consentement"—without her consent—to follow her lover until death:

Je suis venu, belle maitresse,
A fin de vous mener dehors,

(I have come, my beautiful mistress, to take you away)

says the youth, and she responds:

> Je te suivrai jusqu'a la mort.[45]

> (I will follow you till death.)

The second song of this group dealing with escapes from the nunnery carried out with outside help is considerably more piquant than the first one. In it, a youth stopping to pick some flowers in a garden as he strolls down the road one morning in May hears a nun lamenting her fate:

> je di trop envis vespres ne conplies,
>
> . . . .
>
> Elle s'escriait 'com seux esbaihie!
> e deus, ki m'ait mis en ceste abaie!
> maix ieu en istrai per sainte Marie:
> ke ni vestirai cotte ne gonnete.

("I say vespers and compline with distaste.". . . She cried, "How dazed I am! And those who put me in this abbey! But, by Saint Mary, I will leave: I will wear neither tunic nor gown.")

The young man's heart fills with joy at the words of the charming "prisoner" and, coming to the door of the convent, he immediately rescues her from her lonely cell:

> Quant ces amis ot la parolle oie,
> de joie tressaut, li cuers li fremie,
> et vint a la porte de celle abaie:
> si en getait fors sa douce amiete.[46]

(When her friend hears the words, he trembles with joy, his heart thunders, and he comes to the door of this abbey to let out his sweet friend.)

The last song of the group tells of a girl whose father placed her in the cloister because he had found her with a lover of whom he

disapproved; soon after, though, she effects a hilarious escape with
the help of her lover. The young man bribes a worker who has access
to the convent grounds; the worker then feigns an attack of some
strange illness—"Je crois que ma vie va prendr' fin, / Je meurs de mal
au ventre" (I think my life is going to end, I am dying of a stomach
pain)—he cries, and the lovers are reunited soon after:

> Le ramoneur est retourné
> Tout droit au monastère;
> Dans un d'ses sacs a enfermé
> La jolie demoiselle.
>
> . . . .
>
> Il a traversé tout l'couvent
> Avec la mère abbesse,
> Et dans les bras de son amant
> Il a r'mis sa maîtresse.47

(The chimney sweep returns straight ahead to the monastery; in
one of his bags he puts the pretty young woman. . . . He goes
through the convent with the mother abbess, and in the arms of
her lover he places his mistress.)

There is a Piedmontese version of the song which seems a little less
contrived as it describes the young gallant's misery upon hearing of
his lady's distress: "munigheta la völo fè!" (they want to make her a
nun!), he exclaims. He dashes to the convent on his steed,

> A l'è rivà giüst a cul'ura, ch' la bela a intrava 'nt ël munastè.
> —Ch'à scuta sì, madre badëssa, na parolinha chi'i j'ai da dir.—
> An bel dizend-je la parolinha, s'a j'à büta-je l'anel al dì.

(He arrives just as his fair maiden is about to enter the nunnery.
"Listen to me, mother abbess, to one little word I have to say,"
and saying it, he put a ring on her finger.)

The triumphant young woman then exclaims: "—S'ai si chërdio di
far-mi múnia, sun fà-me spusa giojuzament—"48 (They wanted to
make me a nun but I have joyfully become a bride.)

As we have seen, then, the interest aroused in the medieval mind
by the wayward nun is evidenced by the number of songs on the

subject that have come down to us and which the people supposedly sang throughout the last few centuries of the Middle Ages. Some tell of grieving nuns, others of obstinate ones, practically all are sympathetic to the women unwillingly professed, and many look upon the wayward nun with considerable amusement. To the last category belong two dialogues between a mother and a daughter in which the latter refuses to enter the religious life because she would much rather stay in the world and be loved by a young man. The first one, from the French region of Fontenay-le-Marmion is a playful conversation where a fifteen-year-old daughter confesses to her mother she wants a lover, to be told in no uncertain terms that she will go to a convent and learn to read. When the daughter asks if they wear ribbons and beautiful clothes at the convent and whether they go dancing and enjoy themselves, the mother, plainly ignoring the wishful tone of the question, answers that they do not and that all she will need when the time comes will be a white veil and a black robe. The girl then promptly responds that she will not go:

> "Au couvent, ma mère, non je n'irai pas:
> Le garçon que j'aime je ne le quitterai pas;
> Le garçon que j'aime n'est pas loin d'ici,
> Il est à la porte, je le vois veni."[49]

(I will not go to the convent, mother, I will not leave the young man I love; the young man I love is not far from here, he is at the door, I saw him come.)

Equally frivolous is the second dialogue, also from Fontenay-le-Marmion, in which a seventeen-year-old girl pleads with her mother to get a husband for her. Thereupon, the mother shouts that she will get a broomstick instead and will put her daughter in the nunnery which, as we have seen before, could serve as either cell or sanctuary:

> "Voilà bientôt le temps, ma mère,
> Qu'il faut me donner un mari,
> Car j'ai dix-sept ans et demi;
> Maman, cédez à ma prière.
> . . . ."
> "Effrontée, hélas! que vous êtes!
> Si je prends le manche à balai,

> Au couvent de la soeur Babet
> Je te mets pour la vie entière."[50]

("Before long the time will come for me to get a husband,
mother because I am seventeen and a half; mother, listen to my
plea." . . . "Alas, you are a brazen hussy! If I get the broomstick I
put you in the convent of sister Babette for the rest of your life.")

As pointed out earlier, most "chansons de nonne" sing of the
plight of the reluctant nun. Nevertheless, we also know from historical evidence that there were many women who entered the cloister of
their own free will in search of a spiritual refuge when earthly love
failed to fulfill its promise of joy. Thus, in a few songs the convent
appears as a haven for unhappy lovers. In this charming French ditty,
for example, a young man finds his former love after a long search
and to his question—"Où vas tu maintenant?" (Where are you going
now?)—she answers,

> "M'en vois rendre nonnette
> (Helas)
> En un petit couvent.
> Puis que d'aultre que moy
> Vous estes amoureux."[51]

(I am going to become a nun [alas] in a small convent because
you are in love with someone else.)

Most of the time, however, despite its theme, the "chanson's" characteristic spirit of frivolity remains unchanged. In this old French song
the singer regrets having been too coy with her lover; now she has lost
him and all she has left is the nunnery:

> Las! si je le puis revoir,
> Je ne ferais le desdaigneuse,
>
> . . . .
> Je ne m'y marieray jamais,
> Je seray religieuse,[52]

(Alas! If I could see him again, I would not be disdainful, . . . I
will never marry, I will be a nun)

and in the next song, a young maiden now suffers because of her past scorn. She once had fifteen lovers in seven days but is now about to become a nun because she lost them; she was too disdainful:

> Adieu les plaisirs du monde,
> Je m'en vais dans les couvents.
> M'enfermer avec les noires
> Dans des lieux étroitement.[53]

(Goodbye to the pleasures of the world, I am going back to the convent, to seclude myself with the women in black in that narrow place.)

In the next two songs a girl says she will take the veil if her family does not allow her to marry the man she loves:

> Si mes parents le veul' bien
> Pour moi je suis contente;
> Si mes parents ne le veul' pas
> Dans un couvent j'y rentre.[54]

(If my parents like him I will be pleased; if my parents do not like him I will enter a convent.)

In the second song there is actually a new twist to the "threat": if her lover could only join her in her cell, the prospective nun knows that they could be happy together:

> Mon Dieu s'il se pouvoit faire
> Que tous deux ensemblement
> Fussions dans un monastere,
> Pour y passer nostre temps,
> Capuchin et capuchine,
> Nous vivrions tous deux contents.[55]

(My God, if it were possible that the two of us could spend our time together in a monastery as capuchins we would live happily.)

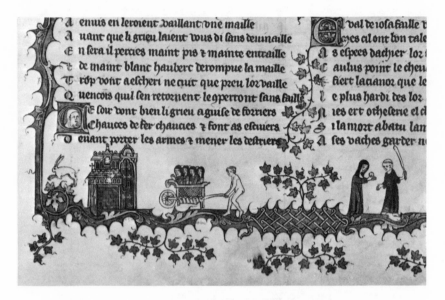

a enuis en leroient baillant one maille
a uant que li grieu laient tous di sans deuinaille
E n sera il percies maint pis et mainte entraille
et de maint blanc hauberc derompue la maille
tu rop vont aeschert ne quit que peu lor vaille
Quenvois quil sen retoruent le operront sans faille
E four vont bien li grieu a guise de forriers
Chauces de fer chauces et font as escuiers
O euant porter les armes et mener les testriers

al del de rosa saille t
yes al ont bon tale
a s espees dachier lor
aulus point le cheu
fiert la cianor que le
e plus hardi des lor
les ert othefenie el d
i la mort abatu lan
a fes vaches garder n

Nuns sitting in wheelbarrow pushed by naked man. Flemish, fourteenth century. MS. Bodley 264, folio 22recto. Whole lower border. Courtesy, Bodleian Library.

Among the variety of medieval "chansons" dealing with the theme of the wayward nun or the nun unwillingly professed there is a quaint group of songs called "jeux de transformation" in which the girl, in an attempt to evade an unwanted lover adopts various shapes. These old "jeux de transformation" are always found in the form of a dialogue between an elusive maiden and her persistent lover and are still popular today. One of the changes that the girl might undergo is to become a nun, whereupon the lover immediately announces that he will, then, become either a priest or a monk and eventually get her. The following are different versions of the stanza in the "jeux de transformation" where the girl proclaims she will enter a convent. The lover's response is included—

From the north of France:

> Si tu te mets en dame dans un couvent,
> Je me mettrai en prêtre, gaillard chantant,
> Confesserai les dames de ton couvent.[56]

(If you become a nun in a convent, I will become a priest, vigorous singer, I will confess the ladies of your convent.)

From Bourbonnais:

> Je m'y mettrai nonne
> Dans un couvent;
>
> . . . .
> Si tu te mets nonne
> Dans un couvent,
> Je m'y mettrai prècheu
> Pour te prècher.[57]

(I will become a nun in a convent, . . . If you become a nun in a convent I will become a priest to preach to you.)

From the Pyrénées:

> Si tu te fais la nonne,
> Nonne dans un couvent,
> Je me ferai prêcheur
> Prêcheur pour te prêcher,
> Je prêcherai
> Par amitié.[58]

(If you become a nun, a nun in a convent, I will become a priest, a priest to preach to you; I will preach for friendship.)

From the Pyrénées also:

> Se tu te fas la mounjo
> D'aquel counbent tant grand,
> Ieu me farèi le mounje,
> T'aurè 'n te counfessant.[59]

(If you become a nun in that big convent, I will become a monk, I will hear your confession.)

From Catalogne:

> Si tu 't tornas una monja,
> en convent te ficarán;
> mes jo 'm tornarè un fraret
> y t' anirè confessant.[60]

(If you become a nun they will put you in a convent; but I will become a friar and I will hear your confession.)

From the area around Brest:

> Si tu te fais nonne
> Dans un couvent
> Je me ferai prêtre
> Pour te confesser.[61]

(If you become a nun in a convent I will become a priest to confess you.)

From Bretagne possibly:

> Si tu te fais nonne
> Dans un couvent
> Je me ferai
> Moine chantant
> Pour confesser la nonne
> Dans le couvent.[62]

(If you become a nun in a convent I will become a singing monk to confess the nun in the convent.)

From England today:

> If you become a nun, dear,
> A friar I will be;
> In any cell you run, dear,
> Pray look behind for me.[63]

It is a significant point that in five of the "jeux" just quoted, the lover announces he will become either a priest or a monk so he can hear the new nun's confession. We have already seen how pernicious the influence of certain unscrupulous confessors was deemed to be, when an irate prelate blames them for a religious woman's alleged misconduct.[64]

Although the "jeux de transformation" invariably depict the female as the elusive one who retires to the convent for a secluded life, in the next three songs the opposite situation is presented: girls who will not give up their lovers appear ready to take the veil when the young men decide to become monks. In the first song a young woman sings:

> Je m'en iray rendre bigotte
> avec les autres,
> et porteray le noir, aussi le gris
> (sont les couleurs de mon loyal amy).[65]

(I will become a nun with the others and wear the black and also the grey, they are the colors of my loyal friend.)

In the second song, a girl who was once very nice and loved music and musicians too, has lost her lover because he became a monk:

> Il était une fille,
> Une fille de bien,
> Qui amait la musique
> Et mieux les musiciens.
>   Hélas! hélas!
> Celui qu'elle amait le mieux,
> Il s'est rendu religieux.

(Once there was a young woman, a nice young woman who loved music and musicians even better. Alas! alas! He whom she loved best has become a monk.)

The priest to whom she confesses that she is lost without her lover gives her most remarkable advice:

Eh bien, ma jeune fille,
Il faut en faire autant,
Prendre la robe grise
Avec le voile blanc.[66]

(Oh well, my daughter, you must do the same, take the grey
robe and the white veil.)

In the third song, a pregnant girl whose lover has become a monk
plans to take the veil for the rest of her life, but he tells her that she is
not as chaste as a nun should be. She remains undaunted, however:

Si je ne fus pas chaste,
Volage,
La faut en est à vous'
Vous en êtes la cause,
Je le serai sans vous.[67]

(If I am not pure, you fickle one, it is your fault; you are the
cause; I would be [pure] without you.)

In a couple of other songs the nunnery is present, not as a haven
for someone crossed in love, but rather as a refuge from marriage:

Monjica en religión
me quiero entrar,
por no malmaridar.[68]

(I want to be a nun because I do not want a bad marriage.)

With a similar idea in mind, this young woman from the French
Pyrénées declares:

Je ne veux plus m'embarrasser
Des tracas du ménage:
Je veux aller au couvent,[69]

(I do not want to be encumbered with the troubles of a household: I want to go to the convent)

and the girl whose father married her against her will to an old man when she was very young will become a nun to pray to the god of love for someone she can love:

> Mon père m'a mariée
> Que je n'estois qu'un enfant;
> A un vieillard m'a donnée
> Qui a près de soixante ans;
> Et moy qui n'en ay que quinze,
> Passeray-je ainsi mon temps?
>
> . . . .
>
> M'irai 'je rendre nonette
> Dans quelque joly couvent,
> Priant le dieu d'amourette
> Qu'il me donne allegement
> Ou que j'aye en mariage
> Celuy là que j'aime tant?[70]

(My father married me off when I was merely a child; he gave me to an old man who is almost sixty years old; I am only fifteen, will I spend my life like this? . . . I will become a nun in some fine convent to pray to the god of love that he give me relief, or that I may have in marriage the one I love so much.)

Less common than the last three songs (which, despite their unusual theme still retain their light-hearted tone) are the few "chansons de nonne" with a tragic or even a semi-tragic denoument, such as the one in which a young woman's decision to become a nun proves ill-fated for her lover. When, after a long absence, he returns to look for his loved one in the nunnery where she is now living, he falls dead at her feet:

> En lui passant son anneau d'or,
> Le pauvre amant a tombé mort.
> Oh! que de pleurs, oh! que de larmes!
> Chacun y deplorait son sort.[71]

(When he gave her his gold ring, the poor lover fell dead. Oh, how much crying! Oh, how many tears! Everyone laments his fate.)

Much to the Church's dismay, as we know, some nuns were constantly breaking their claustration vows.[72] Once out in the world, a nun was exposed to the same dangers and the same temptations as any other member of her sex: she could fall in love or be the object of someone's love and, in either case, be condemned as reprobate. If we trust the historical evidence cited before, a nun often did not need to leave the convent to break her vow of chastity.[73] The following two poems come from the eleventh and thirteenth centuries approximately. Although written by educated men and not the product of the imagination of the people taking shape in a song, these poems are too significant in the context of everything just mentioned regarding the love of religious men and women to be left out. Both are in the form of dialogues in which a nun and a clerk are involved in a matter of love.

In the first poem, generally attributed to a "clericus vagantes" or goliard poet possibly of the thirteenth century, a nun assumes the role of temptress as she endeavors to seduce a clerk. In the best tradition of all the allegedly reprobate nuns of centuries past, she begs the clerk for love in the most passionate terms. Despite her ardent appeal, however, he will not accept her:

> Nun: Deponam velum, deponam cetera quaeque,
>   ibit et ad lectum nuda puella tuum.
>
> Clerk: Ut velo careas, tamen altera non potes esse,
>   et mea culpa minus non foret inde gravis.[74]

> N: I will remove my veil and everything else, and your maiden will go naked to your bed.
> C: Even if you take off your veil, you will still be what you are, and my guilt would not be less.)

In the other dialogue, from the eleventh-century Cambridge Manuscript, the situation is reversed. In this composition, written half in Latin and half in German, a clerk asks a nun to love him. Unfortunately, almost all of the dialogue was deleted with black ink by the monks of St. Augustine, Canterbury, who were in the habit of censoring in this manner any material they considered morally offensive.[75] On the evidence of the few verses which scholars through the centuries have painfully reconstructed, the poem seems to contain the declaration of love to a nun from a clerk who points out that spring is in the air, nature is in bloom, and it is again the time for love. (And a time to lock all the doors of the nunnery, according to certain episcopal injunctions).[76]

This is the text of the dialogue in a transcription by Peter Dronke:

> Suavissima nunna,   ach fertue mir mit wunna!
> Tempus adest floridum,   gruonot gras in erthun.
>
> Quid vis ut faciam?   sago thu mir, iunger man.
> Turpis, hortaris unicam   ferno themo humele dan!
>
> Carissima mea,   coro miner minne!
> Nunc frondes virent silve,   nu singent vogela in walde.
>
> Iam cantet philomela!—   kristes wirt mine sela;
> Cui me devovi,   themo bin ih gitriuwe.
>
> O formosa domina,   sag ic thir mine triuwe—
> Mee sedes anime,   thu engil in themo humele!
>
> Sed angilorum premia   samt gotelicher minne
> Te prement, animam   thines vogeles ver[r]adan.
>
> Carissima nunna,   choro miner minna!
> Dabo tibi super hoc   wereltero dan genuoc.
>
> Hoc evanescit omne   also wolcan in themo humele:
> Solum Christi regnum   thaz bilibit uns in ewun.
>
> Quod ipse regnat credo   in humele so scono:
> Non recusat dare—   thaz gileistit her ze ware!
>
> Nomini amantis,   ther gitriuwe mir ist,
> Tantum volo credere   thaz thu mir wundist mine sinne.
>
> Laus sit Amori   thaz her si bekere,
> Quam penetrabit ut sol,   also si minnen gerno nu sal.

(He: [Sweetest] nun, [ah] trust [me joyfully]! [Blossom]-time has come, the grass is green on [the earth].

She: What do you want me to do, tell me young [man]? You are wickedly urging your beloved [far away from heaven].

He: [My dearest one], put my love to test! [Now] the leaves in the wood [are] green, now [birds] sing in the wood.

She: Let the nightingale sing! [My soul] will be Christ's, to whom I vowed myself, [to whom I shall be true].

He: Oh lovely [lady], I am telling you [my trust], oh dwelling-place of [my] soul, [angel of the heavens]!

She: Yet the rewards of the angels, [together with] love [of God], [will force you] to betray [the soul of your] (little) bird.

He: [Dearest] nun, put my [love] to test! I shall give you, what is more, great [honour] in the world.

She: All such things pass like clouds in the sky: only Christ's kingdom [endures] for ever.

He: I too believe he reigns in heaven so beautifully: he does [not] refuse to give—that indeed [does he grant].

She: [I so want to trust] in the name [of my lover, who is true] to me, [that you are wounding my senses].

Praise [be to Love] that he is converting her, [her whom] he will penetrate [like the sun], as [now] she is eager [to love].[77]

FABLIAUX

Another medieval literary form where the figure of the profligate nun can often be found too is the fabliau or ribald tale. The same stories of misconduct used by the Church in its sermons to illustrate a moral were used by the jongleur to provoke laughter. His business was to tell ludicrous, often crude tales which were eventually put into French verse and became what we know as fabliaux. Numerous collections of these medieval "contes grasses" have come down to us, such as *Les Cent Nouvelles nouvelles* and *Le cento novelle antiche* or *Il novellino*, although the best known stories are those in Boccaccio's *Decameron*.

In *Les Cent Nouvelles nouvelles* there are three extremely coarse tales—numbers 15, 16, and 21—where one or more licentious nuns figure prominently. Number 15, "Nonnain scavante" (The Crafty Nun) tells of the much too friendly relations between two neighbor-

ing houses of monks and nuns, known as "la Grange et les Bateurs:
car Dieu mercy la charité de la maison aux Nonnains estoit si trés
grande que peu de gens estoient escondis de l'amoureuse distribu-
cion"78 (the Barn and the Flailers for, God be thanked, the generosity
of this house of nuns was so very liberal that few men were excluded
from their amorous almsgiving). Tale number 21, "L'Abesse guerie"
(The Abbess Cured) tells the story of a sick abbess who is finally
convinced by the sisters to follow her physician's suggestion and take
a lover in order to regain her health. To ease her conscience, the nuns
volunteer to do the same thing as their spiritual leader and they tell
her: "Affin que vous n'ayez pensée ne imaginacion que où tems
advenir vous en sourdist reproche de nulle de nous . . . A donc furent
mandez moynes, prestres et clercs, qui trouverent bien à besoigner"79
(In this way you need never imagine or fear that in the future any one
of us might reproach you . . . thereupon, monks, priests, and clerks
were summoned, and they had plenty to do). Tale number 16, "Les
Poires payées" (Payment for Pears) begins: "C'è n'est pas chose es-
trange ne peu accoustumée que moins hantent et frequentent voulen-
tiers les Nonnains" (It is not unusual for friars to chase after nuns). We
are immediately told, then, that a Dominican's much too frequent
visits to "une bonne maison de Dames de Religion"80 (a goodly house
of religious women) cause the abbess to give strict orders to prevent
any further contact between the friar and the nun who is the object of
his affections. She has all the access gates to the cloisters locked, a
measure often adopted in real-life convents too, as we know.81 One
day, though, the undaunted friar-lover manages to avoid the abbess's
vigilant eye and finds himself once more inside hallowed—and forbidden—territory. Yet, before he and the nun can carry out their
wicked intent under a pear tree in the garden, they are interrupted by
a visitor to the nunnery who suddenly pelts them with pears. The
Dominican flees the scene and the stranger then takes over, saying to
the nun:

> "Il vous fault payer le fruitier." Elle qui estoit prinse et surprinse
> voyt bien que reffus n'estoit pas de saison si fust contente que le
> fruitier fist ce que frere Aubery avoir laissé en train.82

> ("You have to pay off for the pears." Taken unaware as she was,
> she saw very clearly this was no time for refusal, and agreed to let
> the fruit man complete what Brother Aubrey had left undone.)

Le cento novelle antiche or *Il novellino* is a collection of Italian ribald tales displaying almost the same lack of taste as the French ones just quoted. Novella 62 of *Il novellino* is the story of the abbess and nuns of a convent[83] who were in the habit of entertaining any knights that visited there by providing them with food and companionship. If we keep in mind the eagerness with which some of the inmates received visitors from the outside world,[84] we may find that, though considerably immoral, the situation in Novella 62 could have taken place in any nunnery of the Middle Ages. Once inside the convent, the visitors were asked to choose from among all the sisters the one that pleased them the most—"E la badessa e le suore li veniano incontro, et in sul donneare, quella que più li piacesse, quella il servia, et accompagnava a tavola et a letto"[85] (And the abbess and the sisters would come to meet them and after flirting with them, the one that pleased them the most waited on them and accompanied them to dinner and to bed).

Probably the most notorious nun stories in Italian literature are those in Boccaccio's *Decameron,* such as the tale of the abbess who dashes out of her room one night because she has just been told that one of her nuns has a man in her cell:

> Era quella notte la badessa accompagnata d'un prete il quale ella spesse volte in una cassa si faceva venire. La quale, udendo questo, temendo non forse le monache per troppa fretta o troppo volonterose tanto l'uscio sospignessero, che egli s'aprisse, spacciatamente si levò suso e come il meglio seppe si vestì al buio; e credendosi torre certi veli piegati, li quali in capo portano e chiamangli il saltero, le venner tolte le brache del prete; e tanta fu la fretta, che senza avvedersene in luogo del saltero le si gittò in capo e uscì fuori.[86]

> (That night the abbess was in the company of a priest, whom she often had brought to her in a chest. She was afraid that the nuns in their zeal and haste might beat so hard at the door that it would open; so she got up quickly and dressed herself in the dark. Thinking she was picking up her nun's veil she took the priest's breeches, and, such was her haste, that without noticing it she put them on her head instead of the veil; and came out of her room.

As the harried abbess launches on a heated speech on the sinfulness of the young nun's conduct, everyone notices her curious headdress,

"Ces presentes heures a l'usaige de Rome furet achevez . . ."
Philippe Pigouchet for Simon Vostre, 1498. Engraving. 18.60.
Courtesy, The Metropolitan Museum of Art, Rogers Fund, 1918.

enhanced by the suspenders still attached to the pants and dangling on either side of her head. Naturally, she is now forced to change her tone and she ends up explaining to the sisters that "impossibile essere il potersi dagli stimoli della carne difendere; e per ciò chetamente, come infino a quel dì fatto s'era, disse che ciascuna si desse buon tempo quando potesse."[87] (it is impossible for anyone to defend herself from the appetites of the flesh . . . everyone should secretly, as they had done until then, enjoy themselves when possible).

Another fourteenth-century version of the same story is *Le Dit de le nonnete,* a poem by Jean de Condé, where the sister is imprisoned by the abbess as punishment for her incontinency. Three of her friends attempt to get the abbess to give the nun a reprieve by threatening to disclose that they "vit les laniers qui pendoient / Devant s[en] front. . . ." (saw the straps that hung in front of her forehead). The incident is reported in much the same words as in Boccaccio's tale:

> Laidement au prendre mesprist,
> Car les braies a l'abbe prist,
> Et puis les jetá erranment
> Sour son cief . . .[88]

(In a bad mood, by mistake, the abbot's breeches she took, and then she threw at random on her scarf . . .)

Besides *Le Dit de le nonnete,* there are three other well-known versions of the tale of the abbess. One of them, a scabrous Italian song of the fourteenth or fifteenth century beginning "Kyrie, kyrie, pregne son le monache!" (Kyrie, kyrie, pregnant are the nuns!) tells exactly the same story of the abbess and the breeches as it describes the licentious practices of a group of cloistered nuns:

> Io andai in un monastiero,
> a non mentir ma dir el vero,
> ov'eran done secrate:
> diezi n'eran tute infoiate,
> senza [dir de] la badesa,
> che la tiritera spesa
> faceva con un prete.[89]

(I went to a monastery, not to lie but to tell the truth, where there were consecrated women: ten of them had been deflowered, not to mention the abbess, who spent long hours spinning yarns with a priest.)

The two other versions appear in La Fontaine's tale *Le Psautier*[90] (The Psalter) and in *Albion's England,* a sixteenth-century metrical British history with mythical and fictitious episodes, where the story of the abbess is told as follows:

> It was at midnight when a Nonne, in trauell of a childe,
> Was checked of her fellow Nonnes, for being so defilde;
> The Lady Prioresse heard a stirre, and starting out of bed,
> Did taunt the Nouasse bitterly, who, lifting up her head,
> Said, "Madame, mend your hood" (for why so hastely she rose,
> That on her head, mistooke for hood, she donde a Channon's hose.[91]

Another famous—infamous?—story from the *Decameron* involving profligate nuns concerns a young man by the name of Masetto who pretends to be deaf and dumb in order to be a gardener at a convent. Once there, one of the young sisters who has heard female visitors gossip about certain forbidden pleasures, decides to find out for herself: "e io ho . . . udito dire che tutte le altre dolcezze del mondo sono una beffa a rispetto di quella cuando la femina usa con l'uomo."[92] (I have often heard . . . that all the other pleasures in the world are hollow in comparison with that a woman feels with a man). Since Masetto is believed to be deaf and dumb, the nuns feel quite safe experimenting with him, and as for the young man, he is only too pleased to oblige—"poi, seco spesse volte ragionando, dicevano che bene era così dolce cosa, e più, come udito aveano, e prendendo a convenevoli ore tempo, col mutolo s'andavano a trastullare."[93] (Afterwards, when they talked it over, they agreed that was even more pleasant than they had heard. So henceforth, at suitable times, they enjoyed themselves with the deaf mute). Soon after all this, everyone else in the convent, including the abbess, finds out about Masetto who eventually becomes unable to cope with the nuns' demands for his "attention." He decides, then, to put an end to the deceit. In order to avoid exposure in the community, though, Masetto was allowed to remain in the convent as its steward, and while thus employed "assai monachim generasse" (he begot a large quantity of little nuns) until the death of the abbess, at which time he returned home "vecchio, padre e ricco"[94] (old, rich and a father).

There is a story reminiscent of the one about Masetto in *Del regimento e costumi di done* by the thirteenth-century Italian author Francesco da Barberino. In it a group of Spanish nuns, after having acquired a great reputation for sanctity, have become totally neglectful of their religious duties. In order to test their true spirit, God grants permission to Satan to send there an emissary by the name of Rasis who will tempt the nuns. Rasis disguises himself as an old woman and arrives at the monastery accompanied by three young boys posing as maidens whom Rasis begs the abbess to accept as novices. To make the newcomers more at ease, she decides that all three should take turns sleeping with each of the twelve sisters under her care, although naturally, no sooner is the arrangement carried out than the real nuns discover the true identity of their new companions. Everyone conspires to keep it a secret, however, and "in sei mesi elleno furono tutte gravide"[95] (they were all pregnant). The situation at the convent is kept secret from the outside world until it is no longer possible to hide the condition of the nuns. At this time the abbess threatens to expose them to their families, but being a young woman herself, at the last minute she too succumbs to the charms of the false novices and all is forgiven for a while. When the time comes for everyone's new baby to be born, the three young men inform the sisters that they cannot stay in the nunnery any longer and, with a "sia vostro tutto il tesoro"[96] (let the entire treasure be yours), they leave the convent for good. The story ends with the whole town storming the nunnery after they find out what has happened there, whereupon, in a fit of righteous fury "mettono mano a le pietre; e così li lor parenti come li altri le lapidarono"[97] (they picked up some stones and their parents, as well as others stoned them).

Verse fabliaux where the figure of the unchaste nun plays a significant part are also common in the late Middle Ages. Among these, *Des trois dames de Paris*[98] (The Three Ladies from Paris) and *Des trois chanoinesses de Cologne*[99] (The Three Canonesses from Cologne), both by Watriquet de Brassenal, are two of the most indecent ones. Almost equally ribald is a debate between some aristocratic canonesses and a group of nuns, in which they argue over who has more right to the love of certain amorous knights.[100] When the canonesses,

who call themselves love's "votaries," complain at the court of Venus
that,

> Dames nonains des grises cotes,
> De cuer outrageuses et sotes,
>
> . . . .
> Ne chevalier ne grant seignour
> Mesissent après vous entente?
>
> . . . .
> A vostre amour les atraieis
> Et ensus de nous les traieis. (ll. 805–32)

(Nuns with grey tunics, bold and foolish-hearted, . . . Do either
knights or great lords escape your attention? . . . To your love
you lure them and away from us you pull them.)

The nuns accuse the canonesses of saying "grosses paroles et espesses"
(many arrogant words) and proclaim that the grey nuns

> les commands d'amours maintient.
>
> . . . .
> Il nous samble que nous soions
> Bien dignes d'avoir benefisce
> En amours . . . (ll. 865–932)

(we follow love's commands . . . It seems to us that we are
worthy of having gains in love.)

After much high rhetoric from both sides, Venus delivers a verdict in
favor of the nuns because they are

> douches et amistables
> Et en penser d'amours estables.[101] (ll. 1195–96)

(sweet and friendly and constant in love.)

A religious woman well acquainted with the ways of the world
is also present in *Daz Maere von dem Sperwaere*[102] (The Story of the
Sparrowhawk), a thirteenth-century German version of the popular
French fabliau *De la Grue*[103] *(The Crane)*. In the German poem, much

less offensive than the original tale, an innocent young nun looks over her convent wall one day and sees a knight carrying a sparrow hawk. When she asks him for it, he promises to give it to her in exchange for "love," the meaning of which he proceeds to explain to her. When the novice's schoolmistress-nun hears about the trade, she becomes enraged and berates her for what she has done; the next time the knight rides by, the novice "forces" the knight to return to her the "love" and take the sparrow hawk with him:

> "hebet mich von der mûre nider,
> und gebet mir min minne wider,
> und nemet ir iuwer vogelîn."[104]

(lift me down from the wall, and give me my love again, and take your bird.)

Besides presenting nuns as profligate, some of the late medieval literature seems to have been fond of the theme of the nun impersonator, that is, someone who would pretend to be a religious woman for purposes less than honorable in every case. We met false nuns in the story in Barberino's book; the same idea appears in a song from the Piedmont region, where a prince disguises himself as a religious woman to gain access to the room—and bed—of a maiden:

> S'a l'è lo prinsi di Carignan,
> S'a s'è vestì-se da munigheta
> Pr'andè dürmì cun üna fieta,[105]

(The prince of Carignan disguised himself as a nun to sleep with a maiden)

and also in a Catalan song in which a student does the same thing for the same purpose:

> Lo traidor del estudiant—se'n guarneix una trampeta;
> se'n vesteix de cotò blanch,—com si fos una monjeta.[106]

(The traitorous student played a trick: he dressed in white cotton as if he were a nun.)

A similar theme is found in a few songs from Holland, Germany and France,[107] and also in a long thirteenth-century French didactic poem, *Le Castoiement d'un père a son fils*.[108] (A Father's Punishment of his Son). This time in a work composed for an educated audience, as opposed to the fabliaux aimed at the less literate, the pseudo nun appears in a dishonorable context in one of the stories that make up the long poem. In Number II—"De la male vielle qui conchia la preude Feme" (Of the Old Woman who Ruins the Shrewd Woman)— "une pute vielle" (an old prostitute) "en guise de Nonein velée" (disguised as a nun) gains the confidence of a young wife and talks her into granting her favors to an unworthy suitor, an affair that has the most disastrous results for the young woman:

> Tant fist la vielle mal artouse,
> Que putain fist de bone espouse.[109]

(So much did the crafty old woman do, that she made a whore of the good wife.)

Lewd nuns also appear in a few popular songs, such as these two from the French regions of Angoumois and Poitou called "Le Nez de Martin"[110] (Martin's Nose) and "Il était trois nonnes"[111] (There Were Three Nuns). In the latter,

> Il était trois nonnes
>
> . . . .
> L'une avait un moine,
> L'autre un capucin;
> La troisième enragé
> De n'avoire rien.

(There were three nuns . . . one had a monk, the other a capuchin; the third one was angry because she had no one.)

The third nun, then, pretends to be unable to walk and a physician is called. He leaves his book in a corner, pulls back her sleeve and

> Lui met son remède
> Dans le creux d'la main.

(He puts his medicine in the hollow of her hand.)

In Poitou the last part of the song is slightly different and considerably more malicious:

> Il lui donne une herbe,
> Qui croit dans la main,
> Qui fait pusser l'ventre
> Et grossir les seins.[112]

(He gives her an herb that grows in the hand, makes the belly get large and the breasts too.)

Less explicit than "Il était trois nonnes" but equally piquant is "Le Nez de Martin," alive with the joys of double entendre and where three nuns walking in the woods one day notice a nose attached to a tree. It had apparently been placed there by its owner, Martin the monk, who cut it off after it froze on his face one night in the woods:

> Dans le trou d'un arbre
> Martin le plaça.

(On the trunk of a tree Martin placed it.)

The sisters plan to take the nose with them to the convent; at the end of a pole it will put out the candles in the chapel, or better still, the fires that burn below the sisters' hearts?

> Dans not' monastère
> Il nous servirà,
> Au bout d'une perche
> Les cierges éteindra.
> Ah! quel dommage,
> Quel dommage, Martin,
> Martin, quel dommage![113]

In English literature there are very few examples of ribald tales that make use of the "bad" nun theme, and the two that come to mind

"Two Nuns." Master of the Amsterdam Cabinet, ca. 1480. Drypoint. LI69, LII 71. Courtesy, Rijksprentenkabinet, Rijksmuseum, Amsterdam.

are literary works written for an educated audience. The tale of the abbess and the "breeches" appears in a sixteenth-century piece by Thomas Twyne called *The Schoolmaster,* while a light-spirited fourteenth-century fabliau attributed to John Lydgate tells the story of a prioress and her three frustrated suitors. *The Tale of the Lady Prioress and her Three Suitors,* which scholars have little doubt is a translation from a French fabliau of unknown origin, gives a detailed and hilarious account of the hardships endured by a knight, a priest, and a merchant as they attempt, unsuccessfully, to gain the love of a reluctant—and shrewd—prioress. It is significant that there is no mincing of words in the knight's protestations:

All is for your love, madam, my life would I venture,
So that you will grant me, I have desired many a winter
Underneath your comely cowl to have my intent.[114]

We have merely skimmed the surface of a fascinating chapter of
the literature of the Middle Ages; countless other songs and stories are
still waiting to be told again:

> Adieu vous di, dame nonnain:
> L'en ne parle a vous qu'a dangier,
>
> Dire faut quant on a grant fain:
> Adieu vous di, dame nonnain,[115]

(Good-bye I say to you, lady nun: one speaks to you only
sparingly, speech fails when one is very hungry)

sings a French "trouvère"-poet, but we cannot say goodbye to the
"dame nonnain" yet. In search of the possible truth behind the figures
of the professed women in the "chansons de nonne" and the fabliaux
we will now attempt to trace the pattern of the tradition which
nurtured them a little further. We have seen the figure of the wayward
nun playing a prominent role in four major genres of medieval
literature; by the fourteenth century she had become part of a well-
established literary tradition. The next chapter places her within this
tradition.

Doña Garoza and Madame Eglentyne

"Religiosa non casta es podrida toronja."[1]

(An unchaste nun is like a rotten orange.)

But the historian knows; he has all sorts of historical sources in which to study nunneries, and there he meets Chaucer's Prioress at every turn.[2]

BY THE FOURTEENTH CENTURY, the stereotyped figure of the wayward nun in literature had acquired remarkable notoriety, as the examples from the chansons, the fabliaux, and the moral and satirical works cited in the previous chapters will attest. Although the cultural products of Western Europe were available only to a limited sector of the population, as always, certain current themes and ideas knew no boundaries, and what would today be called a scholarly exchange seems to have taken place among the men of letters, mostly religious men or perhaps those attached to a noble house as poets or tutors. In either case, since "the Goliard, like the Latin tongue, knew no frontiers,"[3] works by wandering scholars or learned authors traveled freely across Europe. For Juan Ruiz, Archpriest of Hita, living out his life (c. 1280–c. 1350) as a minor prelate in a small Spanish town, international exchanges literary or otherwise must have been virtually impossible. Nevertheless, judging from the materials used for the portraits of the two nuns, one in the *Libro de Buen Amor (LBA)* and the other in the *General Prologue* to the *Canterbury Tales,* the Archpriest of Hita seems to have had access to some of the same sources used later by the English poet. As for Chaucer (c. 1340–1400), a man whose library by fourteenth-century standards was vast and whose court contacts took him on several missions to the continent, precisely during his most productive literary years, an acquaintance with the stock literary themes and figures of the period would have been not only logical but inevitable.

It is important to remember here that if we are ready to acknowledge the existence of opportunities of cultural contact between England and the Continent, we must also take into account two highly probable effects of such a contact. The first one is that, regardless of its geographical location or its political environment, no country could be viewed as wholly isolated from prevalent fourteenth-century trends. The second probable effect is that, if the literature produced by learned men could have such ample diffusion despite the scarcity of available books, the songs and the stories that the people loved, more accessible by their very nature, probably reached an even wider public. Let us turn briefly to history once again in an attempt to justify this last assertion. According to the chroniclers, the routine and the hardship of castle and courtyard alike were broken and relieved by the joyful presence of the traveling ministrels and troubadours. By the mere fact of their constant wandering across every land, they unwittingly came to fulfill the role of couriers bearing, not merely messages, but the entire lore of centuries to all corners of the medieval world. Whether repeating the ancient ballads and tales or making up new songs, these old poets of the high road eventually made the creations of the people the common property of every man. Besides the wandering ministrels and troubadours, there was another channel through which stories and songs traveled from place to place and across the ocean to faraway lands, and this was the pilgrimage, one of the most popular endeavors of the Middle Ages, as denoted by history and literature alike: "pilgrimages were incessant; they were made to fulfill a vow as in cases of illness or of great peril, or in expiation of sins."[4] It was well known, however, that the men and women who went on pilgrimages, though ostensibly engaged in a holy venture, "occasionally did they strive to shorten the weary length of the way by song and music. As often as a crowd of pilgrims started to go from one place, they seem always to have hired a few singers and one or two musicians to go with them."[5]

While the most popular pilgrimages were undoubtedly those to the closer, local sanctuaries, the lure of the road and the possibility of seeing other places attracted many English pilgrims to distant shrines.[6] They crossed the Channel to Calais and rode on to Boulogne where they could view the relics of a miraculous virgin, like the Wife of Bath herself had supposedly done, or they went to Amiens to worship a head of St. John the Baptist.[7] Most interesting for our purpose, though, is the fact that there were also Spanish pilgrimages undertaken from England, among which the one to world-famous St. James Compostella was particularly recommended.[8] This would naturally have provided an excellent opportunity for the satire, the song, and the story from the country of the Archpriest of Hita to make their way to the country of Chaucer and vice versa. Furthermore, by the fourteenth century so much material was already shared by so many thinkers, writers, and religious men that it was becoming increasingly difficult to determine sources, and the stock figures of medieval literature such as the Gluttonous Monk, the Disobedient Wife, or the Wayward Nun were known to everyone and held up to ridicule or scorn without compunction by poet and preacher alike.

Among the genres popular in the twelfth through the fourteenth or fifteenth centuries, satire, especially of things religious, seems to have had a particular appeal for the medieval mind. We have already seen in Chapter 2 how cruel and blatant some monastic satires could be, especially those aimed at such well-known targets as monks, friars, and nuns. We must bear in mind, though, that satire is a cousin to caricature and that the smallest foible is often magnified to distortion for the sake of effect, to enhance the incongruities in someone's portrait. Ridicule is an ancient and trusted tool of satire designed by the master satirist himself in his portraits of flawed men and women. It is Horace's immeasurable achievement that a successful satire's "militant irony," "its persuasive voice,"[9] so binds the readers that the point of view of the satirist becomes their own and they begin to share his "emotional strain."[10] Horace's famous "castigat ridendo mores" with its promise of a reasonably mild indictment cut more deeply yet than any invective would, and his vaguely amused tone, totally devoid of either bitterness or anger has successfully exposed the follies of men to countless generations.

It is precisely this gentle sarcasm that marks the satire of the Archpriest of Hita and Chaucer, especially their satire on the figure of the wayward nun. Chaucer's "rippling undercurrent of satire, mellow, amused, uncondemning,"[11] and the Archpriest's painless satire, of the

kind that "does not draw blood,"[12] make their targets risible at times
but always real. While devoid of tears or savage indignation, their
method is, however, astonishingly effective in its portrayal of individ-
uals whose weaknesses are exposed by their own behavior. Chaucer
does not level any general, abstract accusations against religious
women as was traditional in medieval satire, but through the use of
dramatic description causes both the type and the individual to come
alive. The Archpriest, on the other hand, does bring certain charges
against nuns. He invariably tempers them with praise of their accom-
plishments, however, even though these, in agreement with his unfailing attitude of merry criticism are usually in the field of "amor":

> aman falsamente a quantos las amavan;
> son parientes del cuervo: de cras en cras andavan;
> tarde cumplen o nunca lo que afiuzavan;
>
> todo su mayor fecho es dar muchos sometes,
> palabrillas pintadas, fermosillos afeites,
> con gestos amorosos e engañosos juguetes:
> trayen a muchos locos con sus falsos risetes.
>
> Mio señor Don Amor, si él a mí creyera,
> el combit de las monjas aqueste, recibiera;
> todo vicio del mundo, todo plazer oviera:
> si a dormitorio entrara, nunca se arrepentiera.

> (All nuns love falsely whomsoe'er they catch within their claws
> Since nuns are kith and kin of crows who cry, "Ah pause! Ah
>   pause!"
> And late or never yield that thing which trusting lovers draws.
>
> Their greatest feat is foisting off some wretched scurvy trick
> With painted words and blandishments, and pretty rouge laid
>   thick;
> With gestures amorous and smiles that catch one in the quick,
> While they, with bursts of laughter false, a host of lovers pick.)
>   (stanzas 1256 b, c, d–1258)

There is not in either poet any trace of the reformer's zeal, but
rather "a bountiful sense of humor"[13] which leads them to mirror the

life of their time in their work. With characteristic wit, both Chaucer and the Archpriest present portraits of two medieval nuns that resemble many nuns known to their audience, and no attempts are made to embellish or to blacken the pictures created with infinite care as objects of satire. We believe that it is through the manipulation of suggestive detail provided by hundreds of years of literature on the theme of the wayward nun that the Spanish and the English poets create the intriguing figures of Madame Eglentyne and Doña Garoza. They illustrate the very essence of their creators' satirical approach, subtle and intangible, something that "depends on an attitude which cannot be pinned down, which is always escaping to another view of things."[14] It is precisely the carefully wrought ambiguity of both portraits that has baffled critics through the centuries and has led some to pronouncements later deemed invalid by other critics who, in turn, were proved wrong by another group and so on till the present.[15]

The main thing to keep in mind when dealing with descriptions of fourteenth-century nuns is that these women cannot be judged by twentieth-century standards. For medieval man the body was considerably less important than the soul, therefore, the sins of the flesh such as gluttony, vainglory, and even incontinence were regarded as less abominable than those of the spirit, such as apostasy, for example. Because the emphasis in the portraits of Doña Garoza and, particularly, Madame Eglentyne, is on what the Middle Ages would have called venial sins, the satiric intention of the authors is sometimes missed. A closer look, nevertheless, reveals a striking contrast between what the two nuns seem to be and what they should be, the result of "a delicately poised ambiguity"[16] created by a mass of ironic details. For our present purposes, it will be necessary to disassociate the Prioress's portrait from her tale. In the light of our approach to the portrait, any consideration of the relationship between teller and tale would require an analysis of the potentially satiric overtones of the latter, something entirely beyond the scope of this book.

Juan Ruiz, Archpriest of Hita, was born around the year 1280 in a small village near the Spanish city of Alcalá, where he died probably in 1350. Little is known about this "jongleuresque" priest, except that he spent some time in jail by order of the Archbishop of Toledo for writing verses parodying Church rituals. The Archpriest's *LBA* is an unusual work intended to teach success to one whom women have forsaken ("entiende bien mi libro e avrás dueña garrida" [stanza 64d]).

Mingled with the poet's descriptions of his artful seductions of various women there are several poems on the sins and the Passion of Christ, as well as paeans to chastity. "It throbs with lust, yet it is full of moral exempla and of fables rich in practical wisdom. It is a strange medley indeed."17 There is in the Archpriest of Hita a powerful strain of Horatian-Goliardic-Rabelaisian irony but, as has already been noted, no animosity in his satire. Like Chaucer, he displays a profound understanding of human nature and an acquaintance with people in all walks of life despite his restricted provincial background. He shows familiarity with courtly romance and the medieval "ars amatoriae," both of which delight in playing with the distinction between "buen amor" or courtly love (Provenzal "bona amors" and French "bone amors") and "loco amor" or lechery. In the episode of Doña Garoza, the longest in the *LBA* (stanzas 1332–1507), the Archpriest-narrator, whose identity is never revealed, apparently seduces a religious woman with whom he then seems to have a love affair. Nothing is clear cut except the narrator's proclivity for women and the fact that he gains access to the nun through the ministrations of an old bawd, a direct descendant of Ovid's Dipsas and sister to the Duenna of the *Roman de la Rose* and Chaucer's Wife of Bath. Her name, Trotaconventos, is a veritable "coup de maître" and one of the Archpriest's most felicitous satiric touches in the *LBA*. It is made up of the verb "trotar," to trot or run from one place to another and the noun "conventos," convents. Although in translation the word naturally loses some of its original flavor, in Spanish it retains, even today, much of the color and piquancy of the medieval notion—a woman who "trotted" from one religious house to another procuring for her clients:

> messajera de unas negras pecaças
> que usan mucho fraires e monjas e beatas:
> son mucho andariegas, merecen las çapatas;
> estas trotaconventos fazen muchas baratas.

> (from that tribe accursed, some vile, black-hearted bawd
> Employed by nuns and monks and others sanctified by God.
> Such well deserve the shoes they wear in prowlings much
>   abroad—
> There's not a maid these convent-trotters cannot win by fraud.)
>   (stanza 441)

In the episode of Doña Garoza, framed by a discussion of the pro's and con's of loving nuns and thanks to the magic of the Archpriest's superb characterization, the figure of the nun, at first only a mere feature in a general situation, comes alive in action.[18] Religious women participate in the procession gathered to celebrate the arrival of the god of love, an event that coincides with the beginning of spring, and they are in illustrious company:

> mucho omne ordenado que otorga perdones,
> los clérigos seglares con muchos clerizones.
> En la processión iva el abat de Berdones,
>
> órdenes de Cistel con la de Sant Benito,
> la orden de Cruniego con su abat benedito,
> quantas órdenes son: non las puse en escrito;
> . . . .
>
> Todas dueñas de orden, las blancas e las prietas,
> Cistel, pedricaderas e muchas menoretas,
> todas salen cantando, deziendo chançonetas:
> "Mane nobiscum, domine, que tañen a completas."

(For there one saw now hallowed men who pardoned sinners
   pained,
Now brothers lay, now some who wore the cloth but weren't
   ordained,
Besides an abbot marching there who for Saint Bernard
   reigned.

I saw some Blessed Saints and some which I Cistercians
   guessed,
With monks of Cluny, sable-crossed, who brought their abbot
   blest—
Indeed, the orders that I saw can't be in verse expressed.
. . . .

Dear sisters Black and Sisters White and every order went,
Cistercians, querulous Dominics, Francis' nuns love-bent,
All singing as they marched this song which showed their
   hearts' intent.
"Abide with us, oh Lord, "Tis, eve, and far the day is spent.")
   (stanzas 1235 b, c, d; 1236 a, b, c; 1241)

Their attitude on this occasion seems to be in agreement with that reflected in the satires and the fabliaux reviewed: "in a parody of the disciples' invitation to the resurrected Jesus to abide with them, these professional 'brides of Christ,' greet the lord of love and invite him to their beds."[19] It is, then, in the satiric tradition of Jean de Meung, the *Council of Remiremont,* and Boccaccio that religious women are first mentioned in the *LBA;* they remain enveloped in a strange aura of "devotion and lubricity"[20] throughout the entire poem. Thus, when the nuns again approach the god of love to offer their services to him, the sexual innuendo in their words has become more obvious— "señor, vete connusco, prueva nuestro celicio" (Come, dally with us, Sir, awhile, and try our hairy shirts [stanza 1255d]), they say. Avoiding circumlocution, one critic of the *LBA* points out that, in his opinion, the Archpriest's intention here was to create "a double-entendre between the hair shirt or cilix put on by a nun to chasten her nature and that other hairy thing put on by nature to chasten a nun."[21]

The next three stanzas begin what Maria Rosa Lida, the critic par excellence of the *LBA* calls the "game of zigzag" that will continue to the end of the episode, and whose premise is to "lead the reader in one direction, immediately to surprise him with a sudden turn."[22] It is in this spirit, therefore, that we are told it is dangerous to love nuns because, as cited earlier, "aman falsamente a quantos las amavan" (nuns love falsely whomsoe'er they catch within their claws [stanza 1256 b]). Deftly manipulated by the Archpriest, the reader sways between what one critic calls the artistic and the aesthetic poles of a literary work: "the artistic pole is the author's text and the aesthetic is the realization accomplished by the reader." However, as the same critic recognizes, because there is no "face-to-face-situation" when a reader "confronts" a text, he "can never learn from the text how accurate or inaccurate are his views."[23] After pointing out, then, the dire consequences of becoming involved with a religious woman, a circumstance that should be quite familiar to us, having encountered it in a number of monastic satires, the author once more offers a contradictory view. In a complete turnaround, the narrator presents an exceedingly seductive picture of the delights awaiting those who venture into a liaison with a nun—

> todo vicio del mundo, todo plazer oviera:
> si a dormitorio entrara, nunca se arrepentiera.

(Since every pleasure in the world and appetite he'd hent,
For once he found their sleeping quarters ne'er would he
   repent.) (stanza 1258 c, d)

The complexity of the reading process is heightened throughout
this section of the episode by the constant intertwining of the perspectives defining the author's view. The meaning of the text is
filtered through the reader's mind, subject all the time to several
perspectives; in the case of the conflicting opinions on religious
women in the stanzas just quoted, the perspectives at work are those
of the author and narrator, the plot of the episode, and the reader
himself. As readers, our understanding depends on what we assume
to be the cultural code framing the narrative, a code with a previously
accepted significance within a specific cultural context.[24] Returning
to stanza 1258 c, d just quoted above, the satire on the amatory gifts of
some religious women is quite light and does not jolt the reader with
any sudden epithets, while the humor resulting from the incongruity
between matter and style—religious women and goliardic poetry—is
typical of such medieval raillery. What is strikingly different is that,
although in the twelfth, thirteenth, and fourteenth-century poetry of
Italy and France, for instance, love had for a long time been treated
either very solemnly or very casually, Spanish poetry, written almost
exclusively by religious men, had shunned erotic topics. For the
Spanish monks, love was a sin and everything related to it an object of
shame.[25] Again, of course, the irony of the passage—of the entire
episode, in fact—is enhanced because the object ridiculed was so well
known to the medieval reader.
   So far, then, we cannot be sure whether the Archpriest is in
favor of or against loving nuns; we have to wait for seventy-four
stanzas before he ever mentions the subject again and when he does, it
is doubtful once more whether he is praising or admonishing:

   amat a alguna monja e creedme de consejo;
   luego non se casará, nin salirá a concejo,

(Go love a nun; believe me, son make that your one ambition,
For they can't marry afterward, nor dare breathe their
   condition—) (stanza 1332 b, c)

says Trotaconventos to the Archpriest. Feeling lonesome on a day when everyone else is in good company—

> Los que ante eran solos, desque eran casados
> veíalos de dueñas estar acompañados,

(All those who erst were single soon were housed and bedded
  double—
I saw them in the company of girls who loved to bubble—)
  (stanza 1316 a, b)

the Archpriest has just asked his go-between for "alguna tal garrida" (some pretty girl to make my very own [stanza 1317 c]). The old bawd makes two failed attempts at procuring and then, in the stanza cited above (1332 b, c) suggests that he "love a nun," obviously expecting better results from such an affair. Trotaconventos is well acquainted with religious women—"Yo las serví un tiempo, moré i bien diez años" (I once was servant to a nun, God knows how many a year [stanza 1333 a]), she says, and this marks the beginning of one of the best known passages in the whole *LBA,* the famous catalogue of uncommon and wonderful concoctions that religious women reputedly can prepare for their lovers.

> tienen a sus amigos viciosos, sin sossaños;
> ¡quién dirié los manjares, los presentes tamaños,
> los muchos letuarios, nobles e quán estraños!

(And I learned how they kept their sweethearts pampered
  without fear;
Why who could tell what wondrous presents, condiments and
  cheer
They make them with elixirs potent and prescriptions queer,)
  (stanza 1333 b, c, d)

Trotaconventos tells the Archpriest, and the next four stanzas are taken up with a list of exotic substances, many of which were certainly "not intended for mere sweetmeats."[26] After reciting the wonderful electuary with its promise of rapturous delights, Trotaconventos is now determined to break the Archpriest's resistance to having an affair with a religious woman and she talks for four stanzas about the infinite joys awaiting anyone willing to surrender to the love of a nun. In another display of h.s sophisticated control over the audience whose susceptivity he has been manipulating since early in the episode, the Archpriest now has the old bawd describe nuns in the most glowing terms as not only well-mannered and discreet, but also as beautiful, generous, and forthright. They are excellent lovers, she says, thoughtful and responsive, "en noblezas de amor ponen toda su hemencia" (ready to devote all their ingenuity to feats of love).[27] The tirade ends with the comment that "quien a monjas non ama non val maravedí" (a man who loves no nun has wits not worth a copper [stanzas 1338 d, 1339 d]) and is followed by a section listing the pleasures awaiting those who will love a religious woman:

> Sin todas estas noblezas, an mucho buenas maneras:
> mucho encobiertas son, donosas e plazenteras;
> más saben e valen más las sus moças cozineras
> para el amor del mundo, que unas dueñas de sueras;
>
> como imagen pintada, de toda fermosura,
> fijasdalgo muy largas e francas de natura,
> grandes doñeaderas: amor siempre les dura;
> comedidas, cumplidas e con toda mesura;
>
> todo el plazer del mundo e todo buen doñear,
> solaz de mucho sabor e el falaguero jugar,
> todo en las monjas es más que en otro lugar.

(Besides a nun is so well trained that in her sleep she straddles,
Is secretive, yet tutors men just how to dip their paddles.
Why when it comes to worldly love and merry fiddle-faddles,
The servant of a nun knows more than dames with leather
  saddles.

E'en like the Virgin's image painted every wondrous hue
Which men may worship with a kiss that thrills them through
  and through,
The figure of a nun inflames a man to have her too,
And since she knows the art of love, to learn from her to woo.

For every pleasure in the world, the latest syles in whoring—
The peace of sated ecstasy [a bliss you've been ignoring];

All this you'll find in nuns, and thus they'll merit your
adoring.) (stanzas 1340–1342 a, b, c)

The image conjured by Trotaconventos must be just what those
other lovers of medieval nuns mentioned earlier had in mind when
they approached them for their favors, because the Archpriest is
finally convinced. He wants to know now how he could possibly gain
access to one of the keepers of such a garden of delights. Trotaconventos promises she will arrange everything, and soon after we find
her talking with a nun "que avía servida" (whom she had served some
time [stanza 1344 a]). It is not clear in what capacity the bawd had
served this nun, but the Archpriest is careful to envelop their first
meeting with an air of immorality and license that we recognize only
too well: here is a religious woman listening with the utmost familiarity to the advances of a procuress with whom she actually seems to
have a long-standing relationship! Yet, just when we may be ready to
accept the fact that this nun really is like those countless others we
met earlier in other medieval literatures, the poet again chooses to
confuse us. In typical *LBA* fashion the direction of the narrative
changes abruptly[28] and we are told that Doña Garoza does not belong
to the tradition of wayward nuns we have come to know so well—

Aquesta buena dueña avié seso bien sano,
era de buena vida, non de fecho liviano.

(But this good woman certainly was sensible and wise,
And all her life was virtuous and ne'er did sin devise.)
(stanza 1347 a, b)

The next one hundred and twenty-six stanzas find Trotaconventos and Doña Garoza engaged in a rhetorical duel of wits as each
attempts, with all the elements at her disposal, to prove her point.
Trotaconventos wants to convince Doña Garoza that to accept the
Archpriest as a gallant will bring her only joy—the irony here is, of
course, that it would be the wrong kind of joy altogether for a
religious woman. The nun valiantly resists, however, arguing that she
would much rather continue to live in the austerity of the convent
than lose her honor and become an object of scorn:

Más valen en convento las sardinas saladas,
fazer a Dios servicio conas dueñas onradas,
que perder la mi alma con perdizes asadas
e fincar escarnida com'otras deserradas.

(I'd rather in my convent eat sardines preserved in salt,
Accompanied by honest dames [whose lives may God exalt]
Than sell my tail for roasted quail, to one who would not halt,
When I had lost my soul for him, to spurn me for my fault.)
    (stanza 1385)

The lively argument between the two women goes on for many lines
as they both resort to fables whose morals serve to strengthen their
respective positions.[29] Here and there things are said by one or the
other that provide a glimpse of Doña Garoza's past as well as of her
spiritual posture at this particular moment in her life. The following
two stanzas, for instance, throw some light on the old relationship
between Trotaconventos and Doña Garoza, as first the nun and then
the old procuress speak:

tú estavas coitada, pobre, sin buena fama,
onde oviesses cobro non tenías adama;
ayudéte con algo, fui grand tiempo tu ama:
conséjasme agora que pierda la mi alma.

"Señora," diz la vieja, "¡por qué só baldonada?
Quando trayo presente, só mucho falagada;
oy vin manos vazías: finco mal estultada."

(You once were in distress and poor, a woman of ill fame;
You had no livelihood nor e'even a penny to your name;
I gave you money then and long your mistress I became,
Yet now you counsel me to lose my soul and sink in shame.

"My lady," said the crone to her, "why is it I'm reviled?
When formerly I brought you what you wished, on me you
    smiled,
But now you see my empty hands, on me are insults piled.")
    (stanzas 1355–1356 a,b,c)

Nothing further is said about these "gifts" that Trotaconventos used to bring to Doña Garoza, but the old woman's words concerning the nun's fondness for such presents seems to echo those of li Muisis and the *Roman de la Rose*. There, religious women are accused of insatiable greed[30] and of accepting presents from their lovers in exchange for their favors. Little by little, then, through innuendo and suggestion interspersed with bold statements on the false honor of religious women, the figure of Doña Garoza begins to emerge, drawn by the poet with incredible ingenuity in a satirical portrait unparalleled in the Spanish literature of the Middle Ages. The Archpriest has already proved his acquaintance with the stereotyped figure of the wayward nun of previous centuries; that he is also aware of circumstances in a fourteenth-century nunnery becomes strikingly clear too in this brief description of life in the convent for the sisters who choose to ignore the offers of prospective lovers. The picture is one of unredeemed gloom:

> comedes en convento sardinas, camarones,
> berçuelas e lazeria, e los duros caçones,
> dexades del amigo perdizes e capones:
> ¡perdédesvos, coitadas!, mujeres sin varones;
>
> con la mala vianda, con saladas sardinas,
> con sayas d' estameña, passades vos, mesquinas:
> dexades del amigo las truchas, las gallinas,
> las camisas froncidas, los paños de Melinas.

(You munch sardines and prawns within a cheerless monastery.
Chew garden truck, and tough old steaks of shark, in portions
    chary,
While shunning quail with which your lover wants to make you
    merry—
You wreck your lives by shunning men, you wretched dames
    contrary!

With noisome victuals like sardines, besoaked in bitter brine,
You give your bellies punishment—you wear coarse shirts of
    twine,
And scorn you lovers' trout and capons, partridges and wine,
Besides the flouncy gowns they offer, made of fabrics fine.)
    (stanzas 1393–1394)

Also, the nuns always seem to be either singing or reading or else quarreling with one another, this activity an echo of a major complaint in the diocesan bishops' visitation reports.[31]

> ¡señora, qué negra ledanía!
> En aqueste roído vos fallo cada día:
>
> o vos fallo cantando o vos fallo leyendo,
> las unas con las otras contendiendo, reñiendo.

> (God choke that priest, the dull long-winded drone.
> Why do I find you every day attracted by his moan?
>
> I find you singing hymns or prayers [it's always either one]
> Unless it's caterwauling with some other pious nun.)
>   (stanzas 1396 c, d-1397 a, b)

From the beginning of the episode the voice of the satirical narrator has been hinting that Doña Garoza is a nun like many others—hiding beneath a mask of decency two of the most abhorred sins a professed woman might commit: indecency and unchastity. The poet, however, capitalizing expertly on the reader's expectations, has the possibly wayward Doña Garoza suddenly say something apparently quite out of character for a wayward nun: "religiosa non casta es podrida toronja" (an unchaste nun is like a rotten orange [stanza 1443 d]).[32] This is a statement almost on a par in its ferocity with the angriest medieval diatribes against dissolute behavior in the nunnery reviewed in an earlier chapter. Nevertheless, as if to offset such incongruency and to safeguard the satiric intent of his creation, the most salacious comment of the entire episode, one pointing out unmistakably the corruption undermining the old monastic order, comes precisely from Doña Garoza. While telling Trotaconventos the fable of the thief protected by Satan, the nun quotes the devil as saying,

> luego seré contigo, desque ponga un fraile
> con una fraila suya que me diz: "¡traile, traile!"

(I will be with you as soon as I get a friar together with his nun,
who's always nagging me, "Bring him, bring him!".)
   (stanza 1466 a, b)[33]

In view of what happens later and bearing in mind some of the
Archpriest's earlier comments on cloistered women in general, the
reader cannot help but wonder here if this might not be an expression
of Doña Garoza's own subconscious desires. Such an inquiry results
from the attempts the reader must make to fill in what we may call
"gaps" in the narration—the details the author purposefully leaves out
and which stimulate the reader to infer what is meant from what is
not said.[34] The satirical intent is quite clear, though, and the poet's
inspired touch allows the reader to observe the nun in action; as she
and Trotaconventos "are made to reveal themselves through their
spontaneous actions and equally spontaneous language."[35] Proving
once more that she is much wiser in the ways of the world than she
should have been, the nun tells the procuress that it is not customary
for a lady to be the first one to speak of love to a man and that,
therefore, "the most she can do is look at him keenly"[36]—"cumple
otear firme" (stanza 1483 c). She wants to know what he looks like,
and she wants to hear the truth:

> que desse arcipreste me digas su figura:
> bien e atal qual sea, dim toda su fechura;
> non respondas escarnio do t' preguntan cordura.

(See if you can describe this man, his gait, his countenance,
His figure, manner, everything, but mind you don't enhance
And stuff me full of pretty lies, for I take all askance.)
   (stanza 1484 b, c, d)

Doña Garoza's request elicits from the old woman a description
of the poet that has intrigued the critics for centuries now. Is Trotaconventos giving us the real portrait of the Archpriest, is she
describing him as she perceives him herself or, in a further attempt to
encourage the nun to love her client, is the old woman embellishing
the portrait with as many erotic details as possible? Stanzas 1485
through 1489 contain what is known as the portrait of the Archpriest
of Hita and, judging from the growing fervor displayed by Trotaconventos as she proceeds with the description, this is "a man enough to
bedazzle the imagination of any female, pleasurable or not":[37]

¡Par las çapatas mías!
tal omne qal yo digo, no es en todas las erias,

(By my slippers! You could not find his equal anywhere) (stanza
1489)[38]

shouts the old woman at the end, carried away by her own enthusi-
asm. Every detail of the Archpriest's portrait is intended to convey
the image of an exceptionally virile man, from the abundant dark hair
to the long nose regarded by the symbol-loving Middle Ages as
indicative of "the proportions of the male generative member."[39]
That a religious woman might engage in a love affair is no surprise to
us any more; the irony of the Archpriest's portrait lies rather in the
fact that this prospective lover's description pointedly includes certain
traits that the readers of the LBA (as familiar with medieval superstition as Chaucer's audience) would have regarded as signs of extreme
sexual potency—dark hair, long nose, deep voice, strong neck, thick
lips, and large ears.[40] According to the narrator, Trotaconventos has
surpassed herself in her description of the lover to the nun—"A la
dueña mi vieja tan bien que la enduxo" (How exquisitely was this nun
persuaded by my whore [stanza 1490 a]). The old woman now makes
a few general remarks on the dissolute habits of some religious men
and women, and for a brief moment the Archpriest's benevolent
satire becomes a harsh commentary on monastic corruption. This is
tempered, though, as always, by the prevailing mood of almost
irrepressible gaiety which emanates from Trotaconventos and by her
choice of words:

Sodes, monjas, guardadas, deseosas, loçanas;
cobdiciosos, los clérigos desean las ufanas;
¡todos quieren nadar: los peces e las ranas!
a pan de quinze días, fambre de tres semanas.

(You cooped up nuns are passionate, and burning up with lust,
But sporting monks desire to be with gayer women trussed,
Howe'er as all things like to swim, they'll wriggle where they
    must;
For people starved a month will hunger for a week-old crust.)
    (stanza 1491)

At last the nun is ready to accept a visit from the potential lover and openly confirm our suspicions of her profligacy. With his usual flair, though, the poet compounds the irony of the moment of decision by allowing Doña Garoza one more face-saving stratagem that may permit her to retain some sense of propriety: the demand that other nuns be present when she talks to the Archpriest. This request, of course, is the last straw in the long list of satirical touches already observed in the episode; religious women had always wanted to receive their visitors alone, and it was the archbishop who invariably fought for their compliance with the rule that they should have one or more sisters in the room with them.[41] Despite the attempt at a last stand, however, there does not seem to be any doubt in the mind of Trotaconventos that Doña Garoza will accept his advances once she sees the Archpriest in the flesh. After all, nuns are known to be "deseosas" (passionate), and he is a most desirable man, and a priest too.[42]

The poet is now almost through presenting Doña Garoza to the reader. Inspired perhaps by other examples of medieval monastic satire or by reports of real transgressions in the nunnery, the Archpriest adds to the portrait of his nun one more element which could be taken from the long list of complaints made against religious women by the Church: the ease with which lovers' messages traveled in and out of the convent.[43] The Archpriest sends a letter to Doña Garoza through the old bawd who also conveys to him the nun's reply, evidently not quite as inviting as he had hoped but still encouraging:

> guardas tenié la monja más que la mi esgrima,
> pero de buena fabla vino la buena cima.

> (Yet guards she had more than my sword, but guards can't
>   ward off crime
> And pleasant conversation oft results in merry times.)
>   (stanza 1498 c, d)

As with "buen amor," the phrase "buena cima" has caused much controversy among critics for centuries. Nevertheless, Joan Corominas, one of the great twentieth-century scholars of the *LBA* has no doubt that "the phrase 'buena cima' is unequivocal and may not, therefore, be interpreted in a pious sense."[44] For the Archpriest of

Hita, as for all the poets of the courtly tradition, love is an ennobling passion, one which restores a man's youth, sharpens his wit, and renews his spirit:

> al mancebo mantiene mucho en mancebez,
> e al viejo perder faz mucho la vejez.

> (Love keeps a young man in his prime [a physiologic truth];
> Love helps a senile patriarch retain the sap of youth.)
>   (stanza 157 a, b)

The result of "buen amor" à la Archpriest of Hita happens to be "buena cima" or the total enjoyment of the beloved up to but excluding the sexual union, a state seen by the troubadours as "falso amor" (false love).[45]

We are finally near the end of the episode when the eager lover at last gets a glimpse of the up to then elusive nun. We also see her for the first time through his eyes:

> alto cuello de garça, color fresco de grana.

> (Her girlish neck was slim, her face was flowerlike and fair.)
>   (stanza 1499)

The emotion of this first encounter so perturbs the Archpriest that he wrings his hands in frustration at the sight of so much "wasted" loveliness while exclaiming, "desaguisado fizo qui l' mandó vestir lana" (Whoever made her put on sackcloth did her wrong, I swear [stanza 1499 d]). Interestingly enough, this is a complaint that we have heard many times before but always spoken by the "victim" herself, that is, by the young woman forced to become a nun and made to wear the dark forbidding habit against her will by someone who "did her wrong."[46]

> ¡Valme, Santa María!, mis manos me aprieto:
> ¡quién dio a blanca rosa ábito e velo prieto!
> más valdrié a la fermosa tener fijos e nieto
> que atal velo negro, nin que ábitos ciento.

(So help me, Holy Virgin, but I raise my hands, alack,
Who gave a rose as white as she that ugly habit black?
'Twere better that a radiant girl should never children lack
Than take the veil of chastity and fight her yearnings back!)
   (stanza 1500)

This is unmistakably the language of passion. The irony of the
situation is overpowering; here is an Archpriest, himself enjoined by
his own religious vows to shun all physical love falling in love before
our eyes with, of all women, a nun. The next six stanzas are saturated
with the same tenacious ambiguity that characterizes the entire episode; in stanza 1501, the lover-priest, aware of the punishment awaiting those who commit a sin so foul yet overcome with desire, is ready
to transgress as long as there may be promise of forgiveness later. It
seems that neither lover will be able to resist the urge of the carnal
appetite; the words rush out of the narrator's mouth as in a torrent, as
though he were no longer capable of coherent thought:

> Oteóm de unos ojos que parecién candela;
> yo sospiré por ellos, diz mi coraçón: ¡héla!
> Fuime para la dueña, fablóme e fabléla:
> enamoróm la monja e yo enamoréla.

> (She gazed on me with eyes that shone like altar candles bright,
> 'Till like a prayer my spirit rushed out towards her at the sight;
> She spoke to me and I to her as though from some far height,
> And then she loved me with a kind of tremulous delight.)
>   (stanza 1502)

The old "game of zigzag" already in progress early in the
episode[47] is in full swing now. If the stanza just quoted above (1502)
appeared to indicate that all restraints were gone and that Doña
Garoza belonged to the tradition of reprobate nuns mocked and
reviled by Nigellus Wireker and li Muisis among others, in the next
stanza this is no longer clear; the battle between "cupiditas" and
"caritas" may not be quite over after all:

> Recibióme la dueña por su buen servidor:
> siempre le fui mandado e leal amador,

mucho de bien me fizo con Dios en limpio amor;
en quanto ella fue biva, Dios fue mi guiador.

(Still she received me only as her loved retainer true,
And always loyally I did whate'er she'd have me do,
With clean and chastened love my spirit close to God she drew
So that as long as she still lived, that God I loved and knew.)
   (stanza 1503)

Because, as was mentioned above, "limpio amor" like "buen amor"
may be interpreted as the heavenly love of God or one faithful lover's
earthly delights up to the sexual union,[48] the ambiguity that pervades
the entire episode is even more powerful here. If the poet's early
remarks on religious women (stanzas 1340–1342) are to be taken as the
expression of his true beliefs, then stanzas 1503 through 1505 display
his satiric bent even further. Though the language is purposefully and
cunningly veiled, it seems safe to assume that the description of Doña
Garoza and the general comments on nuns that follow were written
tongue in cheek:

> con mucha oración a Dios por mí rogava,
> con su abstinencia mucho me ayudava,
> la su vida muy limpia en Dios se deleitava:
> en lucura del mundo nunca se trabajava;
>
> para tales amores son las religiosas:
> para rogar a Dios con obras piadosas.

(Through many prayers to God for me she did her life exhaust;
She helped me too by abstinence, though passion paid the cost;
She yearned for God, and in His love her spotless soul was
   lost—
Ne'er in this frenzied world's delights her being was engrossed.

For loves like that are holy women made,
That is, for praying God and bringing pious persons aid.)
   (stanzas 1504–1505 a, b)

The lines immediately following are once again familiar and so is the
tone:

"Eve." Gislebertus (Burgundian, born c. late eleventh century). Sculpture fragment. Cathedral of St. Lazare, Autun. Musée Rolin. Photo courtesy of Jet Prendeville.

> que para amor del mundo mucho son peligrosas,
> e son muy escuseras, perezosas, mintrosas.

(as far as sensual love is concerned they are dangerous, hypocrites, idlers and gossips.)[49] (stanza 1505 c, d)

The episode of Doña Garoza ends, then, in the same way in which it began, with a comment on the unseemly habits of certain religious women. It is our contention that the Archpriest's attitude towards them, and towards Doña Garoza in particular, is inspired by the medieval tradition of literary wayward nuns whose existence is documented in countless episcopal visitation records, sermons and injunctions. It is to this same tradition that the figure of Madame Eglentyne also belongs. Through a detailed analysis of her portrait in the *General Prologue* to the *Canterbury Tales*, aided by some of the major criticism of the last eighty years, as well as a review of primary sources old and new, we can view her from a new perspective. The result should be a better understanding of Chaucer's Prioress as heir, with the Archpriest of Hita's Doña Garoza, to what we called earlier that long line of prototypical wayward nuns dating back to the early stages of monasticism.

Madame Eglentyne was "a very conspicuous lady."[50] Her head dress, her manners, her rosary, and her brooch caused her to stand out among the other pilgrims; in fact, her very presence in such company ought to have attracted everyone's attention, since nuns were not allowed to go on pilgrimages by ecclesiastical ruling. Already in the year 791 a council had forbidden religious women to participate in pilgrimages and in 1195 the Council of York had decreed: "In order that the opportunity of wandering may be taken away from nuns, we forbid them to take the path of pilgrimage."[51] The reason for this injunction, aside from the fact that Church authorities were for ever fighting to keep the nuns within their cloister, was that pilgrimages, as mentioned above, were known to be not only religious occurrences but social occasions as well. According to Jacques de Vitry many pilgrims "weary of wayfaring, used to drink themselves tipsy,"[52] and in Roger Bacon's commentary on the *Secretum Secretorum,* cited by Bridges in his edition of the *Opus Majus* (I, 403), Venus is said to be favorable to pilgrimages when in conjunction with the Moon.[53] Besides the morally dangerous consequences risked by anyone going on pilgrimage in the fourteenth century, there were physical perils too, such as highway bandits lurking behind every tree along the road, while illnesses and inadequate lodging also plagued the travelers. Another, and much more important circumstance which should have kept the Prioress from riding to Canterbury on pilgrimage was the fact that she was bound by oath—and papal injunction—to remain within the cloister "sub-perpetua"[54] (forever) instead of wandering into the world, particularly such distance as there was between her presumed nunnery of Stratford atte Bowe and the Canterbury shrine. One critic actually figures that the trip must have taken at least twelve days, as it was approximately three to four days with three overnight stops or three days with two overnight stops; in addition to the three days on the road, there would be one or two days in Canterbury, three days to return to Southwark, and then four days' round trip to and from Southwark to Stratford.[55] This would have meant an exceedingly long absence from her house for any nun, let alone a Prioress, whose behavior, as we know, was meant to set an example for the rest of the congregation. Therefore, we are inclined to agree with Muriel Bowden that "the mere fact that Madame Eglentyne is one of the Canterbury pilgrims is the first point of satire in a portrait that is satiric."[56]

As if the "illegal" presence of the Prioress on a pilgrimage were not already enough to cause a medieval audience to smile in tolerant amusement at a frequent real-life situation—and a well-known literary figure—step by step the next twenty-three lines build a portrait of a nun whose resemblance to a courtly lady of romance grows more and more striking with each succeeding verse:

> Ther was also a Nonne, a Prioresse,
> That of hir smylyng was ful symple and coy;
> Hire gretteste ooth was but by Seinte Loy;
> And she was cleped madame Eglentyne.
> Ful weel she soong the service dyvyne,
> Entuned in hir nose full semely,
> And Frenssh she spak ful faire and fetisly,
> After the scole of Stratford atte Bowe,
> For Frenssh of Parys was to hire unknowe.
> At mete wel ytaught was she with alle:
> She leet no morsel from hir lippes falle,
> Ne wette hir fyngres in hir sauce depe;
> Wel koude she carie a morsel and wel kepe
> That no drope ne fille upon hire brest.
> In curteisie was set ful muchel hir lest.
> Hir over-lippe wyped she so clene
> That in hir coppe ther was no ferthyng sene
> Of grece, whan she dronken hadde hir draughte.
> Ful semely after hir mete she raughte.
> And sikerly she was of greet desport,
> And ful plesaunt, and amyable of port,
> And peyned hire to countrefete cheere
> Of court, and to been estatlich of manere,
> And to ben holden digne of reverence.
> But, for to speken of hire conscience,
> She was so charitable and so pitous
> She wolde wepe, if that she saugh a mous
> Kaught in a trappe, if it were deed or bledde.
> Of smale houndes hadde she that she fedde
> With rosted flessh, or milk and wastel-breed.
> But soore wepte she if oon of hem were deed,
> Or if men smoot it with a yerde smerte;
> And al was conscience and tendre herte.
> Ful semyly hir wympul pynched was,
> Hir nose tretys, hir eyen greye as glas,
> Hir mouth ful smal, and therto softe and reed;
> But sikerly she hadde a fair forheed;

It was almoost a spanne brood, I trowe;
For, hardily, she was nat undergrowe.
Ful fetys was hir cloke, as I was war.
Of smal coral aboute hire arm she bar
A peire of bedes, gauded al with grene,
And theron heng a brooch of gold ful sheene,
On which ther was first write a crowned A,
And after AMOR VINCIT OMNIA.[57]

From "hir smylyng," which was "ful symple and coy," to her superbly polished manners, Madame Eglentyne's figure is drawn from the same sources used by the most famous authors of medieval French romance, such as Deschamps, Machaut, Froissart, and Watriquet de Couvin. In their pages, ladies much like the Prioress smiled in a manner that was "symple and coy" and were often called "Eglantine."[58]

This courtly-lady-"Prioresse," however, had not only chosen a most unlikely name, but "Hire gretteste ooth was but by Seinte Loy." The Benedictine Rule governing all aspects of monastic life in the nunnery urges its followers—"Non jurare, ne forte perjuret"[59] (not to swear lest perchance one foreswear oneself), and even though neither Chaucer nor his audience would have known the exact words of this—or any—section of the Rule, the fact that a religious woman swore, no matter how lightly, would have been understood as a violation of proper monastic conduct. Actually, an oath by Saint Loy can hardly be called swearing, yet critics through the centuries have both vehemently attacked and defended the Prioress's "right" to swear by "Seinte Loy." To the latter, that is, to those who refuse to accept the satiric implications in her portrait, the oath is just another indication of what they call her "daintiness," not seen as in any way affecting her image as a devoted ecclesiastic.[60] Those who consider that it would be highly irregular for a nun, let alone a prioress, to swear, however genteel her oath might be, also point out that St. Loy was invoked then, and is still invoked today by the "petites ouvrières" of Paris when they wish to see in their dreams the image of the man they will marry.[61] (Most likely Chaucer was not aware of the added significance of making the Prioress swear by St. Loy, but the mention of that particular saint's name certainly adds special significance to the line for twentieth-century readers). The fact that Madame Eglentyne swears—albeit so gently—is only one instance of her misconduct in a

portrait that almost reads like a catalogue of infractions to the Benedictine Rule. To go back once more to her "smylyng," it should be
noted that a smile that looked as inviting as the one from a lady of
romance would not only have been most unseemly in a nun, but
could also have been taken as an indication of her desire for further
social contact.

We have now been introduced to Madame Eglentyne and we
know that she has an engaging smile and that she is capable of using a
mild expletive. We are quite ready to hear something about this nun's
religious life, but when that information finally comes, it consists of a
mere reference to the manner in which she sings the "service
dyvyne"—"ful weel" and "entuned in hir nose ful semely," according
to the narrator—and nothing else. It is becoming more and more
obvious that this is the portrait of a religious woman where the
emphasis is not going to be either on religion or the nun's attributes,
but rather on the way in which the narrator perceives them and
presents them. Again, as with Doña Garoza, we receive "messages"
from the narrator intended to help us visualize the character described. At the same time, these "messages" are transmitted in two
ways, since we, as readers, actually receive them by composing
them.[62] The satiric overtone is alternately enhanced and diminished
by the narrator's comments, apparently intended only to create a
picture without any attempt at moral judgement at this point.

> And Frenssh she spak ful faire and fetisly,
> After the scole of Stratford atte Bowe,
> For Frenssh of Parys was to hire unknowe,

is what we are told next, and we may assume that, though only
mildly ironic, the remark about her French is meant to reenforce the
impression of a woman concerned with worldly rather than spiritual
propriety.

The joke, however, is on Madame Eglentyne herself, so preoc-
cupied with being "holden digne of reverence" that she does not
realize her efforts to speak French "ful faire and fetisly" become
ludicrous when the listener detects her provincial accent, acquired at
Stratford and unrefined by lack of contact with the court of Paris.
Actually, as one critic points out, "a certain ineptitude with classical
or foreign languages is a common satirical touch in medieval English
literature."[63] This is a remark which, in the particular case of

Madame Eglentyne is rendered even more poignant by the fact that Stratford, although definitely not a second-rate nunnery,[64] somehow remained in the shadow of the much more prestigious and aristocratic Barking Abbey. Located on a branch of the river Lea in Essex, Stratford atte Bowe was about a mile away from the powerful Abbey of Barking that would have been regarded by the less privileged nuns of Stratford as highly as the Westminster court. Legend has it that an underground passage connected Barking with All Hallow's Barking, a distance of about eight miles. If so, this passage would have permitted the nuns "to travel to and from London unnoticed."[65] In view of the historical evidence reviewed, Madame Eglentyne's proximity to Barking, Chaucer's comments on her lifestyle, and her ambition "to contrefete cheere / of court" would all make her highly suspect of perhaps taking covert trips to London, where her efforts "to been estatlich of manere" would have had a better chance of being appreciated.

The next section of the portrait is a minutely detailed description of the Prioress's perfectly dainty table manners, a refinement hardly expected in a religious woman. The ironic implications of such a passage can hardly be missed; they have been an object of concern to Chaucerian critics for centuries. Here is "a Nonne, a Prioresse," that is, a woman bound by her sacred profession and by what should have been years of austere living in the supposedly stern environment of the convent, indulging in the ritual of eating a meal with the most incredible elegance because, contrary to her vow of humility, "In curteisie was set ful muchel hir lest." Madame Eglentyne must have known, and Chaucer's audience must have suspected that she was not only violating another precept of the Benedictine Rule—"Saeculi actibus se facere alienum"[66] (to avoid worldly conduct)—but that she was in flagrant contravention of a cardinal dictum of the Church proclaiming that, "essus carnium, et potus vini . . . seminarium libidinis est"[67] (the eating of flesh and drinking of wine . . . is the seed of lust). It was considered of extreme importance in the Middle Ages to avoid the sin of gluttony thought to be closely associated with lust. Already in the seventh century St. Gregory had said that "de ventris ingluvie, inepta laetitia, scurrilitas, immunditia, multiloquium, habetudo sensus circa intelligentiam propagantur"[68] (for from gluttony are propagated foolish mirth, scurrility, uncleanness, babbling, dullness of sense in understanding). This is really an accusation that could be more easily leveled at the Monk than at the Prioress, it is true, but of which she may not be regarded as quite free, judging from her exaggerated concern with the politest way to handle food, a concern that was, as already mentioned, more fitting in a worldly lady than a nun:

> She leet no morsel from hir lippes falle,
> Ne wette hir fyngres in hir sauce depe.

What really makes Chaucer's already apparently incriminating words even more damaging when applied to a religious woman is the fact that the description of the much vaunted manners of Madame Eglentyne, carefully rehearsed so as to make her exactly "à la mode"[69] are from Jean de Meung's *Roman de la Rose*.[70] It has been known for centuries now that the lines are part of the advice given by the Duenna—"la Vieille"—to Fair Welcome on how women should behave in order to gain a man's love:

> Il affiert bien qu'el soit a table
> De contenance convenable.
>
> . . . .
>
> Et si bien prenne sa bouchée
> Que sur son pis goutte ne chée
> De souppe ne de saulse noire,
> Et si doit si sagement boire
> Que sur soy n'en espande goutte,
> Car pour trop rude ou pour trop gloute
> La pourroit bien aucun tenir
> Qui ce luy verroit advenir.
> Et garde qu'au hanap ne touche
> Tant qu'elle ait morcel en la bouche
> Laquelle elle doit si bien terdre
> Que point n'y laisse gresse adherdre
> Au moins en la levre dessure,
> Car quant gresse en elle demeure
> Ou vin il gaste las maillettes
> Qui ne sont ne belles ne nettes.[71]

(Fit manners should she have when she's at meat;

. . . .

She should not wet her fingers in the sauce
Beyond the joint, nor soil her lips with soup,
With garlic, or fat meat; nor pile a heap

Of food and then convey it to her mouth.
With tips of fingers should she handle bits
That she should dip in sauce, white, yellow or green,
And very carefully the mouthful lift,
That on her breast no bit of pepper falls,
Or soup or gravy. Then so gracefully
She should her goblet quaff that not a drop
She spills upon her clothes, for far too rude
Or gluttonous men might consider her
If they should see such accident occur.
The common cup should not approach her lips
While yet there is some food within her chops;
And ere she drinks she wipes her mouth so clean
That on her lips no speck of grease adheres,
At least not on her upper lip, for then
Globules of it might float upon the wine.
Which would be most disgusting and not neat.)

As if the Duenna's counsel were not already suspect, it becomes even
more so when we remember that it originally comes from the highly
disreputable procuress in Book III of Ovid's *Amores*. Here, in order to
arm women against the men to whom he has given so much advice in
Books I and II, Ovid tells the ladies some secrets on the art of love:

Carpe cibos digitis: est quiddam gestus edendi:
   Ora nec immunda tota perunge manu.
Neve domi praesume dapes, sed desine citra
   Quam capis; es paulo quam potes esse minus;
Priamides Helenen avide si spectet edentem,
   Oderit, et dicat "stulta rapina mea est."72

(Daintiness matters: be sure to help yourself with your fingers
In the most ladylike way; don't feed your face with a paw.
Don't just pick at your food, as if you had had a big dinner;
Don't, on the other hand, gobble as much as you can.
Even a Helen would seem repulsive, a horrible creature,
Taking too much at a meal, stuffing herself to the ears.)

The last line of the section on the Prioress's table manners—"ful
semely after hir mete she raughte" has traditionally been interpreted

as indicating one more accomplishment—"she reached for her meat daintily"—in the long list of niceties in which Madame Eglentyne seems to excel. The first hint that an extra touch of irony may be implicit in the word "raughte" came in 1914, when a Chaucerian scholar pointed out that "raughte" could be connected with Old English "hroecan," "to spit," and that it should, therefore, be translated as Modern English "retched" instead of "reached." This rather bizarre interpretation actually brings a "little Rabelaisian touch"[73] to the description, one more in keeping with the aura of good-humored mockery surrounding the portrait of this and the other ecclesiastics in the *Prologue*. Although it does, somehow, sound like a most unkind remark for Chaucer to make about this nun who appears to be the object of only mild and amused satire throughout the *Canterbury Tales*, the notion that such a refined lady as Madame Eglentyne could be caught in one of the most elementary psysiological acts, would probably have appealed to the rather primitive sense of humor of a medieval audience.

The portrait goes on:

> And sikerly she was of greet desport,
> And ful plesaunt, and amyable of port,
> And peyned hire to countrefete cheere
> Of court, and to been estatlich of manere,
> And to ben holden digne of reverence.

It is only after reading the lines several times, however, that the full effect of the irony becomes clear: all these marvelous traits, so desirable in a courtly lady are actually being ascribed to a nun. Could what one critic calls "this conflation of the courtly lady and the nun"[74] have been the product of Chaucer's imagination alone or, in the words of Muriel Bowden, "is she drawn from a living model?"[75] If we trust once again the evidence of the historical documents that have come down to us, we must answer yes to the question posed above; we could have met Madame Eglentyne in person in any fourteenth-century nunnery. As for her literary counterparts, we have already met them in the songs and the fabliaux, the sermons, and the satires of the Middle Ages. Besides the collective importance of the lines recently quoted as a confirmation of the general personality of the Prioress, already implied at the beginning of her portrait, there is in them a key word holding the secret to her character, and that is the verb "to countrefete," modern English "to imitate" or "to deceive." If she was "of greet desport, / And ful plesaunt, and amyable of port," then it cannot have been the court of Jerusalem she was trying to imitate but rather that of Babylon, and perhaps, as one critic says, "she follows the Squire and could dance in his garden."[76] As "the unsaid comes to life in the reader's imagination, so the said 'expands' to take on greater significance than might have been supposed,"[77] and we begin to see Madame Eglentyne, not as a bad woman, but as a prioress who is not so good.

It is important to note that at this time in the portrait our original expectations are still unfulfilled, because nothing in the description has so far matched the image of a religious woman we might have entertained. Although no single detail may be taken as exclusively satirical, each one fails to correspond to what we, as twentieth-century readers, may have anticipated when we first knew there was in the assembly "a Nonne." What happens is simply that Madame Eglentyne does not fit the cultural code that would establish her as a religious woman within our own, familiar cultural context. The next line, however, begins with the adversative "but" followed by a mention of the Prioress's "conscience," both of which could be taken to indicate a possible shift in the direction of the portrait:

> But, for to speken of hire conscience,
> She was so charitable and so pitous.

Yet, just when we think that perhaps now, finally, something will be said about this religious woman's spiritual make-up, we are told—

> She wolde wepe, if that she saugh a mous
> Kaught in a trappe, if it were deed or bledde.

This disconcerting "see-saw" technique, where contradictory statements follow one another in rapid succession is strongly reminiscent of the Archpriest of Hita's "modus operandi" when attempting to plant in our minds the image of Doña Garoza as a member of the wayward nun tradition, while cunningly endowing her with exactly the opposite attributes expected in a religious woman of that ilk. In the case of the Prioress's charitableness, our expectations as readers get thwarted once again, when we find out that she cries over dead mice and we wonder what kind of charity hers is. According to St. Thomas, true charity is the friendship of man for God, which may be extended to other human beings.[78] Therefore, since we are prepared for a totally different kind of statement in the portrait, the substitution of mice for men becomes strikingly anticlimactic. Its effectiveness as a source of subtle humor is further enhanced by the poet's anticipatory remarks on Madame Eglentyne's seeming aloofness from spiritual concerns. Her bent towards the mundane, evidenced by her "smylyng," her "ooth," her chosen courtly name, her punctilious manners, and her "amyable port" have all been carefully-casually planted clues. Everything appears to indicate that this nun's desire "to ben holden digne of reverence" may not refer to the respect owed her as a representative of the Church, but rather as a noble lady. It is a striking phenomenon and one more proof of Chaucer's superbly polished craft that the tone of the description remains basically neutral throughout, thus conveying a disturbingly ambiguous picture:

> Of smale houndes hadde she that she fedde
> With rosted flessh, or milk and wastel-breed.
> But soore wepte she if oon of hem were deed,
> Or if men smoot it with a yerde smerte;
> And al was conscience and tendre herte.

This passage, again delivered by the narrator in the most objective manner—as though having dogs were perfectly natural for a nun—actually records, not a mere fact of her lifestyle, but also a clear disregard for the episcopal injunctions against the presence of animals in the convent.[79] Furthermore, not only did Madame Eglentyne violate here another rule, but she seems to have done it with gusto, feeding her "illegal" dogs choice morsels from the nunnery table, such as "rosted flessh" and "wastel-breed."[80] Could this trivial act of disobedience be taken as a sign that if she were capable of breaking one rather minor rule she might perhaps have been tempted to break other, more important ones? The last line speaks of her conscience once more—"And al was conscience and tendre herte"—but this time we are not so easily taken in as before at the mention of the word "conscience" and we no longer expect great things to follow. They do not. Yet, lines 142 and 150 ("But, for to speken of hire conscience . . .

And al was conscience and tendre herte") which provide the framework to the passage on the Prioress's misapplied charity and love may
have a much greater significance than is apparent in the satirical
context of the portrait: they could actually be interpreted as extending
the poet's reproach—no matter how veiled or how temperate—to all
of the religious world. It would be quite fitting, and very much in
tune with Chaucer's fondness for "double entendre," to create an
impression of such ambivalent force that the lines may be taken as a
simple statement of fact about one flawed individual, or as an indictment of the whole ecclesiastic community of his time.

Nothing else is forthcoming on Madame Eglentyne's likely
spiritual qualities, but again the narrator turns from the brief mention
of "conscience" to a detailed description of the Prioress's appearance.
This is another section of the portrait that has caused considerable
controversy among critics, some of whose judgments have ranged
from the extravagant to the ludicrous. In most cases the critics, like
the reader, are struck by the seeming incongruency arising from the
description of the physical charms of a beautiful woman who happens
to be a nun and, as a result, they are left with the uncomfortable
feeling of having somehow found out something that they were not
supposed to know. The Prioress, though, is an attractive woman and
her physical attributes are listed by the narrator according to the
purest canons of medieval rhetoric without the slightest hint of
mockery. Why, then, does her "descriptio pulchritudinis" (description
of beauty) evoke such mixed reactions in the reader, and where does
the discrepancy resulting in some of Chaucer's finest ironic touches
reside? The answer is perhaps that everything hinges on a "misuse" of
the convention formulated by Geofroi de Vinsauf and long accepted
by medieval authors. "If you wish to describe womanly beauty," says
de Vinsauf,

> Praeformet capiti Naturae circinus orbem;
> . . . lilia vernent
> In specula frontis; . . .
>
> . .   .   .
> . . . castiget regula nasi
> Ductum, ne citra sistat vel transeat aequum;
> Excubiae frontis, radient utrimque gemelli
> Luce smaragdina vel sideris instar ocelli;
> Aemula sit facies Aurorae, nec rubicundae

Nec nitidae, sed utroque simul neutroque colore.
Splendeat os forma spatii brevis et quasi cycli
Dimidii; tanquam praegnantia labra tumore
Surgant, sed modico rutilent, ignita, sed igne
Mansueto.[81]

(Let Nature's compass draw the outline of the head; . . . let lilies
grow on the lofty forehead . . . let restraint rule the shape of the
nose, lest if fall short of, or exceed, the proper bounds. Let the
sentinels of the forehead gleam from both sides, twin little eyes
with emerald lights, like a constellation . . . Let the swelling lips
be moderately full, and red, fired with a mild flame.)

The rules that should guide a description of female charms go
on for thirty-seven lines,[82] but what gives the physical portrait of the
Prioress an added ironic measure is the fact that, included in the set of
de Vinsauf's famous "rhetorical injunctions" are two sentences that
might have made some readers of the *General Prologue* blush, had they
known them. The lines probably brought a twinkle of mischief to
Chaucer's eye as he wrote them.

De Vinsauf says:

Pectus, imago nivis, quasi quasdam collaterales
Gemmas virgineas producat utrimque papillas.
Sit locus astrictus zonae, brevitate pugilli
Circumscriptibilis. Taceo de partibus infra:
Aptius hic loquitur animus quam lingua.[83]

(Let the snowy bosom present both breasts like virginal gems set
side by side. Let the waist be slim, a mere handful. I will not
mention the parts beneath: here the imagination speaks better
than the tongue.)

Does not the reader of

Hir nose tretys, hir eyen greye as glas,
Hir mouth ful smal, and therto softe and reed;
But sikerly she hadde a fair forheed;
It was almoost a spanne brood, I trowe;
For, hardily, she was nat undergrowe

feel a twinge of anticipation at what may come next in the description?[84] In the twelfth-century *Speculum Stultorum*,[85] there is a section on religious women where the author hints at "the beauties beneath the gown" in the best rhetorical manner:

> Hae caput abscondunt omnes sub tegmine nigro,
> Sub tunicis nigris candida membra latent.[86]

> (Beneath black veils they all conceal their heads,
> Beneath black skirts they hide their lovely legs.)

In the "recurrent pattern of ambivalence"[87] of the Prioress's portrait, banter carries more weight than sobriety, and what remains unsaid is always more suggestive than what is explicit. Moreover, what is left out does not disappear from view in the process, and changes continue to take place in the reader's mind which prompt him "to adopt a position in relation to the text."[88] In his illuminating article on the subject, "The Art of the Descending Catalogue,"[89] Kevin Kiernan points out that one of the "most shocking" things in the catalogue of the Prioress's physical traits is the realization that Chaucer followed closely Geofroi de Vinsauf's precept—

> Sed ipsa
> Tibia se gracilem protendat; pes brevitatis
> Eximia brevitate sua lasciviat. . . .[90]

(Let beauty descend from the top of the head to the very feet.)

The portrait, Kiernan says, is presented in two installments, and the first half "simultaneously descends and reverts from mouth to nose to fingers to breast to mouth,"[91] while the second half again goes back to the nun's head. In the *General Prologue*, though, the golden hair suggested by the rhetorician is replaced by a wimple. This is a device which almost compels the reader to encircle the subject with his mind's eye, since his gaze is directed around the body with the mention of clothing and, in the case of Madame Eglentyne, her "wympul" and her "cloke."

As so many readers and scholars have been doing for centuries, let us pause for a moment in contemplation of the Prioress's "wympul." Here is an article of clothing pertaining to a religious woman's habit which was not exactly like the one prescribed by the Benedictine order. This "regulation wimple" was supposed to be "not only puritanically plain, but also of Mohammedan amplitude," so as to hide as much of the face as possible, preferably down to the eyebrows.[92] Madame Eglentyne's wimple, however, certainly did not reach her eyebrows, in fact, it barely covered her forehead that "was almoost a spanne brood." This was quite in keeping with the latest medieval fashion,[93] that called for Madonnas and beautiful women to display a very high forehead, with a plucked hairline even, as we can see from many fourteenth-century portraits. Actually, the phrase "she was nat undergrowe" has intrigued scholars for hundreds of years, and while some see her as almost robust—"the Prioress is very large of forehead, and her bodily proportions are quite in keeping"[94]— other critics feel it is merely another ironic stab of Chaucer's at a religious figure who does not live for the spirit alone, as is obvious from the attention she pays to eating.[95] The *Ancrene Riwle*,[96] the thirteenth-century manual for anchoresses says,

> Treowe ancres beoð briddes icleopede. for ha leaueð þe eorðe. Þ is þe luue of alle worltliche þinges. and þurh ȝirn unge of heorte to heouenliche þinges. fleoð uppart toward heouene. . . . Þeo briddes fleoð wel þe habbeð lutel flesch as þe pellican haueð and feole fiðeren. þe strucoín for his muchele flesch. and oþre swucche fuheles makieð a semblant to fleon. and beateð þe wengen. ah þe uet eauer draheð to þer eorðe. Alswa fleschlich ancre þe liueð i flesches lustes and folheð hire eise. þe heuínes se of hire flesch and flesches unþeawes bineomeð hire hire fluht. and tah ha makie semblant and muche nurð wið wengen. oþres nawt hiren. Þ is leote of as þah ha fluhe. and were an hali ancre. hwa se ȝeorne bihalt. lahheð hire to bismere. for hire uét eauer as doð þe strucoins. Þ beoð hire lustes. draheð to þere orðe.[97]

(True anchoresses are called birds because they leave the earth, that is, the love of all worldly things, and because of the longing of their hearts towards heavenly things, fly upward towards heaven. . . . Those birds fly well that have not much flesh, like the pelican, and many feathers. The ostrich and other such birds, because of their great weight of flesh, make only a pretence of flying, beating their wings while their feet remain always near the ground. So with the sensual anchoress who lives for the

pleasures of the body and cultivates her own comfort; the weight
of her flesh and bodily vices prevent her from flying, and though
she makes a pretence and great commotion with wings . . . and
though she has some appearance of flying and looks like a holy
anchoress, whoever looks closely will laugh her to scorn, for her
feet, that is her desires, keep her always near the earth as the
ostriches do.)

It is quite possible that if Chaucer could convey to his audience the
image of a nun who, like "the sensual anchoress" was weighted down
by her flesh, that is, by the magnitude of her carnal appetites, everyone would laugh at her too.[98]
    As we continue scrutinizing the description of the Prioress's head
in the portrait, we must not forget that, highlighting the passage is
the line that introduces it—"Ful semyly hire wympul pynched was."
Critics have often pointed out that these words really provide the
initial surprise of the section, since a "pynched wympul" would
definitely have been improper array for a woman that had forsworn
all worldly adornments. Moreover, lay women also wore wimples in
the fourteenth century (the Wife of Bath had one that was
"ywympled wel"), although they did it to complement their garb and
not in an attempt to keep their faces from men's eyes, but precisely for
the opposite reason. What a wonderful touch of fine Chaucerian
irony to have Madame Eglentyne wear a wimple as a nun naturally
would, but to make it "ful semyly pynched," thus turning an element
of potential monastic reticence into a piece of fashionable attire. At
this point in the portrait, it seems as though the entire passage dealing
with the Prioress's physical looks has been leading up to "Ful fetys
was hir cloke, as I was war"; together with the line on her wimple, it
forms the framework within which Madame Eglentyne's features
come alive before our eyes. Again by a masterful stroke of satiric
innuendo, what should have been merely part of a religious woman's
garb—"hir cloke"—becomes, when described as "ful fetys,"[99] another instance of this particular nun's disregard for the rules of her
order and the propriety which they attempted to enforce. Chaucer
and his audience were well aware (as we are too) of the medieval
Church's fruitless efforts to curb unseemly displays of finery among
its female representatives, since "for more than six weary centuries
the bishops waged a holy war against fashion in the cloister, and they

waged it in vain."[100] No better example, thus, of the failure of the ecclesiastical authorities in this matter than the clothes of the Prioress who, against regulations, wore, not only an elaborately "pynched wympul," but also a "ful fetys cloke." To complete her "un-mona-chal" array,

> Of smal coral aboute hire arm she bar
> A peire of bedes, gauded al with grene,
> And theron heng a brooch of gold ful sheene,
> On which ther was first write a crowned A,
> And after AMOR VINCIT OMNIA.

It would once more highlight the close relationship between the nuns in real life and Chaucer's creation to go back again to the historical evidence provided by certain visitation reports of the diocesan bishops and archbishops, where the matter of improper attire for religious women is discussed:

Year 1314, Keldholme Priory: Archbishop Corbridge issued an injunction against "secular finery and singularity of dress [which] were to be avoided by the nuns."[101]

Year 1397, Nun Monkton Priory: Thomas Dalby, Archbishop of Richmond, ordered the nuns to wear no silk clothes or veils, furs, "nor rings on their fingers, nor tunics pleated, or with brooches."[102]

Year 1445, Goring Priory, from visitation report by an assistant to Bishop Alnwick:

Et deinde, quia dominus vidit oculata fide moniales gerere vela sua vltra et supra frontes extenta, iniunxit eidem priorisse in virtute obediencie prestita quod ipsa gerat et faciat sorores suas gerere vela sua; vsque ad oculos suos extenta.[103]

(And then, because my lord saw with the evidence of his eyes that the nuns do wear their veils spread out on either side and above their foreheads, he enjoined upon the same prioress in virtue of her obedience proffered that she shall wear and cause her sisters to wear their veils spread down to their eyes.)

Year 1440, Langley Priory, from visitation report to Bishop Alnwick:

Domina Johanna Groby dicit quod quedam moniales vtuntur peplis de cerico. . . . Domina Cecilia Pole vtitur peplis de cerico contra constituciones, si cut liquet ad oculum. Domina Margareta Fox vtitur peplis de cerico in capite contra constituciones.[104]

(Dame Joan Groby says that certain nuns do wear silken veils. . . . Dame Cecily Pole wears silken veils against the constitutions, as is clear to the eye. Dame Margaret Fox wears silken veils on her head against the constitutions.)

Year 1441, Ankerwyke Priory, from visitation report by Bishop Alnwick:

. . . priorissa vtitur anulis aureis quamplurimum sumptuosis cum diuersis gemmis et eciam zonis argentatis et deauratis et cericis velis, et nimium eleuat velum supra frontem, quod frons patens totaliter ab omnibus potest videri, et fururis vtitur de vario. Fatetur vsum plurium anulorum et zonarum et velorum cericorum et eleuacionem velorum; fatetur eciam vsum fururarum de vario.[105]

(Also the Prioress wears golden rings exceedingly costly with divers precious stones, and also girdles silvered and gilded over and silken veils, and she carries her veil too high above her forehead, so that her forehead, being entirely uncovered, can be seen of all, and she wears furs of vair. She confesses the use of several rings and girdles and silken veils and the high carriage of her veils; confesses also the use of furs of vair.)

Year 1441, Ankerwyke Priory, from Bishop Alnwick's injunctions:

And also that none of yow, the prioresse ne none of the couente, were no vayles of sylke ne no syluere pynnes ne no gyrdles herneysed wyth syluere or golde, ne no mo rynges on your fyngres then oon, ye that be professed by a bysshope, ne that

none of yow vse no lased kyrtels, but butonede or hole be fore,
ne that ye use no lases a bowte your nekkes wythe crucyfixes or
rynges hangyng by thayme, ne cappes of astate obowe your
vayles.106

The list goes on and it is not difficult to recognize some of Madame
Eglentyne's oddities of dress among those causing so much anxiety to
the visiting dignitaries.

There is in the description of the Prioress's clothes an extraordinary technical stratagem that could, at first, seem intended to disori-
ent, again, the reader who continues to expect certain familiar traits
associated in everyone's mind with a religious woman's garb, no
matter how elegant and refined. However, once more, the modern
reader's expectations in this regard—and, let us assume, the medieval
one's too—will remain unfulfilled: "blackness," the single, most conventional feature of a nun's clothes, is missing from the portrait.
Glaring omission or genial touch? As pointed out earlier, the author's
message is communicated to the reader through a process activated
by a subtle yet cohesive interaction between "the explicit and the
implicit, between revelation and concealment."107 The color black,
customarily chosen by religious women to signify their renunciation
of the world, taken by the Church as a token of unworldliness, and
universally accepted as a mark of the inner meekness and modesty
attributed by the readers' cultural code to the brides of Christ is not
mentioned, and the natural order of things is disrupted:

> Vestibus in nigris prius est induta puella,
> Crinibus abscisis, cum monialis erit;
> Deformat corpus foris, vt sit spiritus intus
> Pulcher, et albescat plenus amore dei.108

(When a girl is to be a nun, first she is clothed in black garments
and her hair cut off. She disfigures her body on the outside in
order that her spirit within may be beautiful and grow pure
white, being filled with love of God.)

However, that humility does not seem to be one of the spiritual
attributes of this Prioress who, on the outside, does not look un-
worldly but stylish. There is no mention of black in her portrait but

rather of other, brighter, more cheerful hues: her eyes are "greye" and her mouth is "reed"; she carries a "coral" rosary decorated with "grene" gauds, and the brooch on it is "of gold ful sheene." All in all, Madame Eglentyne could easily be accused of displaying what the Parson in his sermon calls an "outrageous array of clothyng,"[109] a sign of one of the two kinds of pride he condemns with equal force:

> Now been ther two maneres of Pride: that oon of hem is
> withinne the herte of man, and that oother is withoute. . . .
> But natheles that oon of thise speces of Pride is signe of
> that oother, right as the gaye leefsel atte taverne is signe of the
> wyn that is in the celer. And this is in manye thynges:
> as in speche and contenaunce, and in outrageous array of
> clothyng. For certes, if ther ne hadde be no synne in clothyng,
> Crist wolde nat so soone have noted and spoken of the
> clothyng of thilke riche man in the gospel.
>
>   . . . .
>
> As to the first synne, that is in superfluitee clothynge.[110]

If the Prioress is "good at imitating the right things to do and is much taken by the appearances of things she associates with the fashionable world,"[111] then we might apply to her the words of Hugo of St. Victor—"exterior ergo superfluitas, animi muntiat vanitatem"[112] (superfluity which appears exteriorly is an indication of the mind's vanity)—as well as those others of the Parson's: "Now, as of the outrageous array of wommen, God woot that though the visages of somme of hem seme ful chaast and debonaire, yet notifie they in hire array of atyr likerousnesse and pride."[113]

As much as disobedience, overindulgence was in violation of the Benedictine Rule which cautioned: "delicias non amplecti"[114] (not to seek soft living)—an ancient injunction from the Bible issued by Jesus to his Disciples: "do not be anxious about your life, what you shall eat, nor about your body, what you shall put on."[115] Madame Eglentyne, a prioress on a pilgrimage, wearing clothes more suited to a courtly lady than a nun, carried "aboute hire arm" a rosary made of coral "gauded al with grene." This was an ornament that would have been more proper in the hands of a courtly lady than a nun, since coral rosaries seem to have been fashionable among the aristocratic ladies of the time.[116] By wearing such a fine and costly piece of jewelry, the Prioress is once more violating a major principle of the

Benedictine Rule's "tria substantialis" (fundamental triad)—obedience, claustration, and poverty—and her conduct is, therefore, highly reprehensible. Chaucer's detailed description of the rosary with its veiled reproach at such vanity, is in the best tradition of the French satires on nuns such as li Muisis's *Les Maintiens des nonnains*,[117] where religious women are chastised for their improper attire and obvious lack of humility.

Chaucerian critics have always expressed their concern over the Prioress's rosary. In his perceptive critical study of her portrait, Chauncey Wood remarks that Madame Eglentyne's rosary is not "an outer sign of inner devotion, but an outer sign of inner worldliness."[118] Wood's words immediately bring to mind those from a passage in the "External Rules" section of the *Ancrene Riwle:* "Hwa se wule beon isehen. þah ha atiffi hire nis nawt muche wunder. ah to godes ehnen ha is lufsumre. þe is for þe luue of him. untiffet wið uten."[119] (If anyone wants to be seen, it is no great wonder if she adorns herself, but she who is outwardly unadorned for the sake of God's love, is dearer in His eyes.) A religious woman was to avoid all worldly conduct, yet the Prioress does not appear to follow this injunction either. The result of such behavior is to emphasize the satiric implications of each small, but highly suggestive detail of her description. Attached to Madame Eglentyne's rich rosary there "heng a brooch of gold ful sheene" as if coral beads "gauded al with grene" were not already conspicuous enough "aboute hire arm." "Ring ne broche ne habbe ȝe" (do not wear any ring or brooch),[120] says the author of the *Ancrene Riwle* in an echo of countless episcopal injunctions and almost as if addressing the Prioress; as we know, however, religious women had been unable to eschew wordly finery for many centuries. The nun in the twelfth century "Planctus monialis," the earliest "chanson de nonne" on record, would like to adorn herself:

> Fibula n[on] perfruor,
> flammeum non capio,
> strophium [as]sumerem,
> diadema cuperem,
>   heu misella!—
> monile arriperem
>   si vale[r]em,
> pelles et herm[inie]
>   libet ferre.[121]

(I have no brooch to enjoy, can wear no bridal veil; how I'd long
to put on a chaplet or tiara, woe is me—I'd get hold of a necklace
if I could—and what joy to wear ermine furs!)

The Prioress does have a brooch; though, and a magnificent one
too, with "a crowned A, / And after AMOR VINCIT OMNIA"
written on it according to the narrator, who ends thus the portrait of
Madame Eglentyne with the most controversial of all Latin quotations in the whole *Canterbury Tales*. Ambiguous and provocative, the
motto on the brooch was long ago traced to Virgil's tenth *Eclogue,*
where the soldier-poet Gallus in the role of an Acadian shepherd
bewails the loss of his love, Lycoris, said to have been a famous
actress. "Omnia vincit Amor: et nos cedamus Amori"[122] (Love conquers all: we too must yield to Love), writes the poet, and although in
the early Middle Ages the phrase had been associated with divine
love, by the fourteenth century usage had restored to it its original
Virgilian sense.[123] It is with this latter meaning that we find it in
Gower's *Vox Clamantis*—"sic amor omne domat" (thus love conquers
everything)—in the chapter describing "forman mulieris speciose, ex
cuius concupiscencia illaqueata militum corda racionis iudicio
sepissime destituuntur"[124] (the beauty of a comely woman, for lust of
whom knights' hearts are ensnared). The same phrase appears also in
the section of the *Roman de la Rose* where Venus sets on fire and
overthrows the Tower of Shame. Here, Virgil is quoted as saying,
"Amor, vainc tout la le verrez / Et nous la debvons recepvoir"[125]
(Love conquers all, and we must cede to him). What is significant is
that the phrase "Amor vincit omnia" culminates the refinement of the
Prioress's portrait. Madame Eglentyne may not have known Latin
(though she probably did) but she did know how to draw attention.
An equivocal motto such as the one she wore was sure to turn
everyone's head.

There is another possible reason why it is quite fitting that the
Prioress should have chosen an ambiguous motto for her brooch: it
went very well with her rosary made of coral, a stone supposedly
endowed with highly equivocal properties. On the one hand, coral
was believed to have a strong apotropaic power, that is, it could ward
off the evil spirits from man's own mind, who continually tempt him
to commit sins of the flesh.[126] This particular virtue of coral must
have been known to Chaucer's audience through one of the most

popular encyclopaedias of the fourteenth century, Vincent de Beauvais's *Speculum Naturale* (a book with which the poet was obviously
familiar since he mentions it in *The Legend of Good Women*—"What
Vincent in his Estoryal Myrour?").[127] In his encyclopaedia Vincent
talks about the "moral properties" of coral "daemonibus quoque te-
rribilis est, et hoc forte, quia frequenter ramorum eius extensio crucis
habet"[128] (It is perhaps also terrifying to demons because frequently
the extension of its branches has the form of a cross). Vincent's
encyclopaedia would have been readily available to Chaucer's audience, who could have also come across other reports of the gem's
power in the popular literature of the time, such as sermons and
saints' lives.[129] Furthermore, the red color of coral was thought to
render it doubly effective against demons and evil spirits supposedly
turned off by the threads of red wool that people attached to valuable
property.[130] It is obvious, then, that the tutelar powers of coral made
it an ideal substance for the rosaries of pilgrims and travelers, who
would naturally be exposed to even more dangers and temptations
than those less adventurous souls who did not leave home. The
following portion of the "corale" entry in the *Sloane Lapidary*, a free
translation of the early thirteenth-century *Second Anglo-Norman Prose
Lapidary* confirms the advantages of carrying along some coral object
when on the road: "It geueth man a good beginning and a good
ending what contry yt he taketh."[131] In the *Peterboroug Lapidary*,
however, another property of coral is recorded which, although
beneficial to man's well being, in a way runs counter to the effects just
mentioned above: "whoso bereð ðis stone vpone him or one his
fynger, he schal get love."[132] It is highly probable that Madame
Eglentyne was acquainted with the popular lore associated with coral
both as an apotropaic and an erotic charm, since she seems to have
had a certain knowledge of precious stones—she calls the young boy
martyred by the Jews in her tale "This gemme of chastite, this
emeraude/And eek of martirdom the ruby bright."[133]

There could have been, then, several reasons for the Prioress to
carry a rosary made of coral beads; we are left wondering. Once again
and with characteristic ingenuity, one last detail in Chaucer's portrait
of Madame Eglentyne is magnified and turned by our own reaction
to it into an element of delicate, yet overpowering ambivalence, in the
finest tradition of medieval monastic satire. It is within this tradition
that the figure of the Prioress as well as that of Doña Garoza must be

Angel of the Annunciation. Martin Schongauer (German, before 1440–91. Engraving. Gift of Lydia Evans Tunnard in memory of W. G. Russell Allen. 63.2876. Courtesy, Museum of Fine Arts, Boston.

viewed. The mixture of sympathy and antagonism so evident in the Spanish poet's presentation of the nun, enhanced by his unparalleled sense of humor and the vitality of his style, is also present in Madame Eglentyne's portrait. What gives the ambiguity surrounding the personality of the Prioress a quality of refinement that the character of Doña Garoza seems to lack is the delicate subtlety of her creator's ironic touch. Nevertheless, both nuns come alive before our eyes as authentic satirical characters; enigmatic and luminous, Doña Garoza and Madame Eglentyne will remain dangerously poised for all time between "caritas" and "cupiditas" in the minds of the Archpriest's and Chaucer's readers.

Conclusion

HE SUBJECT of this book, the figure of the wayward nun in the literature of the Middle Ages, has interested me for a long time. At a very early stage in the research, though, the vastness of the material available made it evident that unless I set some attainable goal, the project would be unmanageable. I soon realized that the presence of wayward nuns in medieval literature for so many centuries was too formidable to be only fiction, and to confirm their existence I was forced to venture beyond the confines of literature into wholly unfamiliar territory. Because a sense of history is something that cannot be developed overnight, my incursion into a field as boundless and fascinating as medieval history seemed not only presumptuous but intimidating at first. It still does. However, as more and more real-life wayward nuns continued to emerge from the old documents, my objective became to establish the relationship between their life-stories and their songs. My premise is that the wayward nun of the Middle Ages is not an isolated literary occurrence, but the reflection of the woman in the nunnery.

I have cited in the initial chapter as many instances of misconduct in the convent as I felt could prove my contention without becoming tiresome to the reader. The injunctions issued by the bishops in charge of the spiritual well-being of the nuns take up hundreds of pages of the episcopal records; I would like to have listed many more. I would especially like to have compared the "waywardness" of the sisters with that of the monks, often chastised by the Church even more severely. I had to remain selective, however, to avoid losing sight of the ultimate goal of that section: to identify the real-life models for the literary nuns. As it was, I had to ignore an entire perspective concerning irregular behavior in the nunnery—the

female point of view, the testimony of the women in charge of the
spiritual guidance of others of their sex. Letters from one harried
abbess to another or to the bishop of the diocese, as well as admonitions to an erring sister were consistently—and regretfully—set aside.
I am aware that this apparent neglect may lead to charges of accepting
as unquestioned truth the accusations and recriminations from male
members of the Church, whose misogynistic bias was legendary. The
possible, even probable slant of the episcopal reports is a matter that
warrants further investigation, but which must remain outside the
scope of this book.

Moving from the historical evidence to the didactic and satiric
works of those who made it their task to castigate or to mock the
conduct of profligate nuns again called for considerable selectivity
and restraint. A complete and systematic review of such works would
have been impossible within the confines of a chapter. The degree of
virulence—or the lack of it—with which they either condemn or
lampoon immorality in the convent seemed the best formula to
display the writers' concern with sinful nuns. The selections quoted
are geared to highlight not only the historical evidence submitted
earlier but also the main thrust of the book. It is of crucial importance
to understand that wayward nuns were a common feature of religious
life in the Middle Ages. By the fourteenth century, the old monastic
impulse was on the wane and the Church, led by two popes, hovered
dangerously on the edge of chaos. A true religious vocation was only
one of the reasons leading medieval women to the cloister, which had
become a melting pot of assorted and conflicting personalities.
Strong-willed inmates vied with equally endowed superiors in breaking the centuries-old enclosure regulations and prompting the call
from the bishops for more stringent measures to curb the abuses. It
was the Church's contention that such blatant disregard for monastic
claustration, the mainstay of the religious commitment of the "sponsa
Dei," was the principal cause of the nuns' misconduct.

In an attempt to get one step closer to the wayward nuns of
fiction, I chose examples from the popular literature on the subject
illustrating the enduring fascination of the people with the sisters who
strayed from the path of virtue. The latter was a circumstance that
could not be ignored, and even if the songs and the tales are, in general,
products of the male consciousness (there is, naturally, no sure way to
prove authorship of material that had belonged to the popular imagination from earliest memory), the issue of antifeminism would only

be pertinent in the case of the tales or fabliaux. Dating back from the oldest tradition of popular lore, the tales of profligate nuns abound in all the literatures of medieval Europe. Immensely irreverent and with total disregard for what the Church has always deemed the highest calling, the tales lambast wicked nuns—and monks—in an apotheosis of lewdness and sin.

For centuries—up to the present—stereotypical wayward nuns have continued to amuse, shock, or embarrass successive generations. Did the authors of the fabliaux, by any chance, have access to the documents of the Church? Were the bishops' registers ever open to the scrutiny of the public? I believe we may answer those questions in the negative. We know that the popular imagination has always looked for characters to ridicule, and such stock types as the Nagging Wife, the Henpecked Husband, the Gluttonous Monk, and the Wayward Nun have been the laughing-stock of the jongleurs and their audiences as far back as memory goes.

I mentioned earlier that the possibility of anti-feminism need not be raised in the case of the "chansons-de-nonne." True, they too probably sprang from the male consciousness, yet in tone and content the songs are consistently sympathetic to the plight of the nun unwillingly professed. Whether repentant or defiant, hiding her shame from the world or flaunting her sin in a travesty of religious ideals, the nuns of the "chansons" are as beguiling today as they were centuries ago. Since my ultimate purpose was to trace a pattern of the attitudes toward the wayward nun which make up the literary convention inherited by Chaucer and the Archpriest of Hita, the "chansons de nonne," as well as the Latin poems, were chosen with that particular end in view. For this reason, even though I am fully aware that some of the songs—and also some of the poems, such as the *Spill* and the *Council of Remiremont*—had to be composed tongue-in-cheek (the satire in them is too crude), it was important to include them because their very existence attests to the widespread popularity of the theme of the wayward nun.

From the episcopal injunctions through the satires and the songs, elusive, pathetic, or frivolous, the nun who transgressed looms, intriguing and indomitable, throughout the Middle Ages. Pitied, villified, or mocked then, and a victim of neglect today, as a senior member of a tradition dating back to the beginnings of monasticism she merits much more than a passing mention or a startled commentary. Separated chronologically, Doña Garoza and Madame

Eglentyne share the exceptional distinction of being the refined products of centuries of prototypical wayward nuns. The Archpriest of Hita and Chaucer were fortunate heirs to a powerful and time-honored tradition that furnished them with vividly delineated models for their nuns. Woven into their portraits are the same basic elements provided by models hundreds of years old.

The satirical implications in the figures of the Spanish and the English nuns were recognized long ago. An appropriate way to conclude would be to point out that tracing the historical and fictional ancestry of Doña Garoza and Madame Eglentyne enhances their enigmatic, fascinating figures. I submit this book, then, as a contribution to a better understanding of these two tantalizingly equivocal literary figures.

Notes

Introduction

1. Trans. Elisha K. Kane, *The Book of Good Love* (Chapel Hill: University of North Carolina Press, 1968), stanza 1498 c, d.

2. Among them are Fernando Capecchi, "Il *Libro de Buen Amor* di Juan Ruiz, Arcipreste de Hita," Cultura Neolatina 13 (1954); Brian Dutton, "'Buen Amor': Its Meaning and Uses in Some Medieval Texts," in *"Libro de Buen Amor" Studies*, ed G. Gybbon-Monypenny (London: Támesis Books, Ltd., 1970), and José Amador de los Ríos, *Historia crítica de la literatura española* (Madrid: José Fernández Cancela, 1863).

3. One of these critics is Roger Walker, "A Note on the Female Portraits in the *Libro de Buen Amor*," *Romanischen Forschungen* 77 (1965), for example, who points out that since the Archpriest frames the episode of Doña Garoza with remarks— consistently derogatory—on the love of nuns, and makes no effort throughout the episode to indicate that she is an exception to the rule of what he seems to regard as the characteristically unchaste behavior of religious women, she must belong to that group too.

4. The ambiguity of Doña Garoza's character is such, that even the most perceptive of all the critics of the *Libro de Buen Amor*, María Rosa Lida, "Nuevas notas para la interpretación del *Libro de Buen Amor*," in *Estudios de literatura española y comparada* (Buenos Aires: Editorial Universitaria, 1969, 2nd ed.), views the portrait of the nun—and the rest of the book—as typical of the Archpriest's maliciously clever art of confusing the reader with conflicting statements in order to entertain him. Luis Beltrán, *Razones de buen amor: oposiciones y convergencias en el libro del Arcipreste de Hita* (Valencia: Editorial Castalia, 1977), points out that Doña Garoza obviously had a history of previous love affairs which were known to her old servant and confidante (the Archpriest's own procuress), and that is why the old woman can assure her employer that she will obtain the love of a nun for him even before contacting Doña Garoza. A few critics agree with Lida that the portrait is too ambiguous to risk a definite opinion; among these, James Burke, "Love's Double Cross: Language Play as Structure in the *Libro de Buen Amor*," *University of Toronto Quarterly* 43 (Spring 1974), and Leo Ulrich, *Zur dichterische Originalität des Arcipreste de Hita* (Francfort: Vittorio Klostermann, 1958), offer two of the most interesting theories. According to Burke, it is the perspective of the reader which alone determines whether Doña Garoza had a

sexual liaison with the Archpriest, or chastely served as his inspiration to abandon for a while his wicked amorous ways and think only of God's love. Ulrich thinks the pervasive ambiguity of the episode—and of the figure of the nun herself—unfolds on two parallel levels skillfully designed never to cross: on one level the Archpriest conquers Doña Garoza's resistance and she becomes his paramour; on the other, the affair is covered up by the importance given to "buen amor." Of all the critics quoted, and the scores of others who have attempted to solve the mystery of the figure of Doña Garoza, only Lida hints at her possible literary ancestors, and she lists—in a footnote—a number of poems having to do with nuns unwillingly professed. The possibility of Doña Garoza belonging to a tradition of subtly or overtly wayward nuns does not occur to any other critic.

5. Among these are D. W. Robertson, *A Preface to Chaucer* (Princeton, 1962; 3rd rpt., Princeton, New Jersey: Princeton University Press, 1973), who feels that the Prioress's behavior is not in accordance with the Benedictine Rule principles of proper ecclesiastical behavior and that Chaucer's satirical approach to the nun is very harsh, and Phyllis Hodgson, editor of *"General Prologue" to the "Canterbury Tales"* (London: Athlone Press, 1969), who talks of "acute irony" in the portrait. Graham Landrun, "The Convent Crowd and the Feminist Nun," *Tennessee Philological Bulletin* 13 (1976), finds that the Prioress is not fit to be one as described in the portrait.

6. Helen Corsa, *Chaucer: Poet of Mirth and Morality* (Notre Dame, Indiana: University of Notre Dame Press, 1964), calls Madame Eglentyne an ironic figure because of the tension in her between the secular and the sacred, and Peter Taitt, *Incubus and Ideal: Ecclesiastical Figures in Chaucer and Langland* (Salzburg, Austria: Institut für Englische Sprache, 1975), is sure that Chaucer's conception of the Prioress is only vaguely ironical. Chauncey Wood, "Chaucer's Use of Signs in his Portrait of the Prioress," in *Signs and Symbols in Chaucer's Poetry*, ed. John P. Hermann and John J. Burke, Jr. (Alabama: University of Alabama Press, 1981), believes that the portrait is satirical thanks to the use of what he calls one of Chaucer's most "delicate" devices: omission. By this he means that none of the features, either physical or spiritual that we associate with the figure of a prioress and, therefore, expect the poet to mention, is included in the portrait. In this way the satire comes across as soft rather than harsh.

7. As an example of the ambiguity evoked by the portrait in scholars who have dedicated considerable time to its study, these are two quotations from the same page of Florence Ridley's compendium on critical approaches to Madame Eglentyne until the mid sixties, *The Prioress and the Critics* (Berkeley: University of California Press, 1965): "she is certainly not a devil" and "she is certainly not a saint." They are the words of Howard Patch, *On Rereading Chaucer* (Cambridge, Mass.: Harvard University Press, 1939), and Dom Maynard Brennan, "Speaking of the Prioress," *Modern Language Quarterly* 10 (1949).

8. One of these, for instance, is Alice Kemp-Welch. Her essay on Roswitha the nun in *Of Six Medieval Women* (Mass., 1913; rpt. Williamstown, Mass.: Corner House Publishers, 1972, 2nd. impression 1979) makes no mention of what we see as the close connection between certain religious women in life and literature.

9. An exception to this neglect of such a striking cultural circumstance is historian Eileen Power's study on medieval nuns, *Medieval English Nunneries* (Cambridge, 1922; rpt. New York: Biblo and Tannen, 1964). Although concentrating on the historical aspects of the medieval nunnery in England, Power's book includes a

long and detailed appendix on profligate nuns in the literature of the period, and a chapter on the wayward nun in medieval literature, where the relationship between her presence there and her historical existence is analyzed in some detail.

10. Studies on medieval women in general do not seem to have flourished for many years after the publication of Kemp-Welch's and Power's books until the seventies, when several scholarly works appeared, among them *Women in Medieval Society*, edited by Susan Mosher Stuard (University of Pennsylvania Press, 1976) and *Medieval Women*, edited by Derek Baker (Oxford, 1978; rpt. Oxford: Basil Blackwell, 1981). *Women in Medieval Society* is a collection of nine essays by different scholars on topics relating to female participation in the medieval world, among which the only one dealing with religious women is "Mulieres Sanctae" by Brenda Bolton. Bolton's thesis is that, although large numbers of women were looking for a true spiritual communion with God in the cloister, their male counterparts in religion and the world in general did not regard their vocation seriously. With characteristic prejudice, medieval men insisted on treating nuns too as "femmes fatales," whose company was to be shunned rather than sought. This attitude of hostility towards religious women is also discussed by Sally Thompson, "The Problem of the Cistercian Nuns in the Twelfth and Early Thirteenth Centuries," in *Medieval Women*. Thompson records the efforts of many religiously-oriented women to enter the Cistercian order and the latter's resistance to such efforts. Indiscipline among the sisters, problems arising from their constant breaking of claustration vows, and the danger posed by certain forward nuns to young and inexperienced monks assigned to the congregation as confessors, are cited by the author as the three main reasons for the Cistercians' reluctance to accept women. The study provides an insight into the situation, reflecting a prejudice against religious women that does not seem wholly unjustified, after all. Two other essays in *Medieval Women* also deal with the problems inherent in regulating communities of frequently strong-willed women living together under strict rules. Jacqueline Smith's "Robert de Arbrissel's Relations with Women" follows that famous "procurator mulierum" (guardian of women) as he organizes his itinerant male and female followers into structured groups devoted to religious pursuits. Eventually, de Arbrissel founded what later became the Abbey of Fontevrault as a refuge for women in need of spiritual guidance, but was severely criticized for allowing into his nunnery some whose morals were doubtful at best. In "Aelred of Rievaulx and the Nun of Watton," Giles Constable discusses an episode in the early history of the Gilbertine order in which Aelred had been asked to intervene. Aelred subsequently related how a nun of Watton, placed in the convent at the age of four, had grown up into a dissolute young woman and was involved, together with her priestly lover, in a gruesome episode which ended in castration for him and public dishonor for her and some of her fellow nuns.

1—The Nunnery as a Social Institution

1. Desiderius Erasmus, *Colloquies,* trans. C. R. Thompson (Chicago: University Press, 1965), p. 107.

2. "Fertheremore we monysshe yow and ylke one of yow alle that now are

and shalle be here aftere that ylk one of yow duely kepe and obserue thise our iniunccyones as thai are afore writene vndere payne of cursyng, the whiche we purpose to gyfe in eueryche of your persones that duely obey ne kepe the saide iniunccyones ouere alle the peynes obofe writen." *Records of Visitations held by William Alnwick, Bishop of Lincoln: 1436 to 1439,* Vol. II of *Visitations of Religious Houses in the Diocese of Lincoln,* ed. A. Hamilton Thompson (Lincoln Record Society and Canterbury and York Society, 13–15, Lincoln: 1914–1929), p. 132. The visitation reports appear in the text in the original Latin with their corresponding translation; both versions are from this edition. Bishop Alnwick's injunctions are given only in English in the *Visitations*.

3. Examples of sexual incontinence among religious women are given throughout Chapters 1 and 2.

4. So prevalent was this "horror," that in 1348 the Church issued an injunction to the effect that "all nuns who have given birth to a child are to be kept for the rest of their lives within the nunnery precincts." Cited by G. G. Coulton, *Five Centuries of Religion* (Cambridge: University Press, 1950), I, 405. See also Archbishop Flemyng's reports of his visitations in the Diocese of Lincoln for a staggering number of cases of nuns who were either pregnant at the time of the visitation or who had already given birth to one or more children. *Injunctions and other Documents from the Registers of Richard Flemyng and William Gray: 1420 to 1436,* Vol. I of *Visitations of Religious Houses.*

5. Historically, it is interesting to note that equal time and space were devoted by the guardians of morality in the religious houses to admonish the men in them. The sins of the monks were as heinous as those of the nuns and their misconduct seems to have evoked the same indignant response. A comparative study of the "waywardness" of medieval men and women of the cloth would be quite provocative, as well as serving to assess whether the purportedly objective reports of the church representatives reveal as much anti-feminine bias as so many of the male writings of the time.

6. See Chapters 2 and 3 for detailed discussions of this matter.

7. *Calendar of Documents Preserved in France,* ed. J. Horace Round (London, 1899; rpt. Nendeln, Liechtenstein: Kraus Reprint Ltd., 1967), I, 384.

8. *Registrum Epistolarum Fratris Johannis Peckham, Archiepiscopi Cantuarensis: 1279–1292,* ed. Charles T. Martin (Rolls Series 77, London: Longman and Co., 1882), III, 851.

9. Ibid.

10. The visitation reports contain hundreds of pages of such injunctions.

11. *The Medieval Nunneries of the County of Somerset and Diocese of Bath and Wells,* ed. Thomas Hugo (London: J. R. Smith, 1867), pp. 30–32.

12. Cited by Henry O. Taylor, *The Medieval Mind,* 4th. ed. (London: Macmillan and Co., 1927), II, 495–96. See also *Victoria History of the Counties of England, York* (London: Archibald Constable and Co., Ltd., 1907), III, 85: "It would almost seem that this remote priory served as a kind of reformatory for young women of good family who had strayed from the path of virtue." *The Victoria History of the Counties of England* will appear in subsequent notes as *V. C. H.*

13. *V. C. H., York,* III, 164.

14. "The word 'incest' is used in its religious sense; it was properly used of

intercourse between persons who were both under ecclesiastical vows and thus in the relation of spiritual father and daughter, or brother and sister, but soon came to be used loosely to denote a breach of chastity in which one part was professed." Eileen Power, *Medieval English Nunneries* (Cambridge, 1922; rpt. New York: Biblo and Tannen, 1964), p. 459, n. 2.

15. *V. C. H., York*, III, 164 and 113.

16. E. Vansteenberghe, *Le Cardinal Nicolas de Cues* (1920). Cited in trans. by Coulton, *Five Centuries*, IV, 133.

17. Ibid., I, 408. For more examples of immoral conduct in the nunnery, see Henry C. Lea, *History of Sacerdotal Celibacy in the Christian Church* (London: Williams and Norgate, 1907), I, 343 and Taylor, II, 495–96.

18. *V. C. H., York*, III, 164.

19. Godfrey Giffard, Archbishop of Worcester, *Register: 1268–1302*, ed. J. W. Willis Bund. (Worcester Historical Society: James Parker and Co., 1902), pp. 278–80. See also *Visitations of Religious Houses*, III, 352–55 for a report on the penance and ultimate excommunication of an unrepentant sinner who had a child by a nun of St. Michael's, Stamford in 1442.

20. *Visitations of Religious Houses*, III, 352.

21. In 1311 Clarice de Speton of Arden Priory was found guilty of incest with Geoffrey de Eston, bailiff of Bulmershire. *V. C. H., York*, III, 113.

22. Lina Eckenstein, *Woman Under Monasticism* (Cambridge: University Press, 1896), p. 219.

23. *Visitations of Religious Houses*, I, 84. See also ibid., III, 348 for report on a nun of St. Michael's, Stamford who left the convent in apostasy "cleaving to a harp-player."

24. Cited in trans. by Coulton, *Five Centuries*, II, 546–47. For a humorous treatment of the same subject see also *The Land of Cokaygne*, in *Early English Poems and Lives of Saints*, ed. F. J. Furnivall, Transactions of the Philological Society (Berlin: A. Asher and Co., 1858), pp. 156–61. This poem is reviewed in detail in Chapter 3.

25. Eude Rigaud, Archevêque de Rouen, *Regestrum Visitationum: 1248–1269*, ed. Thomas Bonin (Rouen: Auguste le Brument, libraire-éditeur, 1852), I, 43. My translation. All subsequent translations are mine unless otherwise indicated.

26. *V. C. H., York*, II, 121, 169. See also *Papal Letters*, in *Calendar of Entries in the Papal Registers*, ed. W. H. Bliss (London: Eyre and Spottiswoode, 1893), VI, 55 and *Visitations of Religious Houses*, II, 114, 120, 218.

27. *V. C. H., York*, III, 181.

28. Thomas Gascoigne, *Locie Libro Veritatum*, ed. J. E. Thorold Rogers (1881), p. 231. Cited by Power, p. 447, n. 6.

29. "Fatebatur se carnaliter cognitam a D. B. apud S. in domo habitacionis sue ibidem situata" (confessed that she was carnally known by D. B. in the home of S., located in the same place). *Visitations of Religious Houses*, I, 71.

30. Ibid., II, 47.

31. "Domina Agnes Smyth inquisita dicit quod Simon Prentes cognovit eam et suscitavit prolem ex ea infra prioratum, extra tamen claustru" (Dame Agnes Smyth said upon inquiry that Simon Prentes knew her [carnally] and begat a child with her below the priory, outside the cloister). *Visitations of the Diocese of Norwich: 1492–1532*, ed. August Jessop (Camden Society NS 43, Westminister, 1888), p. 109.

32. Archbishop Eude Rigaud's visitation reports contain two entries that do mention abortions in the nunnery. One is from vol. I, 255 and the other from vol. II, 491:

Visitavimus prioratum monialium Sancti Albini. . . . Item, Agnetem de Ponte misimus apud leprosariam Rothomagensem, quia consensit fornicacioni dicte Eustachie, et etiam procuravit, prout fama clamat, et quia dedit dicte Eustachie herbas bibere, ut interficeretur puer conceptus in dicta Eustachia, secundum quod dicitur per famam. (August 1256)

(We visited the priory of the nuns of Saint Albin. . . . Also sent Agnes de Ponte to the leprosarium of Rouen because she agreed to the fornication of the said Eustacia, and even contributed, so the word went, and because, according to report, she gave the said Eustacia an herb potion so that the child conceived by the said Eustacia might be killed.)

Per Dei gratiam, visitavimus prioratum monialium Sancti Syndonii. . . . Item, fama plurimum laborabat extra contra Nicholaam de Rothomago, cantricem, et dicebatur communiter in villa quod ipsa nundum erat mensis elapsus fecerat abortivum. (June 1264)

(By the grace of God we visited the nuns of Saint Sydon. . . . Also, a report was very much current outside against Nichola of Rouen, songstress, and it was commonly said in the town that not even one month before she had had an abortion.

The following note is added by the editor of Archbishop Rigaud's visitation reports:

"Au moyen âge, les breuvages données pour procurer l' avortement étaient considérés comme un meurtre, et celui qui se rendait coupable de ce crime était puni de la peine capitale." (In the Middle Ages, the potions given to cause an abortion were considered a murderous act, and anyone guilty of such a crime was given capital punishment.)

Regestrum Visitationum, I, 255, n. 1.
    33. *Visitations of the Diocese of Norwich*, p. 109.
    34. *V. C. H. York*, III, 240.
    35. Ibid., p. 189.
    36. Hugo, pp. 31–32.
    37. P.R.O. *Chancery Warrants*, Series 1, File 1759. See also Files 1762, 1764, and 1769, nos. 1, 15, and 18 in *Calendar of Patent Rolls*, 1381–1385, p. 235, and 1401–1405, pp. 418, 472 for more examples. Cited by Power, pp. 442–43, n. 2.
    38. *V. C. H. London*, I, 518.
    39. Prioress Agnes Bowes deserted the convent of St. Michael to which Wothorpe Priory had been annexed in 1354. See *V. C. H., Northampton*, II, 101.
    40. Joan de Fynnemere "is said to have abandoned her habit and returned to a secular life." ibid., p. 126.

41. Ibid., *Oxford*, II, 104. See n. 14 above for religious meaning of word incest.

42. Ibid., *Bedford*, I, 360.

43. Ibid., *Lincoln*, II, 179.

44. "The bishop in 1300 issued a mandate to the archdeacon of Northampton to denounce Isabel de Clouville, Maud Rychemers, and Ermentrude de Newark, professed nuns of Delapré, who had discarded the habit of religion and notoriously lived a secular life, as apostate nuns. . . . In 1311 another sister, Agnes de Landwath, was denounced for apostasy and for forsaking the habit of religion," ibid., *Northampton*, II, 114.

45. *Visitations of Religious Houses*, II, 3.

46. For more incidents of apostasy see diocesan episcopal registers and *V. C. H.*

47. "Mary . . . the youngest of King Stephen's daughters, and the darling both of her father and mother . . . was dedicated by them to the monastic life from very early years. Her birth took place in 1136 and she was, when old enough placed in the convent of St. Leonard's at Stratford-at-Bow." *Records of Romsey Abbey*, ed. G. D. Liveing (Winchester: Warren and Son, Ltd., 1912), p. 54.

48. Coulton, *Five Centuries*, IV, 126. See also ibid., II, 626–27 for an angry pronouncement from the fifteenth-century German prelate Johann Geiler on the subject of child-nuns ("some come [into religion] because, against their own will, they have been cast or thrust in by their parents like puppies for the drowning, for the sole purpose of getting rid of them"), and also H. S. Bennet, "Medieval Literature and the Modern Reader," *Essays and Studies* 31 (1945), p. 8.

49. *Monasticon Anglicanum*, ed. Sir William Dugdale (London: James Bohn, 1846), III, 363. Even as late as the first quarter of the sixteenth century the Dominican Guillaume Pépin complains that " 'many nobles . . . finding themselves burdened with a multitude of children, and unable to make worldly provision for all, send them while they are yet children into Religion'." Cited by Coulton, *Five Centuries*, II, 639.

50. *Visitations of Religious Houses*, II, 5. See also ibid., II, 217; *Testamenta Vetusta*, ed. Nicholas H. Nicolas (London: Nichols and Son, 1826), I, 63, and *V. C. H., London*, I, 518, n. 35 (The papal mandate says, "She was in infancy placed in the monastery and clad in the monastic habit").

51. *V. C. H., Northampton*, II, 125–26.

52. Ibid., *Buckingham*, I, 355. See also ibid., 383.

53. See the following: *Testamenta Vetusta*, I, 116, 121; *Testamenta Eboracensia*, Surtees Society (London, 1836–1902), II, 6, 134, 187; *Cartulary of St. Mary Clerkenwell*, ed. W. O. Hassall, Camden 3rd. ser. 71 (London: Royal Historical Society, 1949), pp. 233, 259; *Calendar of Wills Proved and Enrolled in the Court of Husting*, ed. Reginald R. Sharpe (London: John C. Francis, 1889), I, 97, 107, 126, 148, 229, 238, 300, 638; *V. C. H. York*, III, 172, and *English Register of Godstow Nunnery*, ed. Andrew Clark (Early English Text Society 129–30, London, 1905), p. 49.

54. Jean Baptiste Thiers, *Traité de la Clôture des Religieuses* (Paris: Chez Antoine Dezallier, 1681). Cited by Power, p. 342, n. 3.

55. See, for instance, *Testamenta Vetusta*, I; *Testamenta Eboracensia*, I and II, and *Calendar of Wills*.

56. Male religious houses also suffered economic hardship in the Middle Ages.

57. See *Cartulary of St. Mary Clerkenwell*, pp. 20, 41, 85, 101, 203, 233.

58. Matins: The principal and longest hour of the Divine Office, forming the right office thereof; it is usually joined to Lauds, whether said overnight or early in the morning. Prime: The portion of the Divine Office assigned to the first hour, i.e. about 6 a.m., the approximate time of its recital in monastic churches. Lauds: The second hour of the Divine Office in the Latin rite, taking its name from Psalms 148, 149 and 150 which formerly always formed part of it and in which the word "laudate" (praise ye . . .) often occurs. Vespers: The evening hour of the Divine Office and with Lauds, the most solemn; it is the normal evening service in churches of the Latin rite and in monastic, cathedral and collegiate churches is sung daily between 3 and 6 p.m. *A Catholic Dictionary: The Catholic Encyclopaedic Dictionary*, ed. Donald Atwater, 3rd. ed. (New York: The Macmillan Co., 1962).

59. *Calendar of Wills*, I, 588 and II, 299, 606. See n. 53 above regarding last quotation.

60. *English Gilds*, ed. T. L. Smith (Early English Text Society 40, London, 1870), pp. 194, 340.

61. See n. 62 below.

62. "Sempringham was in high favour with the three Edwards, who sent thither wives and daughters of their chief enemies. Wencilian, daughter of Llewellyn, prince of Wales, was sent to Sempringham as a little child, after her father's death in 1283. . . . In 1322, by order of the Parliament at York, Margaret, countess of Cornwall, was sent to live at Sempringham among the nuns. In 1324, Joan, daughter of Roger Mortimer, was received at the priory. Two daughters of the elder Hugh Despenser were also sent to take the veil at Sempringham." *V. C. H., Lincoln*, II, 184.

63. *Testamenta Eboracensia*, II, 18.

64. Cited by Power, p. 31. No source given.

65. *Visitations of Religious Houses*, II, 4.

66. *V. C. H., London*, I, 518. See also *Cartulary of St. Mary Clerkenwell*, pp. 67, 70, 86, 88, and *Calendar of Wills*, p. 124.

67. *V. C. H., Warwick*, II, 71.

68. See Coulton, *Five Centuries*, II, 300 and also Dimier, "Chapitres generaux d'abbesses Cisterciennes," *Citeaux* 2 (1960), p. 274 for a view of the abbess of the Spanish convent of Las Huelgas, Doña Sancha García (1207–1230), who "even went so far as to take upon herself the same powers as an abbot—including his sacerdotal authority—and presumed to hear confessions and bless novices." Cited by Sally Thompson, "The Problem of the Cistercian Nuns," in *Medieval Women*, ed. Derek Baker (Oxford: Basil Blackwell, 1978), p. 238.

69. Power, p. 42. See also G. G. Coulton, *Medieval Panorama* (Cambridge, 1938; rpt. Cambridge: University Press, 1939), p. 276: "promotion naturally went very often by good birth and good connections."

70. Frances and Joseph Gies, *Women in the Middle Ages* (New York: Thomas Y. Crowell Co., 1978), pp. 65–66.

71. *V. C. H., Bedfordshire*, I, 360; also in *Visitations of Religious Houses*, I, 82–86.

72. *V. C. H., York*, III, 240. See also ibid., *Northampton*, II, 126 for an account of an early sixteenth-century prioress, Agnes Carter of Sewardsley Priory, "whose election was declared void by the bishop on the ground of her manifest unfitness. She

is described as 'mulier corrupta, apostate, et unius proler mater'" (a corrupt woman, an apostate, and the mother of a child).

73. Jo A. McNamara and S. Wemple, "Sanctity and Power: The Dual Pursuit of Medieval Women," in *Becoming Visible: Women in European History*, ed. R. Bridenthal and C. Koonz (Boston: Houghton Mifflin Co., 1977), p. 93.

74. Cited by G. G. Coulton, "The Truth about the Monasteries," in his *Ten Medieval Studies* (Cambridge: University Press, 1930), p. 92.

75. *Visitations of Religious Houses*, II, 3, 5.

76. *V. C. H., Suffolk*, II, 84.

77. Eckenstein, p. 205.

78. Cited in trans. by Coulton, *Five Centuries*, II, 300.

79. Hugo, p. 24.

80. *V. C. H., York*, III, 114.

81. *V. C. H., Suffolk*, II, 84.

82. Hugo, pp. 33, 29. See also *Visitations of Religious Houses*, II, 114.

83. *V. C. H., London*, II, 150. See also *Visitations of Religious Houses*, II, 119, 122, 133, and John de Drokensford, Bishop of Bath and Wells, *Register: 1309–1329* (Somerset Record Society, 1, London, 1887), pp. 60, 126, 167, 287.

84. *Records of Romsey Abbey*, p. 218.

85. Hugo, pp. 62–63. See also ibid., p. 9. Travel restrictions appear throughout the visitation records as the bishops invariably included them in their injunctions to the nuns.

86. Cited in *Records of Romsey Abbey*, pp. 101, 84.

87. William Wickwane, Archbishop of York, *Register: 1279–1285* (Surtees Society 114, London, 1904), p. 141.

88. *Visitations of Religious Houses*, II, 50.

89. Simonis de Gandavo, Bishop of Salisbury: *Register: 1297–1315* (The Canterbury and York Society 40–41, Oxford: University Press, 1934), I, 10–11. Trans. by Power, p. 344. It is interesting to note that a short time after the statute was promulgated, Bishop Dalderby of Lincoln attempted to persuade the nuns of Elstow to comply with it and in response they "hurled the said statute at his back and over his head, . . . following the bishop to the outer gate of the house and declaring unanimously that they were not content in any way to observe such a statute," *Lincoln Episcopal Register Memo. Dalderby*. Cited by Power, p. 352.

90. *Visitations of Religious Houses*, II, 116.

91. Henry of Newark, Archbishop of York, *Register: 1296–1299* (Surtees Society 128, London, 1910), p. 223. See also *Visitations of Religious Houses*, II, 92.

92. *Records of Romsey Abbey*, p. 102. See also *Visitations of Religious Houses*, II, 115.

93. *Papal Letters*, IV, 37–38. See also *Petitions to the Pope*, vol. VI of *Calendar of Entries in the Papal Registers*, p. 534: "Robert de Ufford, Earl of Suffolk. For license to himself and his wife to enter the monasteries of enclosed nuns of St. Clare with a retinue and therein talk, eat, and drink, and stay for three days."

94. *Papal Letters*, IV, 212.

95. Ibid., pp. 38, 59, 394. See also ibid., I, 245, 525; *Petitions to the Pope*, II, 502, 519, 531, 532, 533, 534, and *V. C. H., London*, I, 518.

96. *Papal Letters*, IV, 397.

97. 1318 visitation by Archbishop Melton, *V. C. H., York,* III, 119.

98. Cited by Coulton, *Five Centuries,* I, 404.

99. See Peckham, III, 924. See also *Records of Romsey Abbey,* pp. 84, 102; Archbishop Henry of Newark, *Register,* p. 223, and Hugo, p. 33.

100. *Patrologiae Latinae,* ed. J. P. Migne (Paris: Bibliothecae Cleri Universae, 1863), CCII, 162, col. 1084.

101. Cited in trans. by Coulton, *Five Centuries,* II, 587.

102. *Visitations of Religious Houses,* II, 133–34, 46. See also ibid., p. 1.

103. Ibid., pp. 134–35. See also *V. C. H., York,* III, 117: "If any woman or man were admitted, that person would be expelled from the house, without hope of mercy, and the prioress would be deposed, and any other nuns who agreed would be condemned to fast on bread and water for two months, Sundays and festivals excepted." See also, ibid., pp. 126, 163: "Special features are that the nuns were not to linger in the "hostilaria" or elsewhere for amusement with outsiders after compline . . . No nun, except the "hostilaria," was to eat or drink in the guest-house, unless with worthy people, no secular persons were to sleep in the dormitory." The "hostilaria" was the nun in charge of the guests at the nunnery. For more complaints on the drinking habits of certain nuns see Alnwick's visitations to Ankerwyke Priory (1441) and Catesby Priory (1442), in *Visitations of Religious Houses,* II, 1, 51, and also Eude Rigaud, *Regestrum Visitationum,* I, 43, where the report of one of his visitations to the priory of Villa Arcelli in July, 1249 discloses that "priorissa ebria est fere qualibet nocte" (the prioress is drunk almost any night).

104. *Yorkshire Archaeological Journal* 16, p. 452. Cited by Power, p. 402. See also *Monasticon,* III, 366 and IV, 554; *V. C. H., Durham,* II, 107; *Visitations of Religious Houses,* II, 116, and *Records of Romsey Abbey,* p. 103.

105. *Visitations of Religious Houses,* II, 51. See also Coulton, *Five Centuries,* I, 406.

106. Vansteenberghe, p. 118. Cited by Coulton, *Five Centuries,* IV, 133. See also *Visitations of Religious Houses,* II, 3.

107. *Monasticon,* IV, 554. See also *Visitations of Religious Houses,* II, 47, 77; *Les Maintiens des nonnains* in Chapter 2, and Chapter 4, n. 43.

108. Peckham, II, 664. See also ibid., II, 652; *Visitations of Religious Houses,* II, 120, and *V. C. H., York,* III, 123.

109. A corrody was "a sum of money or an allowance of meat, drink and clothing, granted by the Superior of the House, or exacted by the king to maintain some servant or other dependent," Hugo, p. 36. "A corrody was so called because it corroded or gnawed upon monastic finances," A. Hamilton Thompson, *The English Clergy and their Organization in the Later Middle Ages* (Oxford: Clarendon Press, 1947), p. 17. Sometimes the corrody came from private sources, as usual, eagerly accepted by the nunnery; see, for instance, *Calendar of Wills,* p. 350: Richard de la Bataille left the proceeds of the sale of some property "for the marriage of Alice, daughter of Lucekyna de Foleham, or for the purchase of a corrody in some religious house if she should be unwilling to marry."

110. John de Grandisson, Bishop of Exeter, *Register: 1327–1369,* ed. F. C. Hingeston-Randolph (London: G. Bell and Sons, 1894–99), I, 100.

111. *V. C. H., London,* I, 518.

112. *The Paston Letters,* ed. John Warrington, Everyman's Library (London, 1968), letter no. 298. See also ibid., p. 76, n. 1.

113. *Visitations of Religious Houses,* II, 175.

114. Ibid., p. 185.

115. *Sussex Archaeological Collection,* IX, 18. Cited by Power, p. 415.

116. Hugo, p. 21.

117. *Records of Romsey Abbey,* p. 146. See also *V. C. H., Bedford,* I, 360; ibid., *Lincoln,* II, 179, and *Visitations of Religious Houses,* II, 7, 92 and 4, where the nuns of Ankerwyke Priory "vadunt cum pannis pictaciatis. Patebat domino nuditas monialium" (go about in patched clothes. The threadbareness of the nuns was apparent to my lord).

118. *V. C. H., Hertford,* IV, 427.

119. Power, p. 473.

2—Moral and Satirical Literature

1. *Le Livre des proverbes français,* ed. Antoine J. V. Le Roux de Lincy (Paris, 1859; rpt. Genève: Slatkine Reprints, 1968), II, 327.

2. Guillaume de Lorris et Jean de Meung, *Le Roman de la Rose,* ed. Silvio Baridon (Milano: Istituto Editoriale Cisalpino, 1954), vol 2, ll. 11302–305. Trans. Harry W. Robbins, *The Romance of the Rose* (New York: E. P. Dutton and Co., Inc., 1962), ll. 100–102.

3. Proverb from the copy of the first edition of Caxton's Chaucer in the British Museum, *Reliquiae Antiquae,* ed. Thomas Wright (London and Berlin, 1843; rpt. New York: AMS Press, Inc., 1966), II, 110.

4. Santa Caterina da Siena, *Libro della Divina Dottrina* (Volgarmente detto Dialogo della Divina Provvidenza), ed. Matilde Fiorilli, 2nd. ed. (Bari: Gius. Laterza e figli, 1928), p. 25. Trans. G. G. Coulton, *Five Centuries of Religion* (Cambridge: University Press, 1950), II, 547.

5. Cited in trans. by Coulton, *Five Centuries,* II, 589, 591, 606. St. Catherine of Siena calls the nuns' life "lasciva e miserabile" (lascivious and miserable) and says that an apostate nun sometimes becomes "una publica meretrice" (a public prostitute). Caterina da Siena, p. 261. See also Coulton, *Five Centuries,* II, 504–647.

6. Juan Ruiz, *Libro de Buen Amor,* ed. Joan Corominas (Madrid: Editorial Gredos, S.A., 1967), stanza 1443 d. Trans. Rigo Mignani and Mario A. di Cesare, *The Book of Good Love* (Albany, New York: State University of New York Press, 1970), p. 277.

7. Giraldus Cambrensis, *Opera,* ed. J. S. Brewer, Rolls Series 21 (London: Longman, Green, Longman and Roberts, 1862), vol. 2.

8. Caesarius of Heisterbach, *Dialogus Miraculorum,* ed. Joseph Strange (Cologne: J. M. Heberle, 1851), I, 273–274. Trans. H. von E. Scott and C. C. Swinton Bland, *The Dialogue on Miracles* (London: George Rutledge and Sons, Ltd., 1929), Book IV, 311, 312.

9. *La Bible de Guiot de Provins* in *Fabliaux et contes des poètes françois des xie,*

xiie, xiiie, xive, et xve siècles, ed. Etienne Barbazan (Paris, 1808; rpt. Genève: Slatkine Reprints, 1976), II, 1–4. My translation. All subsequent translations are mine unless otherwise indicated.

10. "Plus bavard que terrible, plus grondeur qu' indigné." C. Lenient, *La Satire en France au Moyen Age* (Paris: Librairie Hachette et Cie., 1893), p. 109.

11. *La Bible Guiot,* in *Fabliaux et contes,* II, 371, ll. 1980–87.

12. Ibid., p. 377, ll. 2067–68.

13. Ibid., p. 378, ll. 2194–98.

14. Gilles li Muisis, *Poésies,* pub. Kervyn de Letterhove (Louvain: Imprimerie de J. Lefever, 1882), I, 209–36. The following seven references from *Les Maintiens des nonnains* will be identified in the text by page number.

15. For Pope Boniface VIII's bull on conventual claustration ("Periculoso") see Chapter 1.

16. See ibid.

17. See ibid.

18. *Oeuvres galantes des conteurs italiens,* ed. Ad. van Bever et Ed. Sansot-Orland (Paris: Societé du Mercure de France, 1908), p. 129. See also Chapter 1.

19. "Prend gravement la plume pour donner une leçon a son siècle." Lenient, p. 110.

20. *La Bible au Seignor de Berzé* in *Fabliaux et contes,* II, 402.

21. Thomas à Becket, "Satire against the Symoniacs," in *Poésies populaires latines du Moyen Age,* ed. Edélestand du Meril (Paris, 1847; rp. Genéve: Slatkine Reprints, 1977), p. 177.

22. John Gower, *Vox Clamantis,* vol IV of his *The Complete Works,* ed. G. C. Macaulay (Oxford: Clarendon Press, 1902), Liber quartus, Cap. XIII, ll. 55–57. Trans. Eric W. Stockton, *The Major Latin Works of John Gower* (Seattle: University of Washington Press, 1962), p. 179.

23. *Constit. Synod. Gilb. Episc. Circestrens.,* ann. 1289. Cited by Henry C. Lea, *History of Sacerdotal Celibacy in the Christian Church* (London: Williams and Norgate, 1907), II, 435, n.2.

24. Desiderii Erasmi Roterodami, *Colloqvia,* in *Opera Omnia,* ed. L. E. Halkin, F Bierlaire and R. Hoven (Amsterdam: North-Holland Publishing Company, 1972), 1–11, 525. Trans. C.R. Thompson, Desiderius Erasmus, *The Colloquies* (Chicago: University Press, 1965), p. 345.

25. The entire quote from the colloquy "ΙχθηφΑτΙΑ" follows:

Salsamentarivs. Accipe par pari relatum. Audies quod ipse nuper vidi, cuique non interfui solum, verum etiam propemodum praefui. Erant duae monachae, quae visebant cognatos suos. Vbi venissent quo volebant, famulus per obliuionem reliquerat codicem precum iuxta consuetudinem ordinis et loci in quo viuebant. Deum immortalem, quanta illic perturbatio! Non audebant coenare, nisi dictis precibus vespertinis, nec sustinebant ex alio codice dicere, quam ex suo. Interim tota domus coenaturiebat. Quid multis? Cantherio recurrit famulus, sub multam noctem adfert relictum codicem. Dicuntur preces, vixque ad decimam coenauimus.

Lanio. Hactenus nihil audio, quod sit magnopere reprehendendum.

Salsamentarivs. Nimirum, dimidium duntaxat audisti fabulae. Inter coenandum coeperunt illae virgines hilarescere vino, tandem risu soluto, iocis parum pudicis perstrepuit conuiuim, sed nemo licentius egit, quam illae quae nisi dictis ex ordinis forma precibus coenare noluerunt. A conuiuio lusus, choreae, cantilenae, reliqua non audeo commemorare. Sed plane vereor, ne quid ea nocte patratum sit parum virgineum, nisi me fallebant prooemia; lasciui lusus, nutus et suauia.

Lanio. Istam peruersitatem non tam imputo virginibus, quam sacerdotibus earum curam gerentibus.

(Fish. Tit for tat; you'll hear what I myself saw recently. I was not only present but almost presided over it too. Two nuns were visiting relatives. When they reached their destination, it turned out that their servant had forgotten and left behind a prayer book according to the use of their order and community. Good Lord, what an uproar! They didn't dare dine unless Vespers were said and they couldn't bear to say them from any other book than their own. Meanwhile the entire household went hungry. To make a long story short, the servant went back on the gelding; late in the evening he brings back the missing book; prayers are said, and at ten o'clock we've hardly had dinner.

But. So far I hear nothing very awful.

Fish. Well, you've heard only half the story. During dinner these virgins began to get gay with wine, and finally when laughter broke out the party roared at jokes that were scarcely modest ones; nobody behaved more loosely than those two who refused to eat dinner unless prayers were said according to the use of their order. After dinner came games, dances, songs, and other things I don't dare mention; but I'm very much afraid what was done that night was hardly virginal, unless the preliminaries, the sexy games, nods and kisses, deceived me.)

Colloqvia, p. 525. Trans. Thompson, *The Colloquies*, pp. 344–45.

26. John Gower, *Mirour de L'omme*, vol. I of *The Complete Works*, ed. Macaulay, p. 106.

27. See Chapter 1, n. 14.

28. Pero López de Ayala, *Rimado de Palacio*, vol I *of Poesías*, ed. Michel García (Madrid: Editorial Gredos, S.A., 1978), p. 104.

29. *El Libro del Caballero Cifar* en *Libros de caballerías españoles*, ed. Felicidad Buendía (Madrid: Aguilar, 1960), p. 160.

30. "Why I Can't Be a Nun," in *Early English Poems and Lives of Saints*, ed. F. J. Furnivall, (Transactions of the Philological Society, Berlin: A Asher and Co., 1862), pp. 138–48. Subsequent references to this poem will be identified in the text by line number.

31. Walter de Chatillon, "Licet eger cum egrotis," in *La poesía de los goliardos*, ed. Ricardo Arias y Arias (Madrid: Editorial Gredos, S.A., 1970), p. 82.

32. *A Luue Ron,* in *Old English Miscellany,* ed. Rev. Richard Morris (Early English Text Society 49, London, 1872), pp. 93, 98.

33. *Of Clene Maydenhod,* in part II of *The Minor Poems of the Vernon Manuscript,* ed., F. J. Furnivall (Early English Text Society 117, London, 1901), p. 467.

34. *Hali Meidenhad,* ed. Oswald Cockayne (Early English Text Society 18, London, 1866), p. 28.

35. Ibid., pp. 24, 34.

36. In the *De Virginibus ad Marcellinam,* a treatise on virginity, Ambrose echoes the attitude of the Church Fathers, first affirming the institution of marriage and then pointing out the disadvantages of the married states, such as pregnancy, morning-sickness, and breast-feeding, among others. Cited in Aldhelm, *The Prose Works,* trans, Michael Lapidge and Michael Herren (Cambridge: D. S. Brewer, Ltd., 1979), p. 53.

37. F. J. E. Raby, *A History of Secular Latin Poetry in the Middle Ages* (Oxford: Clarendon Press, 1934), II, 46.

38. Aldhelm, *De Virginitate,* in *Opera, Monumenta Germaniae Historica* (Berolini: Apvd Weidmannos, 1919), XV, 315. Trans. Lapidge and Herren, *The Prose Works,* p. 125.

39. Eileen Power, *Medieval English Nunneries* (Cambridge, 1922; rpt. New York: Biblo and Tannen, 1964), pp. 533–34.

40. *The Land of Cokaygne,* in *Early English Poems,* ed. Furnivall, pp. 156–61. The next three references to this poem will be identified in the text by line number.

41. The notion of a "food country" was fairly common in medieval literature. It appeared sometimes as part of the legend of a remote golden age, as in the twelfth-century Irish "Vision of Mac Conglinne":

> The fort we reached was beautiful
> With works of custards thick,
>   Beyond the lake.
> Fresh butter was the bridge in front,
> The rubble dyke was fair white wheat,
>   Bacon the palisade.

Selections from Ancient Irish Poetry, trans. Kuno Meyer (London: Constable and Co., 1911), p. 20.

42. *L'Ordre de Bel-Eyse* in *The Political Songs of England from the Reign of John to that of Edward II,* ed. Thomas Wright (Edinburgh: privately printed, 1884), II, 137–48. The following five references to this poem will be identified in the text by line number.

43. The notion had already appeared in the twelfth-century *Speculum Stultorum* by Nigellus Wireker.

44. A reference either to conditions existing in the double monasteries or simply to the much too common—and illegal—relationships between men and women of the cloth.

45. Nigellus Wireker's, *Speculum Stultorum,* and one of Walter Mapes's poems, contained in MS. Cotton. Vespas. A. xiv. fol. 56, r, also ridicule the Grey Monks for this custom.

46. Ed. William Stubbs (Rolls Series 90, London: Eyre and Spottiswode, 1889), II, 510.

47. The possible reason for William of Aquitaine's obvious resentment regarding monasteries may not be totally unexplained, as he could be parodying here the Abbey of Fontevrault, of doubtful reputation at the time, and where his first wife Ermengarde and his second wife Philippa had become inmates. See Power, p. 45. For a picture of a religious house where there is "Murþe and Munstralsy" (mirth and minstrelsy) see also A Disputison by-twene a cristenemon and a Jew, in The Minor Poems of the Vernon MS., ed. Furnivall, II, 484–93.

48. Rutebeuf, Oeuvres Complètes, ed. Edmond Faral et Julia Bastin (Paris: Editions A. et J. Picard et Cie., 1959), 11,389–407. The next reference to La Vie du Monde will be indicated in the text by line number.

49. This last line could very well be a reference to the "bad habit" of certain nuns of becoming pregnant during such outings. See Chapter 1 and n. 13 above.

50. Rutebeuf, "La Chanson des ordres," in vol. II of Fabliaux et contes des poètes françois, ed. Barbazan, p. 300.

51. "Satire on the People of Kildare," in Reliquiae Antiquae, ed. Wright, II, 75.

52. See n. 22 above.

53. William Langland, The Vision of William concerning Piers the Plowman, ed. J. A. W. Bennet (Oxford: University Press, 1972), passus V, ii, 66, p. 41. Trans. J. F. Goodridge, Piers the Ploughman (Penguin Books, Inc., 1974), p. 66.

54. See Chapter 1.

55. Les Lamentations de Matheolus, ed. Anton G. Van Hamel (Bibliothéque de l'Ecole des Hautes Etudes, Paris: Emile Bouillon, éditeur, 1892), I, 89–90, ll.1719–56. The next reference to Les Lamentations will be identified in the text by line number.

56. Nigellus Wireker, Speculum Stultorum, vol. II of Anglo-Latin Satirical Poets, ed. Thomas Wright (London: Longman and Co., 1872), pp. 4, 94, 93. Trans. John H. Mozley, The Book of Daun Burnel the Ass (Notre Dame, Indiana: University of Notre Dame Press, 1963), pp. 24, 115, 114.

57. Ibid., p. 93. Trans. Mozley, pp. 80–81.

58. Fray Ambrosio de Montesino, "Itinerario de la Cruz," in Romancero y cancionero sagrados, ed. Justo de Sancha, (Biblioteca de Autores Españoles 35, Madrid: Imprenta de los Sucesores de Hernando, 1915), p. 428.

59. Fray Iñigo de Mendoza, Coplas de Vita Christi, in his Cancionero, ed. Julio Rodríguez Puértolas (Madrid: Editorial Gredos, S.A., 1968), p. 403.

60. Jacme Roig, Spill o Libre de les dones, ed. Roque Chabás (Madrid: Librería de M. Murillo, 1905). For more on this monstrous nunnery see the entire section (Book II, part 4).

61. Ibid., Book II, part 2, l.3937. Subsequent references to the Spill will be identified in the text by line number.

62. Zeitschrift für Deutsches Altertum 8 (1849), pp. 160–67.

63. "L'oeuvre d'un clerc, mauvais latiniste, mais libertin spirituel, . . . touchant de très pres à la famille de ceux qui allaient prendre, quelques anées plus tard, le nom de goliard." Ernest Langlois, Origins et sources du "Roman de la Rose" (Paris: Ernest Thorin, éditeur, 1890), p. 6.

64. For the complete text of the bull see Charles Oulmont, Les Débats du clerc et du chevalier dans la littérature poétique du moyen âge (Paris: Honoré Champion, 1911),

pp. 55–57. I have incorporated the emendations of the text of the bull made by M. A. Thomas and cited in Edmond Faral, *Recherches sur les sources latines des contes et romans courtois du Moyen Age* (Paris: Librairie Ancienne Honoré Champion, 1913), p. 215, n. 1.

65. *The Council of Remiremont,* in *Les Débats du clerc et du chevalier,* pp. 93–100. All subsequent references to the Latin text of the *Council* are from this edition and will be identified in the text by line number.

66. According to F. M. Warren, the "excommunicatio rebellarum" is given in terms appropriate to pagan mythology. *"The Council of Remiremont,"* *Modern Language Notes* 22 (1907), 139.

3—"Chanson de Nonne" and Fabliau

1. *Chants et chansons populaires des provinces de l'ouest,* ed. Jérome Bujeaud (Niort: L. Clouzot, 1866), I, 263.

2. "Un lieu commune de la littérature amoreuse du Moyen Age." Felix Lecoy, *Recherches sur le "Libro de Buen Amor"* (Paris: Librairie E. Droz, 1938), p. 266. My translation. All subsequent translations are mine unless otherwise indicated.

3. *Chants et chanson populaires,* I, 136–37.

4. *Zeitschrift für romanische Philologie* 5 (1881), 545, No. 28.

5. "Planctus monialis," ed. M. Vatasso, "Contributo alla storia della poesia ritmica latina medievale," in *Studi Medievali* 1 (1904), 124.

6. Peter Dronke, *Medieval Latin and the Rise of the European Love Lyric* (Oxford: Clarendon Press, 1966), II, 357–58.

7. Ibid., pp. 358–59. Dronke's translation is the result of painstaking scrutiny of the original manuscript under ultraviolet lamp: "In my translation, only the words that can neither be read nor accurately inferred from the MS. are in square brackets," p. 356, Paleographical notes.

8. *Altfranzösische Romanzen und Pastourellen,* ed Karl Bartsch (Leipzig: F. W. C. Vogel, 1870), p. 28. Also in *Les Romans de la Table Ronde,* rédigés par Jacques R. Boulenger (Paris: Union Générale d' Editions, 1941), ll, 251–52.

9. *Chants et chansons populaires,* I, 264.

10. T. Casini, *Studi di poesia antica* (Città di Castelo: Casa editrice S. Lapi, 1913), p. 156, No. 21.

11. "Lassa, mays m'agra valgut. . . ," "Del Manuscript 129 de Ripoll del segle xive," ed. J. Rubiò, *Revista de Bibliografia Catalana* 5 (1905), 376. Trans. by William M. Davis, in *An Anthology of Medieval Lyrics,* ed. Angel Flores (New York: The Modern Library, 1962), pp. 374–75.

12. *Alte-Hoch und Niederdeutsche Volkslieder,* ed. Ludwig Uhland (Stuttgart und Tübingen: F. G. Gottascher, 1845), II, 854, No. 328.

13. See Chapter 1.

14. Pedro de Lerma, *Las doze Coplas Moniales* in *Cancionero de obras de burla provocantes a risa,* ed. L. Usoz (Madrid: Luis Sánchez, 1841), p. 221.

15. *Alte-Hoch und Niederdeutsche Volkslieder,* II, 853, No. 327. Trans. by Eileen Power, *Medieval English Nunneries* (Cambridge, 1922; rpt. New York: Biblo and Tannen, 1964), p. 605. See also *Deutsche Liederdichter,* ed. Karl Bartsch (Berlin: B. Behr's Verlag, 1901), p. 379, No. 98.

16. Ibid., II, 854, No. 329.

17. "Dues cançons populars italianes en un manuscrit català quatrecentista," ed. R. Aramón I. Serra, *Estudis Románics* 1 (1948), 180.

18. Eustache Deschamps, "Sur une novice d'Avernay," in vol. IV of *Oeuvres Complètes,* ed. Marquis de Queux de Saint Hilaire (Paris: Librairie de Firmin Didot et Cie., 1834), p. 233, No. 751. See also Chapter 1, n. 64.

19. *Chants et chansons populaires,* I, 262–63.

20. Casini, p. 157, No. 22.

21. *Cansons de la terra: Cants populars catalans,* ed. Francesch Pelay Briz y Candi Candi (Barcelona: Alvar Verdaguer, 1877), II, 171. Also in *Chants populaires de la Provence,* ed. Damase Arbaud (Aix, 1862–64; rpt. Marseille: Lafitte Reprints, 1971), II, 118–21.

22. *Altfranzösische Romanzen und Pastourellen,* p. 29.

23. *Deutsche Liederdichter,* p. 379, No. 98. Trans. by Power, p. 605. For another version of the lied see *Alte-Hoch und Niederdeutsche Volkslieder,* II, 853–54, No. 327.

24. *Poesía española medieval,* ed. Manuel Alvar (Barcelona: Editorial Planeta, 1969), p. 956, no. 444.

25. Ibid., pp. 956–57, No. 457.

26. Ibid., p. 924, No. 383.

27. Ibid., p. 934, No. 411.

28. "¿Quién dio a la blanca rosa hábito, velo prieto?," ed. R. León, *Papeles de Son Armadans* 21 (1961), 172.

29. Ibid., p. 176.

30. Ibid., p. 174. It may be interesting to observe as a sign of the extreme popularity of the theme of the nun unwillingly professed that even a nursery rhyme picks it up:

> Ve para doña Guiomar,
> porqu' al tiempo del rezar
> dice siempre este cantar:
> "No quiero ser monja, no."

(Go to dame Guiomar, because when it is time to pray she always sings: "I don't want to be a nun, no.")

Ibid, p. 175.

31. *Recueil de chansons populaires,* ed. E. Rolland (Paris: Maisonneuve et Cie., 1883), I, 55.

32. Deschamps, IV, 236, No. 752.

33. *Altfranzösische Romanzen und Pastourellen,* p. 29, No. 33.

34. *Poésies populaires de la Gascogne,* ed. Jean-François Bladé (Paris: Maisonneuve et Cie., 1882), III, 373. Another song of which there are Provençal and Catalan versions already quoted in part (see n. 21 above) ends on a sterner note. After the nun has despaired at her fate and cursed those who placed her in the convent, one day the devil appears and takes her away as punishment for her rebelliousness:

> Lou diable a pres la moungeto,
> tant pourideto,

la pourtad' du plus haut des airs
et puis la tracho dins l'infers.

(The devil seized the poor nun, he took her high up in the air and afterwards brought her to hell.)

Cansons de la terra, II, 172. For the Provenzal version see also *Chants populaires de la Provence,* II, 122.

35. *Altfranzösische Romanzen und Pastourellen,* p. 29, No. 33.

36. *Poesía española medieval,* p. 954, No. 439.

37. *L'Ancienne chanson populaire en France,* ed. J. B. Weckerlin (Paris: Garnier Frères, 1887), pp. 354–55. This song is quoted in the Introduction.

38. *Französische Volkslieder,* ed. Morris Haupt (Leipzig: Verlag Von S. Hirzel, 1877), p. 40.

39. *Chants et chansons populaires,* I, 137–38.

40. "Ballate e strambotti del secolo quindici," ed. Vittorio Cian, *Giornale storico della letteratura italiana* 4 (1884), 55.

41. *Recueil de chansons populaires,* I. 253.

42. "Aut virum aut murum oportet mulierem habere" (A woman ought to have either a husband or a wall). See Chapter I, n. 54.

43. Casini, p. 257, No. 87.

44. "Vieilles chansons recueillies en Velay et en Forez," ed. Victor Smith, *Romania* 7 (1878), 72, No. 20.

45. *Chants populaires recueillis dans le pays Messin,* ed. Comte de Puymaigre (Metz: Rousseau-Pallez, 1865), p. 39, No. 10.

46. *Altfranzösische Romanzen und Pastourellen,* pp. 28–29, No. 33. (This song has already been quoted in part. See n. 33 above).

47. *Littérature Orale de la Basse Normandie,* ed. Jean Fleury (Paris: Maisonneuve et Cie., 1883), pp. 315–16.

48. *Canti popolari del Piemonte,* ed. Constantino Nigra (Torino: Ermano Loescher, 1888), p. 410, No. 80. Nigra cites ten other versions of the song from different regions of Italy.

49. "Chansons populaires recueillies en octobre 1876 a Fontenay-le-Marmion," ed. Emile Legrand, *Romania* 10 (1881), 391.

50. Ibid., p. 395.

51. *Französische Vokslieder,* p. 63.

52. *L'Ancienne Chanson populaire,* p. 356.

53. *Chants et chansons populaires,* II, 323.

54. *Recueil de chansons populaires,* p. 227.

55. *L'Ancienne Chanson populaire,* p. 406.

56. "Vieilles chansons," ed. Smith, p. 62.

57. *Chansons populaires des provinces de France,* ed. Champfleury (Paris: Garnier Frères, 1860), p. 90.

58. *Chansons populaires des Pyrénées françaises,* ed. Jean Poueigh (Paris: Honoré Champion, 1926), I, 363.

59. Ibid., p. 364.

60. *Cansons de la terra,* p. 127.

61. *Recueil de chansons populaires,* IV, 33.

62. Ibid., p. 31.

63. Leigh Hunt, "The Nun," in *Home Book of Verse,* ed. Burton E. Stevenson (New York: Holt, Rinehart and Co., 1950), I, 624.

64. See Chapter 2, n. 23.

65. *Französische Volkslieder,* p. 85. A shorter version is in *L'Ancienne Chanson populaire,* p. 297.

66. *Littérature orale de la Basse Normandie,* pp. 317–18.

67. Ibid., p. 323. A slightly different version from Poitou is in *Chants et chansons populaires,* II, 259–61.

68. *Poesía española medieval,* p. 924, No. 380.

69. *Chansons populaires des Pyrénées françaises,* I, 123.

70. *Recueil de chansons populaires,* II, 81.

71. *Littérature orale de la Basse Normandie,* p. 313. Also in "Vieilles chansons," ed. Smith, p. 73 and in *Chants populaires recueillis dans le pays Messin,* pp. 35–36. To these two songs may be compared Schiller's "Le Chevalier de Toggenburg," where a soldier returns from the war to find his love in a convent. He sees her one day at a window, but after waiting in vain for another glimpse, he dies while keeping his lonely vigil.

72. See Chapter 1.

73. See ibid.

74. *Carmina Medii Aevi,* ed. Hermann Hagen (Berne: Apvd Georgivm Frobenivm and soc., 1877), p. 256. A French version of the dialogue is in *Recueil de poésies françoises des xve et xvie siècles,* ed. M. Anatole de Montaiglon (Paris: Chez P. Jannet, Libraire, 1858), VIII, 170–75.

75. See Dronke, p. 356. Later, the dialogue suffered further mutilation by a scholar who applied certain chemicals to the ink. See ibid.

76. See Chapter 1. Dealing with the same subject but in a much lighter vein than the Latin poems, as befits a popular composition, this old song from Flanders also presents a religious man and woman in an amorous context:

> Daer wandeld' ä patertje langst de kant;
> Hy greep ä nonnetje by der hand.
> Het was in den midderen dey,
> Het was in den mey.

(There wandered a little priest along the side of the road; he grasped a little nun by the hand. It was at midday, it was in May.)

Chants populaires des Flamands de France, ed. Edmond de Coussemaker (Lille: René Giard, 1930), p. 339, No. 105.

77. Dronke, pp. 354–55. Trans. by Dronke, p. 355.

78. *Les Cent Nouvelles nouvelles,* nouv. éd. (Cologne: Pierre Gaillard, 1786), I, 97–98. Trans. by Rossell H. Robbins, *The Hundred Tales: Les Cent Nouvelles nouvelles* (New York: Bonanza Books, 1960), p. 58. Subsequent translations from *Les Cent Nouvelles nouvelles* are from this edition and will be noted as follows: Robbins, p. . . . .

79. Ibid., p. 144. Robbins, p. 86. Exactly the same story is told by La Fontaine

in *L'Abbesse,* in *Contes,* ed. Louis Perceau (Paris: Le Livre du Bibliophile, Georges Briffaut, éditeur, 1929), II, 15–20.

80. Ibid., II, 1. Robbins, p. 200.

81. See Chapter 1.

82. *Les Cent Nouvelles nouvelles,* II, 6. Robbins, p. 202.

83. "La localizzazione del monastero varia nelle diverse redazioni, ma sappiamo che si tratta del convento di Rémiremont nel dipartimento dei Vosges, divenuto famoso per la sua vita licenziosa" (The location of the convent varies in the different versions of the tale, but we know it is Remiremont in the Vosges region, notorious for its licentious life). *Novellino e conti del duecento,* ed. Sebastiano Lo Nigro (Torino: Tipografia Torinese, 1963), p. 392, n. 2. See also Edmond Faral, *Recherches sur les sources latines des contes et romans courtois du Moyen Age* (Paris: Librairie Ancienne Honoré Champion, 1913), p. 215, n. 2.

84. See Chapter 1.

85. *Le cento novelle antiche (Il novellino),* ed. Gualteruzzi (Milano: Paolo Antonio Tosi, 1825), pp. 84–85, No. 62. The same story is in *Novellino e conti del duecento,* pp. 392–94, No. 15 (151).

86. Giovanni Boccaccio, *Decameron,* edizione critica secondo l'autografo Hamiltoniano, ed. Vittore Branca (Firenze: Presso l'Accademia della Crusca, 1976), p. 596. Trans. Richard Aldington, *Decameron* (New York: Garden City Publishing Co., Inc., 1949), p. 459. Subsequent translations from the *Decameron* are from this edition and will be noted as follows: Aldington, p. . . .

87. Ibid., p. 460. Aldington, p. 460.

88. *Recueil général et complet des fabliaux des xiii͏e et xiv͏e siècles,* ed. M. Montaiglon et G. Raynaud (Paris, 1890; rpt. Burt Franklin Research and Source Works Series 47, New York, 1964), VI, 267.

89. Casini, pp. 126–27.

90. La Fontaine, II, 42–47.

91. William Warner, *Albion's England* (London, 1597), Book V, Chapter 27. Cited by Power, p. 523.

92. Boccaccio, p. 185. Aldington, p. 137.

93. Ibid., p. 186. Aldington, p. 138.

94. Ibid., p. 187. Aldington, p. 139.

95. Francesco da Barberino, *Del reggimento e costumi di donne,* ed. Carlo Baudi di Vesme (Bologna: Presso Gaetano Romagnoli, 1875), p. 277.

96. Ibid.

97. The same story appears in French in *Oeuvres galantes des conteurs italiens,* ed. Ad. van Bever et Ed. Sansot-Orland (Paris: Société du Mercure de France, 1908), pp. 24–30.

98. *Recueil général et complet des fabliaux,* III, 145–55.

99. Ibid., pp. 137–44.

100. *La Messe des Oisiaus et li plais des chanonesses et des grises nonnains* (The Birds' Mass and the Debate of the Canonesses and the Grey Nuns), ed. Jacques Ribard (Gen`ve: Librairie Droz, 1970). Subsequent references to *La Messe* are from this edit, .. and will be identified in the text by line number.

101. Nuns are said to be the best lovers also in the Archpriest of Hita's *Libro de Buen Amor:*

en noblezas de amor ponen toda su hemencia,

. . . .

mucho encobiertas son, donosas e plazenteras.
(And such their virtues are that passion is by them inflamed.

. . . .

[a nun] is secretive, yet tutors men just how to dip their paddles.
(stanzas 1338 d, 1340 b)
Libro de Buen Amor, ed. Joan Corominas (Madrid: Editorial Gredos, S.A., 1967).
Trans. Elisha K. Kane, *The Book of Good Love* (Chapel Hill: University of North
Carolina, 1968). See Chapter 4 for more on the love of nuns in the *Libro de Buen Amor.*
    102. *Erzählungen und Schwanke,* ed. Hans Lambel (Leipzig: F. A. Brockhaus,
1872), pp. 296–306.
    103. *Nouveau Recueil de fabliaux et contes inédits des poètes français des xiie, xiiie,
xive et xve siècles,* ed. E. Barbazan et D. Méon (Paris, 1823; rpt. Genève: Slatkine
Reprints, 1976), IV 250–55.
    104. *Erzählungen und Schwänke,* p. 303.
    105. *Canti popolari del Piemonte,* p. 407, n. 79.
    106. *Cansons de la terra,* III, 207.
    107. See *Canti popolari del Piemonte,* p. 409.
    108. *Fabliaux et contes des poètes français des xie, xiie, xiiie, xive, et xve siècles,* ed.
Etienne Barbazan (Paris, 1808; rpt. Genève: Slatkine Reprints, 1976), II, 92–98.
    109. Ibid., p. 98.
    110. *Chants et chansons populaires,* II, 288–89.
    111. Ibid., pp. 290–91.
    112. Ibid., p. 291.
    113. Ibid., p. 289.
    114. *Selection from the Minor Poems of John Lydgate,* ed. James O. Halliwell (Percy
Society 2, London, 1840), pp. 109–110.
    115. Deschamps, IV, 88, No. 629.

4—Doña Garoza and Madame Eglentyne

    1. Juan Ruiz, Archpriest of Hita, *Libro de Buen Amor,* ed. Joan Corominas
(Madrid: Editorial Gredos, S.A., 1967) stanza 1443 d. Trans. Rigo Mignani and Mario
A. di Cesare, *The Book of Good Love* (Albany, New York: State University of New
York Press, 1970), p. 277. All references to the *Libro de Buen Amor (LBA)* will be to the
edition by Corominas and will be identified in the text by stanza number and letter.
Translations will follow the Spanish version and will be from *The Book of Good Love,*
trans. Elisha Kent Kane (Chapel Hill: University of North Carolina Press, 1968) unless
otherwise indicated.
    2. Eileen Power, "Madame Eglentyne, Chaucer's Prioress in Real Life," in
her *Medieval People: A Study of Communal Psychology* (Penguin Books, Ltd., 1937), p.
69.
    3. Helen Waddell, *The Wandering Scholars* (Boston and New York, 1927; rpt.
Boston and New York: Houghton, Mifflin and Co., 1929), p. 217.

4. J. J. Jusserand, *English Wayfaring Life in the Middle Ages,* trans. Lucy T. Smith (London, 1890; rpt. Williamston, Mass.: Corner House Publishers, 1974), p. 339.

5. Edward L. Cutts, *Scenes and Characters of the Middle Ages* (London: Simpkin Marshall, Ltd., 1930), p. 179.

6. For detailed information on the number of pilgrimages, their origin and history, see Louis de Sivry et M. de Champagnac, *Dictionnaire, géographique, historique, descriptif, archéologique des pélerinages anciens et modernes,* 2 vols. (Paris: Chez L'Éditeur, 1850–1859). That quintessential pilgrim of the Canterbury Tales, the Wife of Bath, who had been three times to Jerusalem and had visited Rome, Bologne, and Cologne, had also been "in Galice at Saint-Jame." The Wife of Bath's Portrait, *The Canterbury Tales, General Prologue,* In Geoffrey Chaucer, *Works,* ed. F. N. Robinson, 2nd. ed. (Boston: Houghton Mifflin and Co., 1961), l. 466.

7. Jusserand, p. 365.

8. See *Reliquiae Antiquae,* ed. Thomas Wright (London, 1841; rpt. New York: A.M.S. Press, Inc., 1966), I, 2–3 for a poem entitled "Pilgrims on Shipboard (a Pilgrimage to the Shrine of St. James de Compostela) time of Henry VI." See also G. G. Coulton, *Chaucer and his England* (London, 1908; rpt. London: Methuen and Co., Ltd., 1963), pp. 140, 141, 142.

9. Northrop Frye, *Anatomy of Criticism: Four Essays* (Princeton, New Jersey: Princeton University Press, 1957), p. 223.

10. Edward A. and Lillian D. Bloom, *Satire's Persuasive Voice* (London: Cornell University Press, 1979), p. 2.

11. Power, "Madame Eglentyne," p. 69.

12. "De las que no hacen sangre." Julio Puyol y Alonso, *El Arcipreste de Hita: Estudio crítico* (Madrid: Sucesora de M. Minuesa de los Ríos, 1906), p. 111. My translation. All subsequent translations are mine unless otherwise indicated.

13. Samuel M. Tucker, *Verse Satire in England Before the Renaissance* (New York: Columbia University Press, 1908), p. 99.

14. Jill Mann, *Chaucer and Medieval Estates Satire: The Literature of Social Classes and the "General Prologue" to the "Canterbury Tales"* (Cambridge: University Press, 1973), p. 197.

15. For a review of critical approaches to the portrait of the Prioress in the *Prologue,* see Florence H. Ridley, *The Prioress and the Critics* (Berkeley: University of California Press, 1965). There is no comparable work on the portrait of Doña Garoza in the *LBA,* but a helpful anthology of critical essays on the entire *LBA* is *"Libro de Buen Amor" Studies,* ed. G. B. Gybbon-Monypenny (London: Támesis Books, Ltd., 1970).

16. Arthur W. Hoffman, "Chaucer's Prologue to Pilgrimage: The Two Voices," in *Chaucer: Modern Essays in Criticism,* ed. Edward Wagenknecht (New York, 1959; rpt. Oxford: Oxford University Press, 1974), p. 36.

17. Emil Lucki, Vol. IV of his *History of the Renaissance* (Salt Lake City: University of Utah, 1965), p. 34.

18. See María Rosa Lida de Malkiel, "Nuevas notas para la interpretación del *Libro de Buen Amor,*" in her *Estudios de literatura española y comparada,* 2nd. ed. (Buenos Aires: Editorial Universitaria, 1969), pp. 66–67.

19. *The Book of Good Love,* trans. Kane, p. 260, n. 27.

20. "Extraña mezcla de devoción y lubricidad." Claudio Sánchez Albornoz, *España, un enigma histórico,* 2nd. ed. (Buenos Aires: Editorial Sudamericana, 1962), I, 453.

21. *The Book of Good Love,* trans. Kane, p. 261, n. 28.

22. "el zigzagueo del episodio." Lida, p. 71 and "encaminar al lector en una dirección para soprenderle inmediatemente con la opuesta," ibid., p. 69.

23. Wolfgang Iser, "Interaction between Text and Reader," in *The Reader in the Text: Essays on Audience and Interpretation,* ed. Susan R. Suleiman and Inge Crosman (Princeton, New Jersey: Princeton Unversity Press, 1980), p. 106.

24. See Gerald Prince, "Notes on the Text as Reader," in ibid., pp. 225–40.

25. "El amor era un pecado, y lo que con él se relaciona objeto de vergüenza." Puyol y Alonso, p. 131.

26. Elisha K. Kane, "The Electuaries of the Archpriest of Hita, *Modern Philology* 30 (1933), 264. For a detailed analysis of the passage, see ibid., pp. 263–66. The narrator had already demonstrated his acquaintance with aphrodisiacs in stanza 941 a, b, as he wondered by which means Trotaconventos had succeeded in obtaining a certain woman's love for him:

> Si la enfechizó o si l' dio atincar,
> o si le dio rainela o l' dio mohalinar.

(Perhaps she gave my dame a philter, aphrodisiac drug,
A brew of herbs or love's potion from a magic jug.)

The entire electuary follows:

> Muchos letuarios dan a ellos: a las de vezes
> diacitrón, codoñate e letuario de nuezes,
> e otros de más quantía—de çanahorias, rehezes,
> embian unas a otras, cada día, a revezes—;
>
> cominada alixándria, con el buen diagargante,
> el diacitronabatis, con fino jingibrate,
> mielrosado, diacímino, diantosio, vadela[n]te,
> la rosata novela, que devía dezir ante;
>
> adragea e alfenique, con el estomaticón,
> e la gariofilata, con diamargaritón,
> triasándalis muy fino; con diasaturión,
> que es para doñear preciado e noble don.
>
> Sabet que todo açúcar allí anda ballonado:
> polvo, terrón e candi, e mucho del rosado,
> açúcar de confites e açúcar violado,
> e de otras muchas guisas que ya he olvidado.

(They minister a lot of compounds to their lovers oft;
Sharp, pungent citrons, quince, and sometimes pastes of kernels soft,
Of carrots vile, at which perhaps the ignorant have scoffed;
And these they alternate with brews to be at all times quaffed.

Of camphor and of cumin seed they mix a recipe,
Of compound ginger, lemon, honey, equal parts in three;
Or brew with cinnamon and pink, rose-honey tinctured tea,
Or with sharp spice and honey prime their gallants for love's spree.

Sometimes they feed them dragon weed with sugar for a coat,
Or mash of cloves and marigold which burns the tongue and throat,
Or saffron and satyrion which sexual lust promote
And goad a man to go for women like a very goat.

All kinds of sugars with these nuns are plentiful as dirt,
The powdered, lump, and crystallized, and syrups for dessert.
They've perfumed sweetmeats, heaps of candy—some with spice of
    wort—
With other kinds which I forget and cannot here insert.)
    (stanzas 1334–1337)

27. Trans. Mignani and di Cesare, p. 260.

28. See n. 22 above.

29. For a detailed analysis of the Archpriest's fascinating dialectical method see Lida, "Nuevas Notas," pp. 67–73.

30. See Chapter 2.

31. See Chapter 1.

32. Trans. Mignani and di Cesare, p. 277. Quoted at beginning of present chapter.

33. Ibid., p. 281.

34. See Iser, p. 110.

35. Lucki, p. 35.

36. Trans. Mignani and di Cesare, p. 283.

37. "Un hombre para encandilar la imaginación de cualquier hembra placentera o no." Luis Beltrán, *Razones de buen amor: oposiciones y convergencias en el libro del Arcipreste de Hita* (Fundación Juan March, Valencia: Editorial Castalia, 1977), p. 343.

38. Trans. Mignani and di Cesare, p. 284.

39. Elisha K. Kane, "The Personal Appearance of Juan Ruiz," *Modern Language Notes* 45 (1930), 106.

40. For a full analysis of the erotic implications of each one of the Archpriest's purported physical features, see ibid., pp. 103–109.

41. See Chapter 1.

42. We may recall here that in the *Council of Remiremont*, a vast assembly of nuns had decided that priestly lovers were far superior to any others. See Chapter 2.

43. See li Muisis's satiric poem *Les Maintiens des nonnains*, Chapter 2 and also Chapter 1, n. 107.

44. "La frase 'buena cima' es, pues, inequívoca y no cabe entenderla en sentido piadoso." *LBA,* p. 556.

45. For a brief but enlightening analysis of the troubadours' "good" and "false" love, see Francisco Márquez Villanueva, "El buen amor," *Revista de Occidente* 2nd series 9 (1965), 269–77.

46. See chapter 3, n. 8 and 9.

47. See n. 22 above.

48. See note 44 above.

49. Trans. Mignani and di Cesare, p. 286.

50. Benjamin B. Wainwright, "Chaucer's Prioress Again: An Interpretative Note," *Modern Language Notes* 48 (1933), p. 34.

51. Cited by Power in "Madame Eglentyne," p. 89.

52. Jacques de Vitry, cited by Power, *Medieval English Nunneries* (Cambridge, 1922; rpt. New York: Biblo and Tannen, 1964), p. 372, n. 1. No source given.

53. Cited by Frederick Tupper, "St. Venus and the Canterbury Pilgrims," *The Nation* 97 (1913), 354.

54. See Boniface VIII's Bull, Chapter 1.

55. Arthur Sherbo, "Chaucer's Nun's Priest Again," *Publications of the Modern Language Association* 64 (1949), 244.

56. Muriel Bowden, *A Commentary on the "General Prologue" to the "Canterbury Tales,"* 2nd ed. (London, 1948; rpt. New York: The Macmillan Co., 1969), p. 93.

57. Chaucer, *Works,* ll. 118–162. All subsequent references to the Prioress's portrait are from this edition and will appear in the text without line numbers.

58. See "Huéline and Eglantine," in *Fabliaux or Tales Abridged from French Manuscripts of the Twelfth and Thirteenth Centuries,* ed. M. Le Grand d'Aussy, trans. Gregory Lewis Way (London: W. Bulmer and Co., 1796), 1, 93–105. See also, "Bele Aiglentine en roial chamberine," a pastourelle in *La Poésie française du Moyen Age (xie– xve siècles),* ed. Charles Oulmont (Paris: Société du Mercure de France, 1913), pp. 255– 57.

59. *The Rule of St. Benedict,* trans. and ed. John Hunter Blair (Fort Augustus, Scotland: Abbey Press, 1948), pp. 28–29. Subsequent references to the *Rule* and translations from it will be from this edition and will be noted as follows: *Rule,* p. . . .

60. "Eligius, Bishop of Noyon and Master of the Mint to Dagobert I, was once asked by his sovereign to take an oath. When Eligius not only refused to swear but also began to weep, Dagobert was apparently convinced of his integrity and said that he would believe him without an oath. Hales* concluded that to swear by St. Eligius was therefore not to swear at all." James J. Lynch, "The Prioress's Greatest Oath Once More," *Modern Language Notes* 72 (1957), 243. *J. W. Hales was the critic who, in 1891, first pointed out this incident in St. Eligius's life.

61. Wainwright, p. 37.

62. Iser, p. 107.

63. Chauncey Wood, "Chaucer's Use of Signs in his Portrait of the Prioress," in *Signs and Symbols in Chaucer's Poetry,* ed. John P. Hermann and John J. Burke, Jr. (Alabama: University of Alabama Press, 1981), p. 99.

64. For more details on Stratford atte Bowe, see Marie P. Hamilton, "The Convent of Chaucer's Prioress and her Priests," *Philologica: The Malone Anniversary Studies,* ed. Thomas A. Kirby and Henry B. Woolf (Baltimore: The Johns Hopkins Press, 1949), pp. 179–90.

65. Ernest P. Kuhl, "Notes on Chaucer's Prioress," *Philological Quarterly* 1–2 (1922–23), 306, n. 28.

66. *Rule*, pp. 26–27.

67. St. Jerome, *Libros Adversus Jovinianum Admonitio*, in *Patrologiae Latinae*, ed. J. P. Migne (Paris: Bibliothecae Cleri Universae, 1863), vol. 303, col. 297. Trans. Robert B. White, "Chaucer's Daun Piers and the Rule of St. Benedict: The Failure of an Ideal," *Journal of English and Germanic Philology* 70 (1971), 25.

68. St. Gregory, *Moralium Libri*, XXXI, in *Patrologiae Latinae*, vol. 76, col. 621. Trans. by R. B. White, p. 25.

69. For a comparison of the Prioress's manners to those prescribed by a medieval manual on manners, see *The Book of Courtesy*, in *The Babees Book: Medieval Manners for the Young*, ed. Edith Rickert, trans. F. J. Furnivall (New York: Cooper Square Publishers, Inc., 1966), pp. 79–85.

70. Bowden quotes a fragment of this passage in English. See Bowden, pp. 95–96.

71. Guillaume de Lorris et Jean de Meung, *Le Roman de la Rose*, ed. Silvio F. Baridon (Milano: Instituto Editoriale Cisalpino, 1954), vol. 2, ll. 13758–59 and 13790–805. Trans. Harry Robbins, *The Romance of the Rose*, ed. Charles W. Dunn (New York: E. P. Dutton and Co., Inc., 1962), ll. 86 and 101–19.

72. P. Ovidi Nasonis, *De Arte Amatoria*, ed. Paul Brandt (Hildesheim: Georg Olms Verlagsbuchhandlung, 1963), III, ll. 755–60. Trans. by Rolfe Humphries, *The Art of Love* (Bloomington, Indiana: Indiana University Press, 1957), p. 176.

73. C. M. Drennan, "Chaucer's Prioress, Canterbury Tales, Prologue, 136: 'Ful semely after hir mete she raughte'," *Notes and Queries* 11th ser. 9 (1914), 365.

74. Mann, p. 129.

75. Bowden, p. 100.

76. Alan T. Gaylord, "The Unconquered Tale of the Prioress," *Papers of the Michigan Academy of Science, Arts and Letters* 47 (1962), p. 622. Gaylord points out that the Squire is also described in terms taken from *Le Roman de la Rose*.

77. Iser, p. 110.

78. St. Thomas Aquinas, *The Summa Theologica*, trans. Fathers of the English Dominican Province (London: R. and T. Washbourne, Ltd., 1917), II, ii, Q. 44, art. 1–4, pp. 538–45.

79. See Chapter 1.

80. For centuries wastel bread was considered "a superior wheat bread (presumably white), and such no doubt was Chaucer's view of it." Kuhl, p. 303. For more on "wastel breed" see ibid., pp. 302–303.

81. Geofroi de Vinsauf, *The Poetria Nova and Its Sources in Early Rhetorical Doctrine*, ed. and trans. Ernest Gallo (The Hague: Mouton and Co., 1971), ll. 568–81.

82. See ibid., pp. 44–45 for complete Latin and English texts.

83. Ibid., ll. 596–600.

84. This will be especially the case if the reader is unfamiliar with de Vinsauf's rules. See n. 83 above.

85. Nigellus Wireker, *Speculum Stultorum*, ed. John H. M. Mozley and Robert R. Raymo (Berkeley and Los Angeles: University of California Press, 1960), ll. 2371–2400. Trans. Graydon W. Regenos, *The Book of Burnel the Ass* (Austin: University of Texas Press, 1959), p. 115.

86. Ibid., ll. 2390–91. Trans. Regenos, p. 115.

87. Peter S. Taitt, *Incubus and Ideal: Ecclesiastical Figures in Chaucer and Langland* (Salzburg, Austria: Institut für Englische Sprache, 1975), p. 61.

88. See Iser, p. 112.

89. Kevin S. Kiernan, "The Art of the Descending Catalogue, and a Fresh Look at Alisoun," *Chaucer Review* 10 (1975), 1–16.

90. de Vinsauf, ll. 600–602.

91. Kiernan, p. 9.

92. G. G. Coulton, *Medieval Panorama: The English Scene from Conquest to Reformation* (Cambridge, 1938; rpt. Cambridge: University Press, 1939), p. 277.

93. "High foreheads happened to be fashionable among worldly ladies, who even shaved theirs to make them higher." Power, "Madame Eglentyne," p. 84. See also Gordon H. Harper, "Chaucer's Big Prioress," *Philological Quarterly* 12 (1933), 310.

94. Harper, p. 309.

95. See Wood, p. 96.

96. There were so many manuscripts of the *Riwle* in Middle French, Middle English, and Latin circulating in fourteenth-century England, that Chaucer was probably acquainted with at least some of the most conventional ideas.

97. *Ancrene Wisse:* edited from MS. Corpus Christi College Cambridge 402, ed. J. R. R. Tolkien (Early English Text Society 249, London: Oxford University Press, 1962), pp. 69–70. Trans. M. B. Salu, *The Ancrene Riwle: The Corpus MS.: Ancrene Wisse* (London: Burns and Oates, 1955), pp. 58–59.

98. Wood, p. 96.

99. The adverb "ful" meaning "very" is used eleven times in the portrait of the Prioress, and "the net result of all this 'ful'-ness is, if you will pardon the pun, fulsome," according to Chauncey Wood. The effect, he continues, is "overpraise" and "a subtle and very entertaining irony" (p. 90). "Fetys" or "fetis" means "cleverly fashioned, neat, elegant." See *Middle English Dictionary,* ed. Hans Kurath and Sherman M. Kuhn (Ann Arbor, Michigan: University of Michigan Press, 1954–1975).

100. Power, "Madame Eglentyne," p. 84.

101. *Victoria History of the Counties of England, York,* (London: Archibald Constable and Co., Ltd., 1907), III, 168.

102. Ibid., p. 123.

103. *Records of Visitations held by William Alnwick, Bishop of Lincoln: 1436 to 1439,* Vol. II of *Visitations of Religious Houses in the Diocese of Lincoln,* ed. A. Hamilton Thompson (Lincoln Record Society and Canterbury and York Society, 13–15, Lincoln, 1914–1929), p. 45.

104. Ibid., pp. 175–76.

"The reference is to archbishop Langton's constitution AD HAEC: 'Decernimus ut moniales et cetere mulieres divino cultui dedicate velum vel peplum sericum non habeant, nec in velo acus argenteas vel aureas audeant deportare. . . . Et sola monialis consecrata deferat annulum, et uno solo sit contenta.'" (Ibid., p. 176, n. 3)

(We decree for nuns and other women dedicated to divine service, that they should not have a silk veil or tunic, nor should they dare to wear on their veil silver or gold pins . . . And only the consecrated nun alone may wear a ring; and she must be content with only one).

105. " 'Varium' or 'varia pellis' was, as its name implies, a variegated fur."
Ibid., p. 3, n. 4.

106. Ibid., p. 8. Bishop Alnwick's injunctions appear in English in the text of
the *Visitations*. See also *V. C. H., York*, III, 122, 181.

107. Iser, p. 111.

108. John Gower, *Vox Clamantis*, in his *The Complete Works*, ed G. C. Mac-
aulay (Oxford: Clarendon Press, 1902), Liber Quartus, Cap. XIV, ll. 639–42. Trans.
Eric W. Stockton, ed., *The Major Latin Works of John Gower* (Seattle: University of
Washington Press, 1962), Book IV, Chapter XIV, p. 181.

109. *The Parson's Tale*, I, 410, in Geoffrey Chaucer, *Works*. See also Wood,
p. 84.

110. Ibid., I, 409–15.

111. John B. Friedman, "The Prioress's Beads of 'Smal Coral'," *Medium Aevum*
39 (1970), 303.

112. Hugo de Folieto or Hugonis de S. Victore, *De Claustro Anime*, Lib. II.
Cited in the original and in translation by White, p. 19.

113. *The Parson's Tale*, I, 429.

114. *Rule*, pp. 26–27.

115. Luke xii, 22.

116. See Friedman, p. 303. See also *The Book of Courtesy*, p. 102: "Ladies with
beads of coral and amber," and the entries for "bedes" and "coral" in *Middle English
Dictionary*. For more examples of the widespread use of coral rosaries and other
ornaments in the Middle Ages, see collections of old wills cited in Chapter 1.

117. Gilles li Muisis, *Poésies*, pub. Kervyn de Letterhove (Louvain: Imprimerie
de J. Lefever, 1882), I, 209–36.

118. Wood, p. 97.

119. *Ancrene Wisse*, p. 215. Trans. Salu, *The Ancrene Riwle*, p. 187.

120. Ibid. See also n. 103 above.

121. "Plangit nonna fletibus," in *Medieval Latin and the Rise of the European Love
Lyric*, ed. Peter Dronke (Oxford: Clarendon Press, 1966), II, 357, ll. 19–27. For a
detailed discussion of "Plangit nonna fletibus" ("Planctus monialis") see Chapter 3.

122. *The Eclogues, Bucolics or Pastorals*, trans. and ed. Thomas F. Royds (Oxford: Basil Blackwell, 1922), pp. 120–21, l. 69.

123. See Richard J. Schoeck, "Chaucer's Prioress: Mercy and Tender Heart," in
Vol. I of *Chaucer Criticism*, ed. R. Schoeck and J. Taylor (Notre Dame, Indiana:
University of Notre Dame Press, 1975), p. 247.

124. *The Complete Works*, Liber Quintus, Cap. III, l. 147. Trans. Stockton,
Book V, Chapter III, p. 99.

125. *Le Roman de la Rose*, II, ll. 21709–710. Trans. Robbins, *The Romance of the
Rose*, l. 98.

126. See Friedman, p. 302.

127. Chaucer, *Works*, l. 307.

128. Vincent de Beauvais, *Speculum Naturale* (Douai, 1624), Lib. VIII, lvii,
p. 523. Cited by Friedman, p. 304.

129. "An allusion to the protective power of coral certainly would not have
been lost upon a reading audience who owed most of its magical, medical, and
astrological lore to lapidaries and encyclopaedias." Friedman, p. 302.

130. See E. S. Rohde, *The Old English Herbals* (New York: Longmans, Green and Co., 1922), p. 28.

131. *English Medieval Lapidaries,* ed. Joan Evans and Mary S. Serjeantson (Early English Text Society 190, London, 1933), p. 125.

132. Ibid., p. 77. Cited by Francis Manley in "Chaucer's Rosary and Donne's Bracelet: Ambiguous Coral," *Modern Language Notes* 74 (1959), 387.

133. The Prioress's Tale, in Chaucer, *Works,* II. 609–10.

Bibliography

Primary Sources

Aldhelm. *De Virginitate.* In *Opera.* Vol. XV of *Monumenta Germaniae Historica.* Berolini: APVD Weidmannos, 1919.

———. *De Laudibus Virginitatis sive de Virginitate Sanctorum.* In *The Prose Works.* Trans. Michael Lapidge and Michael Herren. Cambridge: D. S. Brewer, Ltd., 1979.

Alonso, Dámaso and José Manuel Blecua, ed. *Antología de la poesía española: lírica de tipo tradicional.* Madrid: Editorial Gredos, S.A., 1969.

Alvar, Manuel, ed. *Poesía española medieval.* Barcelona: Editorial Planeta, 1969.

Andreas Capellanus. *The Art of Courtly Love.* Ed. and trans. John Jay Parry. Columbia University Press, 1941; rpt. New York: Frederick Ungar Publishing Co., 1959.

Arbaud, Damase, ed. *Chants populaires de la Provence.* Aix, 1862–1864; rpt. Marseille: Laffitte Reprints, 1971, Vol. II.

Arias y Arias, Ricardo, ed. *La poesía de los goliardos.* Madrid: Editorial Gredos, S.A., 1970.

Banks, Mary Macleod, ed. *An Alphabet of Tales.* 2 vols. Early English Text Society 126–127. London, 1904.

Barbazan, Etienne, ed. *Fabliaux et contes des poètes français des xie, xiie, xiiie, xive et xve siècles.* Paris, 1808; rpt. Genève: Slatkine Reprints, 1976, Vol. II.

———, and Dominique-Martin Méon, ed.. *Nouveau Recueil de fabliaux et contes inédits des poètes français des xiie, xiiie, xive et xve siècles.* 4 vols. Paris 1823; rpt. Genève: Slatkine Reprints, 1976.

Barberino, Francesco da. *Del reggimento e costumi di donne.* Ed. Carlo Baudi di Vesme. Bologna: Presso Gaetano Romagnoli, 1875.

Bartsch, Karl, ed. *Alfranzösische Romanzen und Pastourellen.* Leipzig: F. C. W. Vogel, 1870.

————, ed. *Deutsche Liederdichter des zwölften bis vierzehnten Jahrhunderts*. Berlin: B. Behr's Verlag, 1901.

Bithell, Jethro, ed. *The Minnesingers: Translations*. New York: Longmans, Green and Co., 1909.

Bladé, Jean-Francois, ed. *Poésies populaires de la Gascogne*. Paris: Maisonneuve et Cie, 1882. Vol. III.

Blair, Oswald Hunter, ed. *The Rule of St. Benedict*. Fort Augustus, Scotland: Abbey Press, 1948.

Bliss, W. H., ed. *Papal Letters (A.D. 1198–1304)*. In *Calendar of Entries in the Papal Registers Relating to Great Britain and Ireland*. 13 vols. London: Eyre and Spottiswoode, 1893.

————, ed. *Petitions to the Pope*. In *Calendar of Entries in the Papal Registers Relating to Great Britain and Ireland* (1342–1419). London: Eyre and Spottiswoode, 1896, Vol. I.

Boccaccio, Giovanni. *Decamerone*. Edizone critica secondo l'autografo Hamiltoniano. Ed. Vittore Branca. Firenze: Presso l'Accademia della Crusca, 1976.

————. *The Decameron*. Trans. Richard Aldington. New York: Garden City Publishing Co., Inc., 1949.

————. *The Decameron*. Trans. and ed. Mark Musa and Peter E. Bondanella. New York: W. W. Norton and Co., Inc., 1977.

Boulenger, Jacques R., ed. *Les Romans de la Table Ronde*. Paris: Union Générale d'Editions, 1941, Vol. II.

Brakelman, Jules, ed. *Les plus Anciens Chansonniers français (xiie siècle)*. Paris: Emile Bouillon, Libraire-éditeur, 1870–1891.

Breul, Karl, ed. *The Cambridge Songs: A Goliard's Song Book of the Eleventh Century*. Cambridge: The University Press, 1915.

Bryan, W. F., and Germaine Dempster, ed. *Sources and Analogues of Chaucer's Tales*. Chicago: The University of Chicago Press, 1941.

Buendía, Felicidad, ed. *El libro del Caballero Cifar*. In *Libros de caballerías españoles*. Madrid: Aguilar, 1960.

Bujeaud, Jérome, ed. *Chants et chansons populaires des provinces de l'Ouest*. 2 vols. Niort: L. Clouzot, 1866.

Bulst, Walther, ed. *Carmina Cantabrigiensia*. Heidelberg: Carl Winter, Universitatsverlag, 1950.

Caesarius of Heisterbach. *The Dialogue on Miracles*. Trans. H. von E. Scott and C. C. Swinton Bland. 2 vols. London: George Rutledge and Sons, Ltd., 1929.

————. *Dialogus Miraculorum*. Ed. Joseph Strange. 2 vols. Cologne: J. M. Heberle, 1851.

Carducci, Giosuè, ed. *Cantilene e ballate, strambotti e madrigali nel seccolo tredici e quattordici*. Pisa: Nistri, 1871.

Casini, T. *Studi di poesia antica*. Città de Castello: Casa editrice S. Lapi, 1913.

Caterina da Siena, Santa. *Libro della Divina Dottrina* (Volgarmente detto Dialogo della Provvidenza. Ed. Matilde Fiorilli. 2nd ed. Bari: Gius. Laterza e figli, 1928.

Catholic Dictionary: The Catholic Encyclopaedic Dictionary. Ed. Donald Atwater. 3rd ed. New York: The Macmillan Co., 1962.

(Les) Cent Nouvelles nouvelles. Nouv. éd. 3 vols. Cologne: P. Gaillard, 1786.

Champfleury, ed. *Chansons populaires des provinces de France.* Paris: Garnier Fréres, 1860.

Chaucer, Geoffrey. *The Complete Works, Notes to the Canterbury Tales.* Ed. Walter W. Skeat. 2nd ed. Oxford, 1900; rpt. Oxford: Clarendon Press, 1963.

————. *Works.* Ed. F. N. Robinson. 2nd ed. Boston: Houghton Mifflin Co., 1961.

Chaucer's Poetry: An Anthology for the Modern Reader. Ed. E. T. Donaldson. New York: The Ronald Press Co., 1958.

Chronicon Adae de Usk (A.D. 1377–1421). Ed. and trans. Sir Edward M. Thompson. London: Henry Frowde, 1904.

Cian, Vittorio, ed. "Ballate e strambotti del secolo quindici." *Giornale storico della letteratura italiana* 4 (1884): 1–55.

Clark, Andrew, ed. *The English Register of Godstow Nunnery.* 2 vols. Early English Text Society 129–130. London, 1905.

————, ed. *Lincoln Diocese Documents: 1450–1544.* Early English Text Society 149. London, 1914.

Cockayne, Oswald, ed. *Hali Meidenhad.* Early English Text Society 18. London, 1866.

Corbridge, Thomas of, Archbishop of York. *Register: 1300–1304.* 2 vols. Surtees Society 138, 141. London, 1925.

Coussemaker, Edmond de, ed. *Chants populaires des Flamandes de France.* Lille: René Giard, 1930.

Coulton, G. G., ed and trans. *A Medieval Garner: Human Documents from the Four Centuries Preceding the Reformation.* London: Constable and Co., Ltd., 1910.

Deschamps, Eustache. *Oeuvres Complètes.* Ed. Marquis de Queux de Saint Hilaire. Paris: Librairie de Firmin Didot et Cie., 1834. Vol. IV.

Drokensford, John de, Bishop of Bath and Wells. *Register: 1309–1329.* Somerset Record Society 1. London, 1887.

Drouart la Vache. *Li Livres d'amours.* Ed. Robert Bossuat. Paris: Librairie Ancienne Honoré Champion, 1926.

Dugdale, Sir William ed. *Monasticon Anglicanum: A History of Abbies and other Monasteries, Hospitals, Frieries and Cathedral and Collegiate Churches with their Dependencies in England and Wales.* 6 vols. London: James Bohn, 1846.

du Meril, Edélstand, ed. *Poésies populaires latines du Moyen Age.* Paris, 1847; rpt. Genève: Slatkine Reprints, 1977.

Erasmi, Desiderii Roterodami. *Opera Omnia.* Ed. L. E. Halkin, F. Bierlaire and R. Hoven. Amsterdam: North Holland Publishing Company, 1972, Vol. I–III.

Erasmus, Desiderius. *The Colloquies.* Trans. C. R. Thompson. Chicago: University Press, 1965.

Fleury, Jean, ed. *Littérature orale de la Basse Normandie.* Paris: Maisonneuve et Cie., 1883.

Flores, Angel, ed. *An Anthology of Medieval Lyrics.* New York: The Modern Library, 1962.

Furnivall, F. J., ed. *Early English Poems and Lives of Saints.* Transactions of the Philological Society. Berlin: A. Asher and Co., 1862.

———. ed. *Fifty Earliest English Wills in the Court of Probate,* London. Early English Text Society 55. London, 1882.

———, ed. *The Minor Poems of the Vernon Manuscript.* Early English Text Society 117. London, 1901.

Gandavo, Simonis de, Bishop of Salisbury. *Registrum: 1297–1315.* 2 Vols. The Canterbury and York Society 40–41. Oxford University Press, 1934.

Gaselee, Stephen, ed. *The Oxford Book of Medieval Latin Verse.* Oxford: Clarendon Press, 1928.

Gasquet, Cardinal, trans. *The Rule of St. Benedict.* London, 1925; rpt. New York: Cooper Square, 1966.

Geofroi de Vinsauf. *The Poetria Nova and Its Sources in Early Rhetorical Doctrine.* Ed. and trans. Ernest Gallo. The Hague: Mouton and Co., 1971.

Giffard, Godfrey, Archbishop of Worcester. *Register: 1268–1302.* Ed. J. W. Willis Bund. Worcester Historical Society: James Parker and Co., 1902.

Giffard, Walter, Archbishop of York. *Register: 1266–1279.* Surtees Society 109. London, 1904.

Giraldus Cambrensis. *Gemma Ecclesiastica.* Vol. II of *Opera.* Ed. J. S. Brewer. Rolls Series 21. London: Longman, Green, Longman, and Roberts, 1862.

Gower, John. *The Complete Works.* Ed. G. C. Macaulay. 4 vols. Oxford: Clarendon Press, 1902.

———. *The Major Latin Works.* Ed. Eric W. Stockton. Seattle: University of Washington Press, 1962.

Grandisson, John, Bishop of Exeter. *Register: 1327–1369.* Ed. Rev. F. C. Hingeston-Randolph. 3 vols. London: G. Bell and Sons, 1894–1899.

Greenfield, William, Archbishop of York. *Register: 1306–1315.* 5 vols. Surtees Society 145, 149, 151–153. London, 1931.

Gualteruzzi, ed. *Le Cento novelle antiche (Il novellino).* Milano: Paolo Antonio Tosi, 1825.

Guillaume de Lorris et Jean de Meung. *Le Roman de la Rose.* Ed. Silvio F. Baridon. 2 vols. Milano: Istituto Editoriale Cisalpino, 1954.

————. *The Romance of the Rose*. Ed. Charles W. Dunn and trans. Harry W. Robbins. New York: E. P. Dutton and Co., Inc., 1962.

Hagen, Hermann, ed. *Carmina Medii Aevi*. Berne: Apvd Georgivm Frobenivm and soc., 1877.

Halliwell, James, ed. *Selection from the Minor Poems* of John Lydgate. Percy Society 2. London, 1840.

Hart, William Henry, ed. *Cartularium Monasterii de Rameseia*. 3 vols. Rolls Series 79. London: Longman and Co., 1886.

Hassall, W. O., ed. *Cartulary of St. Mary Clerkenwell*. Camden Third Series 71. London: Royal Historical Society, 1949.

Haupt, Morris, ed. *Französische Volksleider*. Leipzig: Verlag von S. Hirzel, 1877.

(The) Holy Bible: Revised Standard Version Containing the Old and New Testaments. New York: Thomas Nelson and Sons, 1953.

Hugo, Thomas, ed. *The Medieval Nunneries of the County of Somerset and Diocese of Bath and Wells; Together with the Annals of their Impropriated Benefices, from the Earliest Times to the Death of Queen Mary*. London: J. R. Smith, 1867.

Idung. *De Quatuor Quaestionibus; Monacho-Clericorum et Sanctimonialium Virginum Statum Spectantibus*. In Vol. II of *Thesaurus Anecdotorum Novissimus*. Ed. B. Pez (Bernardo Pezio). Sumptibus Philippi, Martini, et Joannis Veith Fratrum, Anno 1721.

Jean de Condé. *La Messe des Oisiaus et li plais des chanonesses et des grises nonains*. Ed. Jacques Ribard. Genève: Librairie Droz, 1970.

Jerome, St. *Lettres*. Trans. Jerome Labourt. Paris: Societé d'édition "Les Belles Lettres," 1949, Vol. I.

Jessopp, Rev. Augustus, ed. *Visitations of the Diocese of Norwich: 1492–1532*. Camden Society NS 43. Westminster, 1888.

Knowles, David, C. N. L. Brooke, and Vera C. M. London, ed. *The Heads of Religious Houses: England and Wales (940–1216)*. Cambridge: University Press, 1972.

Kock, Ernst A., ed. *Three Middle English Versions of the Rule of St. Benedict and Two Contemporary Rituals for the Ordination of Nuns*. Early English Text Society 120. London, 1902.

LaFontaine, Jean de. *Contes*. Ed. Louis Perceau. 2 vols. Paris: Le Livre du Bibliophile, Georges Briffaut, éditeur, 1929.

Lambel, Hans, ed. *Erzählungen und Schwanke*. Leipzig: F. A. Brockhaus, 1872.

Langland, William. *Piers the Ploughman*. Trans. J. F. Goodridge. Penguin Books, Inc., 1974.

————. *The Vision of William Concerning Piers the Plowman*. Ed. J. A. W. Bennett. Oxford: University Press, 1972.

Lee, A. C., ed. *The Decameron: Its Sources and Analogues*. London: David Nutt, 1909.

Legrand, Emile, ed. "Chansons populaires recueillies en octobre 1876 a Fontenay-le-Marmion." *Romania* 10 (1881): 365–96.

Le Grand D'Aussy, M., ed., and Gregory Lewis Way, trans. *Fabliaux or Tales Abridged from French Manuscripts of the Twelfth and Thirteenth Centuries.* London: W. Bulmer and Co. Shakespeare-Press, 1796, Vol. I.

León, Rafael, ed. "¿Quién dio a la blanca rosa hábito, velo prieto?" *Papeles de Son Armadans* 21 (1961): 163–76.

Lerma, Pedro de. *Las doze Coplas Moniales. In Cancionero de obras de burla provocantes a risa.* Ed. L. Usoz. Madrid: Luis Sánchez, 1841.

Le Romeyn, John, Archbishop of York. *Register: 1286–1296.* 2 vols. Surtees Society 123, 128. London, 1910.

Le Roux de Lincy, Antoine J. V., ed. *Le Livre des proverbes français.* Paris, 1859; rpt. Genève: Slatkine Reprints, 1968.

li Muisis, Gilles, *Poésies.* Ed. Kervyn de Letterhove. Louvain: Imprimerie de J. Lefever, 1882. Vol. 1.

Lindsay, Jack, ed. *Medieval Latin Poets.* London: Elkin Mathews and Marrot, Ltd., 1934.

Liveing, Henry G. D., ed. *Records of Romsey Abbey.* Winchester: Warren and Sons, Ltd., 1912.

London, Vera C. M., ed. *Cartulary of Canonsleigh Abbey.* Devon and Cornwall Record Society NS 8. Torquay, 1965.

Lo Nigro, Sebastiano. *Novellino e conti del duecento.* Torino: Tipografia Torinese, 1963.

López de Ayala, Pero. *Rimado de Palacio.* Vol. I of *Poesías.* Ed. Michel García. Madrid: Editorial Gredos, S.A., 1978.

McCann, Abbot Justin, ed. and trans. *The Rule of St. Benedict.* London: Macmillan and Co., 1952.

Martin, Charles T., ed. *Registrum Epistolarum Fratris Johannis Peckham, Archiepiscopi Cantuarensis: 1279–1292.* 3 vols. Rolls Series 77. London: Longman and Co., 1882.

Matheolus. *Les Lamentations.* Ed. Anton G. Van Hamel. 2 vols. Paris: Bibliothéque de l'Ecole des Hautes Études, 1892.

Mendoza, Fray Iñigo de. *Coplas de Vita Christi. In his Cancionero.* Ed. Julio Rodríguez-Puértolas. Madrid: Editorial Gredos, S.A., 1968.

Meyer, Kuno, trans. *Selections from Ancient Irish Poetry.* London: Constable and Co., 1911.

Migne, J. P., ed. *Patrologiae Latinae.* 221 vols. Paris: Bibliothecae Cleri Universae, 1863.

Moncrieff, C. K. Scott, trans. *The Letters of Abelard and Heloise.* New York: Alfred A. Knopf, 1926.

Montaiglon, Anatole de, ed. *Recueil de poésies françoises des xve et xvie siècles.* 13 vols. Paris: Chez P. Jannet, Libraire, 1855–1858.

———— and Gaston Raynaud, eds. *Recueil général et complet des fabliaux des xiiie*

et xive siècles. 6 vols. Paris, 1890; rpt. Burt Franklin Research and Source Works Series 47. New York, 1964.

Montesino, Fray Ambrosio de. *Cancionero.* In *Romancero y Cancionero Sagrados.* Ed. Justo de Sancha. Biblioteca de Autores Españoles, 35. Madrid: Imprenta de los sucesores de Hernando, 1915.

Morris, Rev. Richard, ed. *Old English Miscellany.* Early English Text Society 49. London, 1872.

Newark, Henry, Archbishop of York. *Register: 1296–1299.* Surtees Society 128. London, 1910.

Nicolas, Nicholas H., ed. *Testamenta Vetusta: Being illustrations from wills of manners, customs, etc. as well as of the descents and possessions of many distinguished families from the reign of Henry II to the accession of Queen Elizabeth.* 2 vols. London: Nichols and Son, 1826.

Nigra, Constantino, ed. *Canti popolari del Piemonte.* Torino: Ermano Loescher, 1888.

Oulmont, Charles, ed. *La Poésie française du Moyen Age (xie–xve siècles).* Paris: Société du Mercure de France, 1913.

Ovidi, Publius Nasonis. *De Arte Amatoria.* Ed. Paul Brandt. Hildesheim: Georg Olms Verlagsbuchhandlung, 1963. Vol. III.

——. *The Art of Love.* Trans. Rolfe Humphries. Bloomington, Indiana: Indiana University Press, 1957.

Pelagius, Alvarus. *De Planctu Ecclesiae.* Ulm: Johann Zainer, 1474. Microfilm copy made in 1963 of the original in the Vatican Library.

Pelay Briz, Francesch and Candi Candi, ed. *Cansons de la terra: Cants populars catalans.* 5 vols. Barcelona: Alvar Verdaguer, 1877.

Percy, Thomas, ed. *Reliques of Ancient English Poetry.* London: Swan Sonnenschein and Co., Ltd., 1910.

Perry, George G., ed. *Religious Pieces in Prose and Verse.* Early English Text Society 26. London, 1914.

Poueigh, Jean, ed. *Chansons populaires des Pyrénées françaises.* Paris: Honoré Champion, 1926. Vol. I.

Puymaigre, Cte. de, ed. *Chants populaires recueillis dans le pays Messin.* Metz: Rousseau-Pallez, 1865.

Quiller-Couch, Arthur, ed. *The Oxford Book of Ballads.* Oxford: Clarendon Press, 1920.

Raby, F. J. E., ed. *The Oxford Book of Medieval Latin Verse.* Oxford: Clarendon Press, 1959.

Rickert, Edith, ed. and F. J. Furnivall, trans. *The Babee's Book: Medieval Manners for the Young.* New York: Cooper Square Publishers, Inc., 1966.

Rigaud, Eude, Archevêque de Rouen. *Regestrum Visitationum: 1248–1269.* Ed. Thomas Bonin. 2 vols. Rouen: Auguste le Brument, Libraire-Éditeur, 1852.

Robbins, Rossell H., trans. *The Hundred Tales: Les Cent Nouvelles nouvelles.* New York: Bonanza Books, 1960.

Roig, Jacme. *Spill o Libre de les dones.* Ed. Roque Chabás. Madrid: Librería de M. Murillo, 1905.

Rolland, E., ed. *Recueil de chansons populaires.* 6 vols. Paris: Maisonneuve et Cie., 1883.

Ross, Woodburn O. *Middle English Sermons.* Early English Text Society 209. London, 1940.

Round, J. Horace, ed. *Calendar of Documents Preserved in France Illustrative of the History of Great Britain and Ireland.* London, 1899; rpt. Nendeln, Liechtenstein: Kraus Reprint, Ltd., 1967. Vol. I.

Rubiò, J., ed. "Del Manuscript 129 de Ripoll del segle xiv." *Revista de Bibliografía Catalana* 5 (1905): 376.

Ruiz, Juan, Arcipreste de Hita. *Libro de Buen Amor.* Ed. Giorgio Chiarini. Documenti di Filologia, 8. Milano-Napoli, 1964.

――――. *Libro de Buen Amor.* Ed. Joan Corominas. Madrid: Editorial Gredos, S.A., 1967.

――――. *The Book of Good Love.* Trans. Elisha Kent Kane. Chapel Hill: University of North Carolina Press, 1968.

――――. *The Book of Good Love.* Trans. Rigo Mignani and Mario A. di Cesare. Albany, New York: State University of New York Press, 1970.

Rutebeuf. *La Vie du monde.* In *Oeuvres complètes.* Ed. Edmond Faral and Julia Bastin. Paris: Editions A. et J. Picard et Cie., 1959, Vol. I.

Salu, M. B., trans. *The Ancrene Riwle (The Corpus Manuscript: Ancrene Wisse).* London: Burns and Oates, 1955.

Serra, R., Aramón I., ed. "Dues cançons populars italianes en un manuscrit català quatrecentista." *Estudis Románics* 1 (1948): 159–88.

Sharpe, Reginald R., ed. *Calendar of Wills Proved and Enrolled in the Court of Husting, London (A.D. 1258–1688).* 2 vols. London: John C. Francis, 1889.

Smith, T.L., ed. *English Gilds.* Early English Text Society 40. London, 1870.

Smith, Victor, ed. "Vieilles Chansons recueillies en Velay et en Forez." *Romania* (1878): 52–84.

Smith, W. Carew, ed. *English Proverbs and Proverbial Phrases Collected from the Most Authentic Sources.* London: John Russell Smith, 1869.

Stevenson, Burton E., ed. *Home Book of Verse.* New York: Holt, Rinehart and Co., 1950. Vol.I.

Sussex Archaeological Collection 9 (Sussex Archaeological Society, 1848–1873).

Symonds, John Addington, ed. *Wine, Women and Song: Medieval Latin Students' Songs Now First Translated into English Verse.* London: Chatto and Windus, 1931.

Tanner, Thomas. *Notitia Monastica or An Account of all the Abbies, Priories, and Houses of Friers formerly in England and Wales and also of all the Colleges and Hospitals founded before* A.D. *MDXL*. Cambridge: University Press, 1787.

Testamenta Eboracensia or Wills Registered at York from the year 1300 Downwards. 7 vols. Surtees Society 4, 30, 45, 53, 79, 106. London, 1836–1902.

Thomas, St. Aquinas. *The Summa Theologica.* Trans. Fathers of the English Dominican Province. London: R. and T. Washbourne, Ltd., 1917, Vol. II.

Thompson, A. Hamilton, ed. *Visitations of Religious Houses in the Diocese of Lincoln.* 3 vols. Lincoln Record Society and Canterbury and York Society 13–15. London: Horncastle and Lincoln, 1914–1929.

Tolkien, J.R.R., ed. *Ancrene Wisse:* Edited from MS. Corpus Christi College Cambridge 402. *Early English Text Society* 249. London, 1962.

Uhland, Ludwig, ed. *Alte-hoch und Niederdeutsche Volkslieder.* 2 vols. Stutgart and Tübingen: F. G. Gottascher, 1845.

van Bever, Ad. and Ed. Sansot-Orland, ed. *Oeuvres galantes des conteurs italiens.* Paris: Société du Mercure de France, 1908.

van den Boogaard, Nico H. J., ed. *Rondeaux et refrains du xiie siècle au debut du xive.* Paris: Klincksieck, 1969.

Vatasso, M., ed. "Planctus Monialis." In "Contributo alla storia della poesia ritmica latina medievale." *Studi Medievali* 1 (1904): 124.

Victoria History of the Counties of England. 140 vols. London: Archibald Constable and Co., Ltd., 1907.

Virgil. *The Eclogues, Bucolics or Pastorals.* Ed. and trans. Thomas Fletcher Royds. Oxford: Basil Blackwell, 1922.

Waitz, Georg, ed. "Das Liebesconcil." *Zeitschrift für Deutsches Altertum* 8 (1849): 160–67.

Warner, William. *Albion's England.* London: Printed by the Widow Orwin for I. B[rome], 1597. University Microfilms.

Warrington, John, ed. *The Paston Letters,* 2 vols. London: Everyman's Library, 1967.

Weckerlin, Jean Baptiste, ed. *L'Ancienne Chanson populaire en France.* Paris: Garnier Frères, 1887.

————, ed. *Chansons populaires des provinces de France.* Paris: Garnier Frères, Libraires-Éditeurs, n.d.

Wickwane, William, Archbishop of York. *Register: 1279–1285.* Surtees Society 114. London, 1904.

Wilhelm, James J., ed. and trans. *Medieval Song: An Anthology of Hymns and Lyrics.* New York: E. P. Dutton and Co., Inc., 1971.

William of Malmesbury. *De Gestis Regum Anglorum.* Ed. William Stubbs. 2 vols. Rolls Series 90. London: Eyre and Spottiswoode, 1889.

Wills and Inventories Illustrative of the History, Manners, Language, Statistics, etc. of the Northern Counties of England from the Eleventh Century Downwards. Surtees Society [2], 38, 112, 142. London, 1835.

Winny, James, ed. *The Prioress's Prologue and Tale*. London: Cambridge University Press, 1975.

Wireker, Nigellus. *Speculum Stultorum*. Ed. John H. Mozley and Robert R. Raymo. Berkeley and Los Angeles: University of California Press, 1960.

———. *The Book of Burnel the Ass*. Trans. John H. Mozley. Notre Dame, Indiana: University of Notre Dame Press, 1963.

———. *The Book of Burnel the Ass*. Trans. Graydon W. Regenos. Austin: University of Texas Press, 1959.

Wright, Thomas, ed. *Anglo-Latin Satirical Poets and Epigrammatists of the Twelfth Century*. 2 vols. In *Chronicles and Memorials of Great Britain and Ireland*. Rolls Series 59. London: Longman and Co., 1872.

———, ed. *The Political Songs of England from the Reign of John to that of Edward II*. Edinburgh: privately printed, 1884. Vol. II.

———, ed. *Reliquiae Antiquae*. 2 vols. London, 1841 and 1843; rpt. New York: A.M.S. Press, Inc., 1966.

Zeitschrift für Romanische Philologie 5 (1881): 545, no. 28.

Zeydell, Edwin H., trans. *Vagabond Verse: Secular Latin Poems of the Middle Ages*. Detroit: Wayne State University Press, 1966.

Secondary Sources

Allen, Philip Schuyler, "Medieval Latin Lyrics." *Modern Philology* 5 (1908): 1–54.

Artz Frederick B. *The Mind of the Middle Ages (A.D. 200–1500): An Historical Survey*. New York: Alfred A. Knopf, 1953.

Auerbach, Erich. *Literary Language and Its Public in Late Latin Antiquity and in the Middle Ages*. Trans. Ralph Manheim. Bollingen series, 74. New York: Pantheon Books, 1965.

Aungier, George James. *The History and Antiquities of Syon Monastery, the Parish of Isleworth and the Chapelry of Hounslow*. London: J. B. Nichols and Son, 1840.

Baker, Derek, ed. *Medieval Women*. Oxford, 1978; rpt. Oxford: Basil Blackwell, 1981.

Baum, Paull F. *Chaucer: A Critical Appreciation*. Durham, North Carolina: Duke University Press, 1958.

———. "Chaucer's Puns." *Publications of the Modern Language Association* 71 (1956): 225–46.

Beltrán, Luis. *Razones de buen amor: oposiciones y convergencias en el libro del Arcipreste de Hita*. Fundación Juan March. Valencia: Editorial Castalia, 1977.

Bennett, H. S. "Medieval Literature and the Modern Reader." *Essays and Studies* 31 (1945): 7–18.

Bloom, Edward A., and Lillian D. *Satire's Persuasive Voice*. London: Cornell University Press, 1979.

Bowden, Muriel. *A Commentary on the "General Prologue" to the "Canterbury Tales."* 2nd ed. London, 1948; rpt. New York: The Macmillan Co., 1969.

Boyd, Beverly. "Chaucer's Prioress: Her Green Gauds." *Modern Language Quarterly* 11 (1950): 404–16.

Brennan, Dom Maynard J. "Speaking of the Prioress." *Modern Language Quarterly* 10 (1949): 451–57.

Brewer, D. S. "The Ideal of Feminine Beauty in Medieval Literature." *Modern Language Review* 50 (1955): 257–69.

Browne, Matthew. *Chaucer's England*, 2 vols. London: Hurst and Blackett Publishers, 1869.

Bullough, Vern L., and James Brundage, ed. *Sexual Practices and the Medieval Church*. Buffalo, New York: Prometheus Books, 1982.

Burke, James. "Love's Double Cross: Language Play as Structure in the *Libro de Buen Amor.*" *University of Toronto Quarterly* 43 (Spring 1974): 231–62.

Capecchi, Fernando. "Il *Libro de Buen Amor* di Juan Ruiz, Arcipreste de Hita." *Cultura Neolatina* 13 (1954): 135–64.

———. "Il *Libro de Buen Amor* di Juan Ruiz, Arcipreste de Hita." *Cultura Neolatina* 14 (1954): 59–90.

Castro, Américo. *España en su historia: cristianos, moros y judíos*. Buenos Aires: Editorial Losada, 1948.

———. *La realidad histórica de España*. Mexico, D.F: Editorial Porrúa, S.A., 1954.

———. *The Structure of Spanish History*. Trans. E. King. Princeton: University Press, 1954.

Cawley, A. C. "A Note on Chaucer's Prioress and Criseyde." *Modern Language Review* 43 (1948): 74–77.

Cita-Malard, Suzanne. *Religious Orders of Women*. Trans. George Robinson. New York: Hawthorn Books-Publishers, 1964.

Clark, Thomas B. "Forehead of Chaucer's Prioress." *Philological Quarterly* 9 (1930): 312–14.

Coghill, N. *The Poet Chaucer*. London: Oxford University Press, 1949.

Constable, Giles, ed. *Medieval Monasticism: A Select Bibliography*. Toronto: University of Toronto Press, 1976.

Cook, G. H. *English Monasteries in the Middle Ages*. London: Phoenix House, Ltd., 1961.

Corsa, Helen S. *Chaucer: Poet of Mirth and Morality*. Notre Dame, Indiana: University of Notre Dame Press, 1964.

Coulton, G. G. "Catholic Truth and Historical Truth." *The Contemporary Review* 88 (July–December, 1905): 808–17.

————. *Chaucer and his England*. London, 1908; rpt. London: Methuen and Co., Ltd., 1963.

————. *Five Centuries of Religion*. 5 vols. Cambridge: University Press, 1950.

————. *Life in the Middle Ages*. 2 vols. 3rd ed. Cambridge: University Press, 1967.

————. *Medieval Panorama: The English Scene from Conquest to Reformation*. Cambridge, 1938; rpt. Cambridge: University Press, 1939.

————. "The Truth about the Monasteries." In his *Ten Medieval Studies*. Cambridge: University Press, 1930.

Crawford, William R., ed. *Bibliography of Chaucer* (1954–63). Seattle: University of Washington Press, 1967.

Crook, Margaret B. *Women in Religion*. Boston: Beacon Press, 1964.

Curry, Walter Clyde. *The Middle English Ideal of Personal Beauty; as Found in the Metrical Romances, Chronicles, and Legends of the Twelfth, Thirteenth, Fourteenth, and Fifteenth Centuries*. Baltimore, 1916; rpt. New York: A.M.S. Press, Inc., 1972.

Curtius, Ernst Robert. *European Literature and the Latin Middle Ages*. Trans. Willard R. Trask. New York, 1953; rpt. New York: Harper and Row Publishers, 1963.

Cutts, Edward. L. *Scenes and Characters of the Middle Ages*. London: Simpkin Marshall, Ltd., 1930.

Davies, R. T. "Chaucer's Madame Eglantine." *Modern Language Notes* 67 (1952): 400–402.

Dawson, Christopher. *Medieval Religion and Other Essays*. London: Sheed and Ward, 1934.

Deanesley, Margaret. *A History of the Medieval Church (590–1500)*. 8th ed. London, 1925; rpt. London: Methuen and Co., Ltd., 1957.

Delasanta, Rodney K. "The Horsemen of the *Canterbury Tales*." *Chaucer Review* 3 (1968): 29–36.

de los Ríos, José Amador. *Historia crítica de la literatura española*. Madrid: José Fernández Cancela, 1863.

Deyermond, A. D. *A Literary History of Spain: The Middle Ages*. London and New York: E. Been, Ltd.-Barnes and Noble, Inc., 1971.

Dickinson, T. C. *Monastic Life in Medieval England*. London: Adam and Charles Black, 1961.

Donaldson, E. Talbot. *Chaucer's Poetry*. 2nd ed. New York: Ronald Press Co., 1975.

————. *Speaking of Chaucer*. New York: W. W. Norton and Co., Inc., 1970.

Drennan, C. M. "Chaucer's Prioress, *Canterbury Tales, Prologue*, 136: 'Ful semely after hir mete she raughte'." *Notes and Queries* 11th ser. 9 (1914): 365.

Dronke, Peter. *Medieval Latin and the Rise of the European Love Lyric*. 2 vols. Oxford: Clarendon Press, 1966.

———. *The Medieval Lyric*. Cambridge: University Press, 1977.

Dunn, Peter. "Verdad y verdades en el *Libro de Buen Amor*." In *Actas del Tercer Congreso Internacional de Hispanistas* 26–31 August, 1968. Mexico, D.F.

Dutton, Brian. "'Con Dios en buen amor'": A Semantic analysis of the title of the *Libro de buen amor*." *Bulletin of Hispanic Studies* 43 (1966): 161–76.

Eckenstein, Lina. *Woman under Monasticism*. Cambridge: University Press, 1896.

Elliott, Robert C. *The Power of Satire: Magic, Ritual, Art*. Princeton, New Jersey: Princeton University Press, 1960.

Engelhardt, George J. "The Ecclesiastical Pilgrims of the *Canterbury Tales:* A Study in Ethology." *Medieval Studies* 37 (1975): 287–315.

Evans, Joan, and Mary S. Serjeantson, ed. *English Medieval Lapidaries*. Early English Text Society 190. London, 1933.

———. *A History of Jewellery (1100–1870)*. Great Britain, 1953; rpt. Boston: Boston Book and Art, Publisher, 1970.

———. *Magical Jewels of the Middle Ages and the Renaissance particularly in England*. Oxford: Clarendon Press, 1922.

Faral, Edmond. *Les Jongleurs en France au Moyen Age*. 2nd ed. Paris: Champion, 1964.

———. *Recherches sur les sources latines des contes et romans courtois du Moyen Age*. Paris: Librairie Ancienne Honoré Champion, 1913.

Feinberg, Leonard. *Introduction to Satire*. Ames, Iowa: Iowa State University Press, 1967.

Freyre, Jaime. "El *Libro de Buen Amor:* Introducción a un estudio." *Revista de Letras y Ciencias Sociales* 6 (1907): 197–213.

Friedman, John Block. "The Prioress's Beads of 'Smal Coral'." *Medium Aevum* 39 (1970): 301–304.

Frye, Northrop. *Anatomy of Criticism: Four Essays*. Princeton, New Jersey: Princeton University Press, 1957.

Fyler, John M. *Chaucer and Ovid*. New Haven, Connecticut: Yale University Press, 1979.

Gariano, Carmelo. *El mundo poético de Juan Ruiz*. Madrid: Editorial Gredos, S.A., 1968.

Gaylord, Alan T. "The Unconquered Tale of the Prioress." *Papers of the Michigan Academy of Science, Arts, and Letters* 47 (1962): 613–36.

Gerould, Gordon Hall. *Chaucerian Essays*. Princeton, New Jersey: Princeton University Press, 1952.

Gies, Frances, and Joseph. *Women in the Middle Ages*. New York: Thomas Y. Crowell Co., 1978.

Green, Otis. "Medieval Laughter: *The Book of Good Love*." In his *The Castilian Mind in Literature from El Cid to Calderón*. Vol. I of *Spain and the Western Tradition*. Madison: University of Wisconsin Press, 1963.

———. "On Juan Ruiz's Parody of the Canonical Hours." *Hispanic Review* 26 (1958): 12–34.

————. *The Literary Mind of Medieval and Renaissance Spain.* Lexington: University Press of Kentucky, 1970.

Griffith, Dudley D., ed. *Bibliography of Chaucer: 1908–1924.* University of Washington Publications: Language and Literature 4 (1926): 3–141.

Guzmán, Jorge. *Una constante didáctico-moral del "Libro de Buen Amor."* Iowa University Studies in Spanish Language and Literature 14. Mexico, D.F., 1963.

Gybbon-Monypenny, G. B. "Autobiography in the *Libro de Buen Amor* in the Light of Some Literary Comparisons." *Bulletin of Hispanic Studies* 34 (1957): 63–78.

————, ed. *"Libro de Buen Amor" Studies.* London: Támesis Books, Ltd., 1970.

Hamilton, Marie Padgett. "The Convent of Chaucer's Prioress and her Priests." In *Philologica: The Malone Anniversary Studies.* Ed. Thomas A. Kirby and Henry Bosley Woolf. Baltimore: The Johns Hopkins Press, 1949.

Hannay, James. *Satire and Satirists: Six Lectures.* London: David Brogue, 1854.

Harper, Gordon H. "Chaucer's Big Prioress." *Philological Quarterly* 12 (1933): 308–10.

Hentsch, Alice Adèle, ed. *De la Littérature didactique du Moyen Age s'addressant specialement aux femmes.* Paris, 1903; rpt. Genève: Slatkine Reprints, 1975.

Heer, Friedrich. *The Medieval World: Europe 1100–1350.* Trans. J. Sondheimer. London: Weidenfeld and Nicholson, 1961.

Herlihy, David. "Women in Medieval Society." *The Smith History Lecture.* Houston: University of St. Thomas, 1971.

Hodapp, Marion. "El Arcipreste y Chaucer." In *Actas del I Congreso Internacional sobre el Arcipreste de Hita: el libro, el autor, la tierra, la época.* Barcelona: S.E.R.E.S.A., 1973.

Hodgson, Phyllis, ed. *"General Prologue" to the "Canterbury Tales."* London: Athlone Press, 1969.

Hoffman, Arthur W. "Chaucer's Prologue to Pilgrimage: The Two Voices." In *Chaucer: Modern Essays in Criticism.* Ed. Edward Wagenknecht. New York, 1959; rpt. Oxford: Oxford University Press, 1974.

Hostia, Sister Mary. "The Prioress and her Companion." *College English* 14 (1952–53): 351–52.

Howard, Donald. *Writers and Pilgrims: Medieval Pilgrimage Narratives and their Posterity.* Berkeley and Los Angeles: University of California Press, 1980.

Huizinga, Johan. *The Waning of the Middle Ages.* New York: Doubleday, 1954.

Huppé, Bernard F. *A Reading of the Canterbury Tales.* New York: State University, 1967.

Jeanroy, Alfred. *Les Origins de la poésie lyrique en France au Moyen Age*. Paris: Librarie Ancienne Honoré Champion, Edouard Champion, 1925.

Jessopp, Rev. Augustus. "Ups and Downs of a Norfolk Nunnery." In his *Frivola, Simon Ryan and Other Papers*. London: T. Fisher Unwin, 1907.

Jones, H. S. V. "The Plan of the Canterbury Tales." *Modern Philology* 13 (1915): 45–58.

Jusserand, J. J. *English Wayfaring Life in the Middle Ages (Fourteenth Century)*. Trans. Lucy T. Smith. London, 1890; rpt. Williamston, Massachusetts: Corner House Publishers, 1974.

Kane, Elisha K. "The Electuaries of the Archpriest of Hita." *Modern Philology* 30 (1933): 263–66.

———. "The Personal Appearance of Juan Ruiz." *Modern Language Notes* 45 (1930): 103–109.

Kemp-Welch, Alice. *Of Six Medieval Women: To which is added a note on Medieval Gardens*. Massachusetts, 1913; rpt. Williamston, Massachusetts: Corner House Publishers, 1972, 2nd impression 1979.

Kernan, Alvin B. *The Plot of Satire*. New Haven and London: Yale University Press, 1965.

Kiernan, Kevin S. "The Art of the Descending Catalogue, and a Fresh Look at Alisoun." *Chaucer Review* 10 (1975): 1–16.

Kinney, Muriel. " 'Vair' and Related Words." *Romanic Review* 10 (1919): 322–63.

Kittredge, George Lyman. *Chaucer and his Poetry*. Cambridge: Harvard University Press, 1915.

Knight, S. T. " 'Almost a Spanne Brood'." *Neophilologus* 52 (1968): 178–80.

Knoepflmacher, U. C. "Irony Through Scriptural Allusion: A Note on Chaucer's 'Prioresse'." *Chaucer Review* 4 (1970): 180–183.

Knowles, David, and R. Neville Hadcock. *Medieval Religious Houses in England and Wales*. London: Longmans, Green and Co., 1953.

———, and J. K. S. St. Joseph. *Monastic Sites from the Air*. Cambridge: University Press, 1952.

———, and Dimitri Obolensky. *The Middle Ages*. Vol. II of their *The Christian Centuries*. New York: McGraw-Hill Book Co., 1968.

———. *The Monastic Order in England: 940–1216*. Cambridge: University Press, 1963.

———. *The Religious Orders in England*. 2 vols. Cambridge: University Press, 1955.

Knox, E. V. "The Mechanism of Satire." *The Leslie Stephen Lecture*. Cambridge: University Press, 1951.

Knox, Norman. "The Satiric Pattern of *The Canterbury Tales*." In his *Six Satirists*. Carnegie Series in English 9. Pittsburgh: Carnegie Institute of Technology, 1965.

Krapp, George P. *The Legend of Saint Patrick's Purgatory: Its Later Literary*

History. Dissertation, Johns Hopkins, 1900. Baltimore: John Murphy, 1900.

Kuhl, Ernest P. "Notes on Chaucer's Prioress." *Philological Quarterly* 1–2 (1922–23): 302–309.

Kurath, Hans, and Sherman M. Kuhn, ed. *Middle English Dictionary.* Ann Arbor, Michigan: University of Michigan Press, 1954–1975.

Landrum, Graham. "The Convent Crowd and the Feminist Nun." *Tennessee Philological Bulletin* 13 (1976): 5–12.

Langdon-Davies, John. *A Short History of Women.* New York: Literary Guild of America, 1927.

Langlois, Charles-Victor. *La Vie en France au Moyen Age d'après quelques moralistes du temps.* Paris: Librairie Hachette et Cie., 1911.

Langlois, Ernest. *Gui de Mori et le "Roman de la Rose."* Bibliothèque de l'Ecole des Chartes, 68. Paris: Librairie Alphonse Picard et fils, 1907.

———. *Origins et sources du "Roman de le Rose."* Paris: Ernest Thorin, éditeur, 1890.

Lea, Henry C. *History of Sacerdotal Celibacy in the Christian Church.* 2 vols. London: Williams and Norgate, 1907.

Lecoy, Félix. *Recherches sur le "Libro de Buen Amor" de Juan Ruiz, Archiprêtre de Hita.* Paris: Librairie E. Droz, 1938.

Le Gentil, Pierre. *La Poésie lyrique espagnole et portugaise à la fin du Moyen Age.* 2 vols. Rennes: Plihon, éditeur, 1953.

Le Goff, Jacques. *La Civilisation de l'Occident médiéval.* Paris: Arthaud, 1965.

Lenient, C. *La Satire en France au Moyen Age.* Paris: Librairie Hachette et Cie., 1893.

Lida de Malkiel, María Rosa. "Nuevas notas para la interpretación del *Libro de Buen Amor.*" In her *Estudios de literatura española y comparada.* 2nd ed. Buenos Aires: Editorial Universitaria, 1969.

Lewis, C. S. *The Allegory of Love.* London: University Press, 1959.

Logan, Donald. *Excommunication and the Secular Arm in Medieval England: A Study in Legal Procedure from the Thirteenth to the Sixteenth Century.* Toronto: Pontifical Institute of Medieval Studies, 1968.

Lowes, John Livingston. *Convention and Revolt in Poetry.* Boston and New York: Houghton Mifflin Co., 1924.

———. "Simple and Coy: A Note on Fourteenth-Century Poetic Diction." *Anglia* 33 (1910): 440–51.

———. "The Prioress's Oath." *The Romanic Review* 5 (1914): 368–85.

Lucki, Emil. "Dante, J. Ruiz, Petrarch and Chaucer." In his *History of the Renaissance.* Salt Lake City, Utah: University of Utah, 1965. Vol. IV.

Lumiansky, R. M. *Of Sondry Folk: The Dramatic Principle in the "Canterbury Tales."* Austin: University of Texas Press, 1955.

Lynch, James J. "The Prioress's Greatest Oath Once More." *Modern Language Notes* 72 (1957): 242–49.

McCarthy, Sister Brigetta. "Chaucer's Pilgrim-Prioress." *The Benedictine Review* 6 (1951): 38–40.

Mackaye, Percy. *The Canterbury Pilgrims.* New York: Macmillan and Co., Ltd., 1908.

McNamara, Jo Ann, and Suzanne F. Wemple. "Sanctity and Power: The Dual Pursuit of Medieval Women." In *Becoming Visible: Women in European History.* Ed. Renate Bridenthal and Claudia Koonz. Boston: Houghton Mifflin Co., 1977.

Madden, William A. "Chaucer's Retraction and the Medieval Canons of Seemliness." *Medieval Studies* 17 (1955): 173–84.

Madeleva, Sister Mary. *A Lost Language and Other Essays on Chaucer.* New York: Sheed and Ward, 1951.

Malone, Kemp. *Chapters on Chaucer.* Baltimore, 1951; 3rd rpt. Baltimore: The Johns Hopkins Press, 1964.

Manley, Francis. "Chaucer's Rosary and Donne's Bracelet: Ambiguous Coral." *Modern Language Notes* 74 (1959): 385–88.

Manly, John Matthews. *Some New Light on Chaucer.* New York: Henry Holt and Co., 1926.

Mann, Jill. *Chaucer and Medieval Estates Satire: The Literature of the Social Classes and the "General Prologue" to the "Canterbury Tales."* Cambridge: University Press, 1973.

Márquez Villanueva, Francisco. "El buen amor." *Revista de Occidente* 2nd ser. 9 (1965): 269–91.

Menéndez Pidal, Ramón. *Poesía juglaresca y orígenes de las literaturas románicas.* Madrid: Instituto de Estudios Políticos, 1957.

Montalembert, Count of. *The Monks of the West from St. Benedict to St. Bernard.* New York: P. J. Kennedy and Sons, 1905, Vol. II.

Moorman, John R. H. *Church Life in England in the Thirteenth Century.* Cambridge: University Press, 1945.

Morewedge, Rosemarie T., ed. *The Role of Woman in the Middle Ages.* Albany: State University of New York Press, 1975.

Mundy, John H. *Europe in the High Middle Ages: 1150–1309.* London: Longman Group, Ltd., 1973.

Oliver Asín, Jaime. "Historia y prehistoria del castellano 'alaroza'." *Boletín de la Real Academia Española* 30 (1950): 389–421.

Ornstein, Jacob. "Misogyny and Pro-feminism in Early Castilian Literature." *Modern Language Quarterly* 3 (1942): 221–34.

Oulmont, Charles. *Les Débats du clerc et du chevalier dans la littérature poétique du moyen age.* Paris: Honoré Champion, 1911.

Owst, G. R. *Literature and Pulpit in Medieval England: A Neglected Chapter in the History of English Letters and of the English People.* 2nd ed. New York: Barnes and Noble, Inc., 1961.

Paiewonsky Conde, Edgar. "Polarización erótica medieval y estructura del *Libro de Buen Amor.*" *Bulletin Hispanique* 74 (1972): 331–52.

Painter, Sidney. *Medieval Society.* Ithaca, New York: Cornell University Press, 1960.

Pantin, W. A. *The English Church in the Fourteenth Century.* Cambridge: University Press, 1955.

Patch, Howard R. "Characters in Medieval Literature." *Modern Language Notes* 40 (1925): 1–4.

――――. *On Rereading Chaucer.* Cambridge, Massachusetts: Harvard University Press, 1939.

Payne, F. Anne. *Chaucer and Menippean Satire.* Madison, Wisconsin: University of Wisconsin Press, 1981.

Peers, Edgar A. *Spain, the Church and the Orders.* London: Eyre and Spottiswoode, 1939.

Pérez de Urbel, Justo. *El monasterio en la vida española de la Edad Media.* Barcelona: Editorial Albor, S.A., 1942.

Peter, John. *Complaint and Satire in Early English Literature.* Oxford: Clarendon Press, 1956.

Power, Eileen. *Medieval English Nunneries (c. 1275 to 1535).* Cambridge, 1922; rpt. New York: Biblo and Tannen, 1964.

――――. "Madame Eglentyne, Chaucer's Prioress in Real Life." In her *Medieval People: A Study of Communal Psychology.* Penguin Books Ltd., 1937.

――――. "The Position of Women." In *The Legacy of the Middle Ages.* Ed. C. G. Crump and E. F. Jacobs. Oxford: Clarendon Press, 1951.

Preston, Raymond. *Chaucer.* London and New York: Sheed and Ward, 1952.

――――. "Chaucer, his Prioress, the Jews and Professor Robinson." *Notes and Queries* 206 (1961):7–8.

Puyol y Alonso, Julio. *El Arcipreste de Hita: Estudio crítico.* Madrid: Sucesora de M. Minuesa de los Ríos, 1906.

Raby, F. J. E. *A History of Secular Latin Poetry in the Middle Ages.* 2 vols. Oxford: Clarendon Press, 1934.

Raed, José. *Arcipreste de Hita: Precursor del Renacimiento.* Buenos Aires: Editorial Devenir, 1975.

Rickert, Edith, comp. *Chaucer's World.* New York: Columbia University Press, 1948.

Ridley, Florence H. *The Prioress and the Critics.* Berkeley: University of California Press, 1965.

Robertson, D. W. *A Preface to Chaucer.* Princeton, 1962; 3rd. rpt. Princeton, New Jersey: Princeton University Press, 1973.

Robinson, A. Mary F. *The End of the Middle Ages: Essays and Questions in History.* London: T. Fisher Unwin, 1889.

Rohde, E. S. *The Old English Herbals.* New York: Longmans, Green and Co., 1922.

Rolt-Wheeler, Ethel. *Women of the Cell and Cloister.* London: Methuen and Co., Ltd., 1913.

Root, Robert Kilburn. *The Poetry of Chaucer.* Boston and New York: Houghton, Mifflin and Co., 1906.

Rowling, Marjorie. *Everyday Life in Medieval Times.* London and New York: Putnam's Sons—B. T. Batsford, Ltd., 1968.

Sánchez Albornoz, Claudio. *España, un enigma histórico.* 2nd ed. Buenos Aires: Editorial Sudamericana, 1962. Vol. I.

Savine, Alexander. "English Monasteries on the Eve of the Suppression." In *Oxford Studies in Social and Legal History* 1. Ed. Paul Vinogradoff. Oxford: Clarendon Press, 1909.

Schoeck, Richard J. "Chaucer's Prioress: Mercy and Tender Heart." In Vol. I of *Chaucer Criticism.* Ed. R. Schoeck and J. Taylor. Notre Dame, Indiana: University of Notre Dame Press, 1975.

Scholberg, Kenneth R. *Sátira e invectiva en la España medieval.* Madrid: Editorial Gredos, S.A., 1971.

Shannon, Edgar F. *Chaucer and the Roman Poets.* Harvard Studies in Comparative Literature 7. Cambridge, Massachusetts: Harvard University Press, 1929.

Shelly, Percy Van Dyke. *The Living Chaucer.* Philadelphia: University of Pennsylvania Press, 1940.

Sherbo, Arthur. "Chaucer's Nun's Priest Again." *Publications of the Modern Language Association* 64 (1949):236–46.

Simmons, Rita D. "The Prioress's Disobedience of the Benedictine Rule." *College Language Association Journal* 12 (1968):77–83.

Sivry, Luis de, and M. de Champagnac. *Dictionnaire, géographique, historique, descriptif, archéologique des pélerinages anciens et modernes.* 2 vols. Paris: Chez L'Éditeur, 1850–1859.

Sobejano, Gonzalo. "Escolios al 'buen amor' de Juan Ruiz." *Studia Philologica, Homenaje a Dámaso Alonso.* Madrid: Editorial Gredos, S.A, 1963. Vol. III.

Speirs, John. *Chaucer the Maker.* London, 1951; rpt. 2nd ed. Northampton: John Dickens and Co., Ltd., 1964.

Spitzer, Leo. "En torno del arte del Arcipreste de Hita." In his *Lingüística e historia literaria.* 2nd ed. Madrid: Editorial Gredos, S.A., 1961.

Steadman, John M. "'Hir gretteste ooth': The Prioress, St. Eligius, and St. Godebertha." *Neophilologus* 43 (1959):49–57.

———. "The Prioress's Brooch and St. Leonard." *English Studies* 44 (1963):350–53.

———. "The Prioress's Dogs and Benedictine Discipline." *Modern Philology* 54 (1956):1–6.

Stenton, Doris M. *The English Woman in History.* London: George Allen and Unwin Ltd., 1957.

Strayer, Joseph R. *Western Europe in the Middle Ages.* New York: Appleton-Century Crofts, Inc., 1955.

Stuard, Susan Mosher, ed. *Women in Medieval Society.* University of Pennsylvania Press, 1976.

Stuart, Gilbert. *A View of Society in Europe, in its Progress from Rudeness to Refinement.* Edinburgh: Hohn Bell, 1778.

Suleiman, Susan R. and Inge Crossman, ed. *The Reader in the Text: Essays on Audience and Interpretation.* Princeton, New Jersey: Princeton University Press, 1980.

Taitt, Peter S. *Incubus and Ideal: Ecclesiastical Figures in Chaucer and Langland.* Salzburg, Austria: Institut für Englische Sprache, 1975.

Tannenbaum, María Anita G. "Attitudes on Illicit Love in Literature from Pagan Latinity to the Christian Middle Ages." Dissertation, Ann Arbor, Michigan, 1976.

Tatlock, J. S. P. "Medieval Laughter." *Speculum* 21 (1946):289–94.

Tavard, George H. *Woman in Christian Tradition.* Notre Dame, Indiana: University of Notre Dame Press, 1973.

Taylor, Henry Osborn. *The Medieval Mind: A History of the Development of Thought and Emotion in the Middle Ages.* 2 vols. 4th ed. London: Macmillan and Co., 1927.

Thompson, A. Hamilton. *The English Clergy and their Organization in the Later Middle Ages.* Oxford: Clarendon Press, 1947.

Thompson, James Westfall. *The Literacy of the Laity in the Middle Ages.* University of California Publications in Education 9. Berkeley: University of California, 1939.

———. *The Medieval Library.* Chicago: University of Chicago, 1939.

Torres, Federico. *El Arcipreste de Hita: Estudio y antología.* Madrid: Compañía Bibliográfica Española, S.A., 1963.

Tuchman, Barbara W. *A Distant Mirror.* New York: Alfred A. Knopf, 1978.

Tucker, Samuel M. *Verse Satire in England Before the Renaissance.* New York: Columbia University Press, 1908.

Tupper, Frederick. "Chaucer's Sinners and Sins." *Journal of English and Germanic Philology* 15 (1916):56–106.

———. "St. Venus and the Canterbury Pilgrims." *The Nation* 97 (1913):354–56.

Ulrich, Leo. *Zur dichterische Originalität des Arcipreste de Hita.* Francfort: Vittorio Klostermann, 1958.

Waddell, Helen, ed. *Medieval Latin Lyrics.* 2nd ed. London: Constable and Co., Ltd., 1930.

———. *The Wandering Scholars.* Boston and New York, 1927; rpt. Boston and New York: Houghton Mifflin and Co., 1929.

Wainwright, Benjamin B. "Chaucer's Prioress Again: An Interpretative Note." *Modern Language Notes* 48 (1933):34–37.

Walker, Roger M. "A Note on the Female Portraits in the *Libro de Buen Amor.*" *Romanische Forschungen* 77 (1965):117–20.

————. "Juan Ruiz's Defence of Love." *Modern Language Notes* 84 (1969):292–97.

————. "Towards an Interpretation of the *Libro de Buen Amor.*" *Bulletin of Hispanic Studies* 43 (1966):1–10.

Walsh, James J. *High Points of Medieval Culture.* Milwaukee: The Bruce Publishing Co., 1937.

Warren, F. M. "*The Council of Remiremont.*" *Modern Language Notes* 22 (1907):137–40.

Watt, Francis. *Canterbury Pilgrims and their Ways.* London: Methuen and Co., 1917.

Wenk, J. C. "On the Sources of the Prioress's Tale." *Medieval Studies* 17 (1955):214–19.

White, Robert B. "Chaucer's Daun Piers and the Rule of St. Benedict: The Failure of an Ideal." *Journal of English and Germanic Philology* 70 (1971):13–30.

Whitmore, Sister Mary Ernestine. *Medieval English Domestic Life and Amusements in the Works of Chaucer.* Washington, D.C.: The Catholic University of America, 1937.

Windeatt, Barry. "Gesture in Chaucer." In *Medievalia et Humanistica.* Ed. Paul M. Clogan. *Studies in Medieval and Renaissance Culture* NS 9. Cambridge: Cambridge University Press; 1979, pp. 143–61.

Witte, Stephen P. "'Muscipula Diaboli' and Chaucer's Portrait of the Prioress." *Papers on Language and Literature* 13 (1977):22–37.

Wood, Chauncey. "Chaucer's Use of Signs in his Portrait of the Prioress." In *Signs and Symbols in Chaucer's Poetry.* Ed. John P. Hermann and John J. Burke, Jr. Alabama: University of Alabama Press, 1981.

Wood, Susan. *English Monasteries and their Patrons in the Thirteenth Century.* Oxford: University Press, 1955.

Woolf, Rosemary. "Chaucer as a Satirist in the General Prologue to the *Canterbury Tales.*" *Critical Quarterly* 1 (1959):150–57.

Worcester, David. *The Art of Satire.* Cambridge, Massachusetts: Harvard University Press, 1940.

Workman, Herbert B. *The Church of the West in the Middle Ages.* 2 vols. London: Charles H. Kelly, 1900.

Wrenn, C. L. "Chaucer's Knowledge of Horace." *Modern Language Review* 18 (1923):286–92.

Wright, Thomas. *Womankind in Western Europe from the Earliest Times to the Seventeenth Century.* London: Groombridge and Sons, 1869.

Yunck, John A. *The Lineage of Lady Meed: The Development of Medieval Venality Satire.* Publications in Medieval Studies 17. Notre Dame, Indiana: University of Notre Dame Press, 1963.

Zahareas, Anthony N. *The Art of Juan Ruiz, Archpriest of Hita.* Madrid: Estudios de literatura española, 1965.

Index

WAYWARD NUNS IN MEDIEVAL LITERATURE

was composed in 10½-point Mergenthaler Linotron 202 Bembo and leaded 2½ points
by Coghill Book Typesetting Co.;
with display type in Freehand by Typotronics Inc.;
and ornaments provided by Jōb Litho Services;
printed by sheet-fed offset on 50-pound, acid-free Glatfelter Antique Cream,
Smyth-sewn and bound over binder's boards in Joanna Arrestox B,
also adhesive bound with paper covers
by Maple-Vail Book Manufacturing Group, Inc.;
with dust jackets and paper covers printed in 2 colors by Philips Offset Company, Inc.;
designed by Mary Peterson Moore;
and published by

SYRACUSE UNIVERSITY PRESS
SYRACUSE, NEW YORK 13244-5160